Cinema: the Beginnings and the Future

Univ
C

Essa _____ ing the Centenary of the First Film Show
Proj _ced to a Paying Audience in Britain

Edited by Christopher Williams

UNIVERSITY OF WESTMINSTER PRESS, LONDON

First published in 1996 by the University of Westminster Press
309 Regent Street, London W1R 8AL, United Kingdom

Cinema: the Beginnings and the Future

Essays Marking the Centenary of the First Film Show Projected to a Paying
Audience in Britain

British Library Cataloguing in Publication Data
A catalogue record for this book is available from the British Library

ISBN 1 85919 012 X hardcover
ISBN 1 85919 007 3 paperback

Cover design: Christine Lewsey based on the CD-ROM *Virtual Nightclub*, designed by
Olaf Wendt, © Prospect Management (1996), *Arabesque* by David Pizzanelli (1989),
after Eadweard Muybridge's gravure animation series (1887), and the Lumière film
The London Fire Brigade at Southwark/Alerte de pompiers à Londres (1896), BFI
Stills, Posters and Designs.

Additional design and typesetting: Christine Lewsey, Nick Saunders, Siân Cardy

Set in Bookman 8.5pt type on 12pt leading and Argo

Produced by the Corporate Communications Office, University of Westminster,
15-18 Clipstone Street, London W1M 8JS, U.K.

Printer: Linneys Colour Print, Nottingham

CONTENTS

INTRODUCTION

Christopher Williams

This book has an obvious commemorative purpose. But it also aims to establish the grounds for an argument about the future of cinema.

The celebration encompasses the centenary of the film medium in general and the centenary of one specific moment in its birth. As several of the contributors point out, cinema was not invented. It was the result of a complicated process which had begun about three centuries earlier; a process which mixed science, entertainment, popular culture and the other media, story-telling, business and education in varying proportions. It follows from this that it could not have been the product of one showman or inventor, nor even of two French businessmen with strong interests in science and photography. We owe the cinema to the accumulated efforts of different groups of individuals. They finally brought it into being in a period of general technological and cultural change – the second industrial revolution – from which point it developed into the most popular art form of the twentieth century.

The main innovation of the Lumière brothers – our two French businessmen – was the provision of an adequate mechanism for projecting film to an audience. In 1894 and early 1895 they worked on the development of their Cinématographe, a combined camera, printer and projector, later demonstrating it in film screenings to learned and professional societies and finally to paying audiences.

Thus it was that about eleven months after its first showing to the French Société d'Encouragement à l'Industrie Nationale, and less than two months after its first commercial screening (also in Paris), the Cinématographe was demonstrated to representatives of the British press on February 20 and exhibited to the first public audience for a projected film show in Britain on the next day, Friday, February 21, 1896. The venue for these two events was the Great Hall of the Polytechnic Institution in Regent Street, London. This is the specific moment the book commemorates.

The historical appropriateness of the Polytechnic location emerges clearly from the essays by Roberta McGrath, Mervyn Heard and Joost Hunningher in Part One of this book. But there is also a contemporary reason for noting this appropriateness. Known variously as the Regent Street Polytechnic or just 'the Poly', and more recently as the Polytechnic of Central London or PCL, the Polytechnic has now become the University of Westminster. The University, at the forefront of media education, is proud that the first projected film exhibition to a paying audience in this country took place on its premises.

The argument of the book concerns the survival of cinema. Its second century is beginning in a period more disturbed than the decade of its birth though perhaps as exciting. The cinema in Britain reached its apogee (in terms of support via public attendance at cinemas) in 1946. Since then other technologies and media – most notably, television and video, computing, digitalisation and multimedia – have grown up alongside it. These years have seen reductions both in the volume of films made and the size of audiences at the traditional point of consumption, but the new media seem dependent on film and cinema for the provision of a major part of the product with which they hold the attention of audiences and users.

Should the development of these technologies be seen as threats to film or cinema, or as possibilities for their enhancement? The debate needs to consider cinema's relations with each of these new technologies. Firstly, cinema and television. The two have coexisted as hostile siblings for about 40 years. They are now interwoven with each other, as the essays by Mark Shivas and myself in Part Three show. It is probable there are some things each medium does better than the other. But in any case hybridity – the mixing, deliberate or unconscious, of forms and diction originating in each medium – is already a significant aesthetic force. Its existence does not mean that original and appropriate work cannot be produced in cinema formats. Rather it confirms the multiplicity and adaptiveness of moving-image based forms. On the level of government and institutions, it might be preferable if each small or medium-sized state, or grouping of states, had the cultural or political will to sustain its own film industry and market. But where the will to intelligent state or market intervention has been lacking, the involvement of television has proved a potent and valuable means of support and development for film.

It is clear that in many societies, including our own, large numbers of people prefer to stay home and watch either television-originated material or physically reduced versions of cinema-originated material. At the same time there are audiences which are not prepared to abandon the larger-screen, higher-definition, more luminous experience of emotional intensity and visual stimulation in the framework of the shared, social space of cinema. They may have been helped in this commitment by such different measures as the development of multiplexes, which has led to the rediscovery of cinema by younger adult audiences, and moderate levels of national or local government support. The production of adequately stimulating work for showing at television or video levels would not survive without the cinema audience's demand for what Sylvia Harvey, in the essay which concludes the book, calls 'a private experience in a social space'. From these factors I think we can conclude that cinema, television and video stimulate and enhance each other.

The relations between cinema and the computer – which brings in its wake the digital domain, multi-media, interactivity and virtual reality – are more complicated. The democratic version of computing posits an individual in control, using the technology to manipulate materials, organise knowledge, create new experiences, and (perhaps) communicate with other, similarly empowered individuals. The changes these factors imply for cinema are discussed in Part Three by Barry Salt, Paul Schrader and David Mingay. Could computer games replace the 'private, social' experience of film? Could multiple choices in the provision of computer narratives lead users toward the feeling that they are constructing their own narratives or contributing to the construction of others? Is the possibility of free movement in artificial worlds more exciting than guided movement in artistically-constructed ones?

It is not difficult to offer tentative answers to at least the first two of these questions. For many people computer games are already an acceptable alternative to film or television; but not for everybody, and not as a total alternative. The experience of computer games also draws on the universe of cinema (in particular, on cartoons and the action-adventure genre) and sometimes on pre-existing literary and philosophical modes. Thus, as with the film/television relationship, one is dealing with an expansion into a plurality of languages which feed on each other, not with the replacement of one idiom by another. It is also possible to imagine the marketing of collaborations between computer software writers and users on forms of narrative elaboration and development. For some users this may be a satisfying development of their pre-existing involvement with film or television, for others it may be 'only a game', for yet others perhaps frustrating, in that they want the creators to set the parameters and for their own participation to be the response. We have to remember (and the celebration of early cinema acts as a useful reminder in this regard) that since its beginnings cinema has been an interactive medium, in at least one important sense: it has always solicited and depended on the active responses of its spectators. By the same token, one may argue that digitalisation is more a refinement than a transformation. Cinema spectators knew that the photographic medium transformed what they were shown. This happened already with the re-presentation of the signs of analogy; the re-constitution or construction of everything through breaking it down into digits serves mainly to confirm the change.

Thus cinema's second century begins with it occupying an interesting but by no means fixed position in the midst of a group of other media. If it is no longer the miracle amazement of the early years, nor the institutional monarch of popular entertainment which it was between the 1920s and the 1960s, it is impossible to imagine popular culture or the other media making much sense without it. It has preserved its radical qualities, but perhaps most of all its propensities are still for the heightened emotional response and the mixing of public and private experiences.

To juxtapose, as we do here, the youth of cinema with its mature interaction with the newer media is not to pursue an 'essence' of the medium. It is, rather, to acknowledge and salute the active work of recovery and interpretation begun by the scholars and enthusiasts of early cinema since the 1970s, many of whom have been linked since 1985 through the Domitor Association for the study of early cinema. And to want to integrate the outcomes of this work – or at the very least, bring them into an active, ongoing relationship – with the tasks of thinking about both the theory and history of film in general, and of interpreting the continuing potential of cinema.

Auguste and Louis Lumière, circa 1895

The essays which follow show how exciting research into the aesthetic and historical dimensions of early cinema has become, suggest how much more they still have to teach us and indicate their relevance to the study of the media of the future. One can sense this work beginning, at least in filigree, in many of the essays which follow.

The structure in which they are presented is pragmatic but logical. Part One, *Around a Première*, consists, firstly, of three essays which establish the context for early cinema in popular culture, entertainment and education and culminate in David Robinson's summary of its technical pre-history. These are followed by six pieces discussing different aspects of the work of the Lumière brothers and their Cinématographe: its career in Britain, the diction of the films made for it, the role which fell to the Lumières in the development of a French national mythology of cinema. Together with pieces by John Barnes and Richard Brown I am glad to be able to include international contributions by John L. Fell, Roland Cosandey, and André Gaudreault, the Honorary President of Domitor.

Part Two, *Early Cinema – Then and Now,* includes five essays which make social and cultural observations about early cinema, looking at its importance in terms of interaction and exchange (Simon Popple), its treatment of sport (Luke McKernan), its fascination with trick effects (Michael Chanan), and the assumption that it could only be a 'flash in the pan' (Stephen Bottomore). This strand culminates in Roberta E.

Pearson's piece charting the differences between textual and historical approaches to early cinema studies and to cinema studies in general. The strand is punctuated by two other essays which are very specific in their foci: Martin Sopocy's discussion of international differences in intertitling practice and their implications, and Stephen Herbert's account of how he and his colleagues at MOMI re-created for public experience eight early modes of film exhibition and presentation.

Part Three, *Towards the Future,* begins with Barry Salt's discussion of basic film language and technique, which leads into a consideration of how they relate to CD-ROM and computer games. We then move on to the four pieces about cinema and television, cinema and the new technologies already mentioned. These are followed by John Chittock's account of technological changes in cinema production and exhibition. Finally Sylvia Harvey draws several strands together with a re-evaluation of André Bazin's view of the special qualities of the cinematic image, a survey of the basic contours of cinema as a European institution and a critical interpretation of four contemporary films. I am happy that this section contains essays by distinguished practitioners of film, television and multimedia alongside pieces from more academic writers.

An impulse towards comprehensiveness makes me want to mention two other essays about the Lumière films which could not be included here, for the very good reason that they have already appeared in book form in earlier collections. They are: Marshall Deutelbaum, 'Structural Patterning in the Lumière Films', in *Wide Angle,* vol. 3, no. 1, 1979 and ed. John L. Fell, *Film before Griffith,* California University Press, 1983; and Dai Vaughan, 'Let there be Lumière', in *Sight and Sound,* Spring 1981 and ed. Thomas Elsaesser, *Early Cinema,* BFI, 1990. Each seems to me to have very interesting things to say about the Lumière films; things which complement the last six essays in Part One of this book.

I want to thank all the contributors for their support and helpfulness. The book was conceived alongside the University of Westminster's Lumière Festival, 1996 (director: Joost Hunningher). Some of its concerns were developed in meetings of the University's Criticism and Creativity Research Group. I also want to thank Michael Harvey of the National Museum of Photography, Film and Television, John L. Fell, Roberta E. Pearson, Paul Schrader, David Herbert and Mary Doherty, who each came to my aid on one or more specific problems. For general editorial, design and technical advice, Joost Hunningher, Christine Lewsey, Carol Homden, Chris Fowler, Ronald Gow, David Faddy, Stephen Bottomore, David Mingay, John Chittock, Sylvia Harvey, and Edward Buscombe. I am grateful to Stephanie McKnight and Clementine Williams for allowing me to steal some family time to complete the editing.

PART
ONE

AROUND A
PREMIÈRE

1 NATURAL MAGIC & SCIENCE FICTION: Instruction, Amusement & the Popular Show 1795-1895

Roberta McGrath

Royal Polytechnic: Notice to everybody: If you want science, you can have it. If you want instruction you can have it. If you prefer amusement, you can have it. You can have either or all three by paying the admission fee of one shilling.[1]

In this essay I argue that the early histories of film and photography lie in the rise of consumer culture in the first industrial period which necessitated a re-negotiation of the relations between the human body and geographical space. These histories are located in several professional disciplines, élite artefacts and communal activities. They have their roots in medicine, anatomy and the body; in optical instruments and spectacular entertainments, in cabinets of curiosities and in newly established institutions of instruction and amusement. It is in these multiple and conflictual sites of 'natural magic' and 'philosophical toys' that spectres and human bodies converge.

This framework rejects distinct boundaries in history, disciplines and the body. The period between 1795 and 1895 represents a bridge between an old world and a new. What is significant in current cultural debates is the return of older terms: the illusion, the phantasmagoria, the curiosity, as well as a more general interest in magic and the existence of other worlds. These have come back to haunt our own time because the human body once again threatens to disappear before our very eyes; it is a mark of our own postmodern fragmentation and sense of dislocation in the age of post-mechanical reproduction, and our desire to keep in touch with what is human in a post-human world. In cyber-space questions of fantasy and sexuality have once again taken centre stage. And just as in the late eighteenth and early nineteenth centuries amusement and education were bound together, in the hands of private commerce, we are now told that we live in a period of convergence where entertainment and communications are bundled together in the hands of large corporations. We live in the age of 'edutainment'; but this is not, of itself, new. By tracing the history of convergence and later the divergence of amusement and instruction in the nineteenth century we can begin to understand natural magic as a precursor to science fiction.

I want to begin my narrative in the late eighteenth century, at a moment before the separation of art from science, the optical from the chemical, the world of fiction from the world of fact. These disciplines met in the emerging public arena of popular amusements linked to industrialised technology. There was no clear division between scientific instruments and the apparatus of magic.[2] We cannot understand the emergence of photography and film in the nineteenth century without an understanding, not only of optical technologies such as magic lanterns, phantasmagoria, and dioramas, but also of the spaces of anatomical museums, cabinets of curiosities, galleries of science and temples of health. For a time these spectacles were interlinked. Directories of the period show that many photographic studios and film houses took over from older cabinets and anatomical displays. Indeed, in the very early days some of these older shows still ran alongside the new businesses. Most standard histories of film and photography recall phantasmagoria and dioramas, but this is commonly represented as pre-history, background firmly fixed in the realm of a purely optical teleology, rather than as part of much wider and more complex social (and perhaps more important) *bodily* shifts.

During the period of early industrialisation a cluster of mechanical inventions blurred the boundaries between the human and the mechanical, the real and artificial. These objects simulated human movement and sound. They included automata, early replicants which were known as androids.[3] Among the most popular was a Turkish chess player whose arms moved and an Invisible Girl, who spoke.[4] There were also prosthetic body parts such as speaking heads and writing hands.[5] Simultaneously, audiences were entertained by a number of portable optical instruments and toys and comprehensive visual spectacles such as phantasmagoria and panoramas which appeared on the market.[6] These encompassed the fields of both irrational magic and rational science. Gradually irrational phantasmagoria were replaced by more rational topographic and architectural panoramas and dioramas, although significantly they were still known as 'miracle rooms'.[7] Here spectators, placed in semi-darkness at the centre of a circular painting illuminated from above, lost 'all judgment of distance and space'.[8]

In the sixty years from 1830 onwards audiences were treated to images with unusual veracity and the illusion of life alongside an increasing abstraction. The invention of stereoscopy and photography in the 1830s ran parallel with the oxyhydrogen microscope and spectacles such as the Kineorama (a combination of expansive panorama and illusory diorama). All these technologies meant a new and heightened sense of three-dimensionality and visual tangibility.[9]

By the early 1890s, the perfection of the illusion of physical movement was within grasp. Demenÿ's photophone of 1892 predicted sound.[10] Edison's Kinetoscope was first shown in Britain in Oxford Street in 1894.[11] This marked the realisation of a 'long standing human yearning for entering different realms'.[12] Earlier automata had relied on a concealing of the human within the mechanical; now the mechanical reproduction of human actions was possible.

The first 'moving picture' relied on a defect of the human eye to create the illusion of movement. However, to the nineteenth century viewer the flickering of early film must have resembled spectral magic lantern and phantasmagoric shows that had conjured up images out of nowhere. It is hardly surprising to discover that it was those same magical powers that the earliest photographs, and later film, were said to possess. In the popular press writers referred to photography as 'the black art' declaring that it was 'difficult to express intelligently the charm felt on beholding these pictures' or that 'the effects are perfectly magical'.[13] Photography and film owe much to magicians, conjurers, illusionists, charlatans – people who relied on the world of fantasy and imagination as much as on reality and fact.

These new technologies and amusements entailed not only the reorganisation of the public space, but a reorganisation of the private internal space of the observer. The cinema is the space in which bodies and spectres, both real and fantastic, meet. It is the space of a new becoming-body. The space of the temple, gallery, showroom, museum – all words that were interchangeable – signalled a gradual dismantling of the older body, a displacement of an outmoded model of the subject, and the production of a new observer-consumer.[14]

NATURAL MAGIC

The discourses of photography and film are wider than their histories of invention. David Brewster's *Letters on Natural Magic* first published in 1832 was one of many works written in the nineteenth century which aimed to demystify optical and auditory tricks. For Brewster the eye was not the organ of truth or knowledge but 'the most *fertile* source of mental illusions'; next to the eye 'the ear is the most fertile source of illusions'.[15] In *Natural Magic*, he recalls Philipstal's Phantasmagoria in Edinburgh in 1802 with its startling optical and auditory tricks: 'thunder and lightning, ghosts, skeletons and known individuals [whose] eyes and mouths were made to move by shifting and combined slides'.[16] According to Brewster, many were 'of the opinion that they could have touched the figures'.[17]

The Magazine of Science and School of Arts described the use of the magic lantern within the phantasmagoria as 'a powerful instrument in the hands of the crafty and designing used for the worst purposes of superstition and trickery'.[18] Brewster's work, like many others', aimed to unmask in true Enlightenment fashion the techniques of illusion. However, the result was to 'simply collapse the older model of power onto a single human subject, transforming each observer into simultaneously the *magician* and the *deceived*'.[19] The strategy of industrial rationalisation and demystification did not vanquish illusionary images, but led to their re-enchantment, re-location and survival within the human body. Illusions breed within the human subject.

The magic lantern was an 'obvious mechanical analogue of the human brain, in that it made illusionary forms and projected them outward'.[20] From this moment onwards, the image was not external and outside the subject, but internal, private and within the subject's imagination. This takes us into the realm of the optical unconscious, fantasy, desire. It was this spectre which was to haunt the scientific imagination of the nineteenth century. There was, in fact, no clear division between the eye of artistic illusion and the eye of scientific truth. Having escaped 'the timeless incorporeal order of the camera obscura, the visible was lodged in another apparatus, the unstable physiology and temporality of the human body'. In a reversal of roles, instead of the human body concealed within the machine, the machine was re-located within the human body.[21] It was Brewster who suggested that 'in order to perfect the art of representing phantasms, the objects must be living ones; and in place of chalky ill-drawn figures imitating humanity by the most absurd gesticulations, we shall have phantasms of the most perfect delineation, clothed in real drapery and displaying all the movements of life'.[22] Within a short space of time this would be achieved through the film and the phonograph and, eventually, 'the world's eyes and ears would come to be shaped by Hollywood'.[23]

Photography and film must then be seen as part and parcel of the new culture of capital and the commodity, creating in Benjamin's words, 'not democracy, but a phantasmagoria of equality'.[24] With the camera it is possible for the first time to bring 'remotest objects within the grasp of the observer'.[25] This heralds an increasing acceleration in consumer demand for ownership: 'every day the need to possess the object close up in the form of a picture, or rather a copy becomes more imperative'.[26] The mechanical image imposes a new order upon the world, fragmenting and pulverising knowledge. It was late eighteenth century scientific belief which had established objectivity, and therefore truth, 'as synonymous with the absence of any *sign* of manufacture'.[27] The invention of photography marked the realisation of such a philosophical ideal in the age of mass production. Its trick was to conceal the signs of manufacture and thus for the first time to abolish the distinction between a natural and manufactured world, between real and fake. From the moment of their invention photographs were passed off as portions of nature. Placed on the threshold between an old natural magical world and a newly emergent manufactured universe, the technologies of photography and film represented a dream of the simulacral: the copy without an original; the sign without a referent, ultimately a signifier severed from its signified. The transition took less than 100 years.

LONDON AND THE POPULAR SHOW

Richard Altick's fascinating account *The Shows of London* documents the area around Oxford Street and Regent Street as the heart of the new centres of consumption and display and the location of numerous new museums and exhibitions established between 1770 and 1850.[28] These were a stone's throw from the entertainments flourishing in Regent Street, Oxford Street and in Leicester Square. Within the show-rooms, the secrets of life and death and most importantly of all, sex, which brought both, were explored in displays of wax models, *tableaux vivants*, and body-parts preserved in spirits. These showrooms were instructional. 'Advice' was one of their prime functions and most held 'lectures'. They hovered on the very edge of what was legitimate.

Altick lists two in Margaret Street: James Graham's Temple of Health, with its 'real' goddess of youth and celestial bed dedicated to procreation, and Sarti's establishment which exhibited models of Adonis and Venus that could be taken apart. They were surrounded by an array of smaller models illustrating organs of the senses, the foetus and the breast, the pelvis, viscera of both male and female, the nature of extrauterine pregnancy and the appearance of cholera victims. Later Sarti set up a museum of Pathological Anatomy. Both these establishments, like many others, held separate ladies' and men's sessions. In Berners Street there was Mme Caplin's Anatomical and Physiological Gallery (for ladies only), and Dr Beale Marston's Museum of Science, Anatomy and the Wonders of Nature. Reimer's Anatomical and Ethnological Museum (for men only) displayed wax models of Embryology ('The origin of Mankind from the smallest particle of vitality to the perfectly formed foetus'), Obstetric Operations, and Branches of Midwifery. Dr Kahn's Anatomical Showroom, which had come from 'the continent', contained both wax models and specimens preserved in spirits. Exhibited alongside an embryological exhibit consisting of 103 microscopical figures from fertilised ovum to birth were specimens showing the terrible effects of debauchery in the form of syphilis.

By 1862 however, its name had been changed to the more reputable Dr Kahn's Museum and Gallery of Science.[29] The emphasis on waxworks and specimens gave way to instruments, particularly the oxyhydrogen microscope. By then there had been a tussle over the proper use of wax figures, or worse, the other staple, *poses plastiques*. One writer acerbically commented that while 'Figures of beautiful boys in wax adorned the bedrooms of the Greeks, (..) wax figures the size of life which are often praised for their likeness overstep the proper limits of the fine arts'.[30] The point here is that boundaries between entertainment and instruction were not, as yet, clearly defined. Showrooms like Madame Tussaud's[31] jostled for trade alongside both medical museums such as the Pathological Society in Regent Street or the Royal Institute of Anatomy and Science in Oxford Street.[32]

Between the early and mid nineteenth century many of these buildings changed use from medicine to shows. The area around Leicester Square, for example, is telling. At the turn of the century, the area was a well-known site of indecent print shops.[33] Panton Street was a centre for conjuring, and numerous small museums such as Bullock's held magic shows with magnetic conjuring boxes and automaton soothsayers.[34] It was in Castle Street, just off Leicester Square, that Robert Barker's Panorama had opened in 1792. Barker had lived opposite the anatomist John Hunter, whose museum would later become the Royal Panopticon of Arts and Science. In the mid nineteenth century it housed a photographic studio with a lift which transported customers to the roof. This became the Alhambra and is now the site of the Odeon Cinema, Leicester Square.[35]

THE POLYTECHNIC

Within this milieu, the Polytechnic represented a microcosm of commerce and manufacture. It drew no distinction between art and science, amusement and instruction. Many of the functions of the older shows and cabinets were continued and supplemented with newer, larger, more legitimate public attractions. Its location in Regent Street placed it at the heart of the popular show-rooms, new centres of consumption and transport. It was therefore at the very centre of competition. For forty years it dominated the field.

The Polytechnic Institution Gallery of Sciences opened on August 6, 1838. The original bill describes it as 'An Institution for the advancement of the Arts and Practical Science especially in connexion with agriculture, manufactures and other branches of industry'.[36] In those first few months there were demonstrations of wax-figure making and automata. The machinery which was then in place

Polytechnic Institution programme, February 1862

included: 'letter-press printing, optician's apparatus for polishing lenses, etc, a glass furnace for melting, blowing, and working glass; machinery for cutting, polishing, and engraving'.[37] The potential importance of a mass industrial manufacturing print culture, both visual and textual, was enshrined in these new technological advancements.

The visitor to the Polytechnic entered into a great hall of manufacture which was dominated by a symbolic 'colossal' *papier mâché* eye and ear (one hundred and forty-four times the size of life) at each end.[38] The prime function of the institution was to educate the visitor through seeing, which was epitomised in an overwhelming visual display, and listening, enshrined in the lectures. The Polytechnic continued this latter tradition established by its precursors, though the lectures were no longer about sex, but about more 'rational' topics. However, as the hand-bills show, magic ran parallel with science.

The Hall itself was a miniature industrial world. It contained canals, dockyards, watermills, locks, reservoirs, a miniature train supported on pillars that travelled around the gallery, and a diving bell, which held six people.[39] These dis-

A Spectre Drama at the Polytechnic Institution, May 1863

played new engineering and mechanical and industrial powers to plumb depths and scale heights, as well as increasing speed which would make the world more rapidly accessible.

Around the hall were located 'glass cases or presses containing useful, rare or curious models, clocks and anatomical models'. A programme for 1840 lists exhibits such as a skull, a tin case of preserved mutton, alongside Dr Arnott's hydrostatic bed and Mr Curtis's acoustic chair, 'designed not only for the use of deaf persons but also conveying intelligence from one house to another'.[40] Accounts of the acoustic chair, which suggested the possibility of the communication of sound over long distances, appeared in numerous magazines.[41]

Below the great hall lay a laboratory which had been 'adapted for private patentees and experimentalists who may require assistance in chymical researches'.[42] Above was located a lecture hall which seated

500 (by 1860 it seated 1,000) with a projection room which housed 15 magic lanterns.[43] Childe's grand phantasmagoria opened at the Polytechnic Gallery in 1838.[44] From the 1840s onwards the advertisements and reports of the activities list the 'Dircksian' phantasmagoria, cosmoramic views, panoramas, thaumotropes, kalotropes, phenakistoscopes, zoetropes, photodromes, aetheroscopes, choreutoscopes, and stereoramas.[45] They also included the physioscope, by which the human face is enlarged to a gigantic size, and the oxyhydrogen microscope,[46] described as 'the largest ever constructed, covering an area of some 425 sq ft'.[47] Magic and science were not so far apart, and the scopic devices of enlargement and distortion would be taken up by both photography and film.

A review of the oxyhydrogen microscope at The Gallery of Natural Magic at the Colosseum in Regent's Park described projections of the 'larvae of the water-beetle, gnats and other insects' multiplied four and a half million times. One reviewer claimed, 'Since the discovery of this wonderful world of microscopic life, it has been represented by fanciful writers as a world of spirits, pooled by forms not to be compared with those of the visible world. [Even] in 1820, an otherwise respectable writer described in detail the magic powers with which some of those forms were said to be endowed.'[48]

On September 20, 1839 the Royal Polytechnic Institution advertised: 'The process of photogenic drawing illustrated'.[49] While the rival Adelaide Gallery charged an extra shilling to see the new Daguerreotype process, the Polytechnic displayed it at no extra charge.[50] By 1840, it was advertising 'an exhibition of one hundred Daguerreotypes of the first class, part of a series of 1,100 works of art and ingenious scientific inventions; among them specimens showing the process of Birmingham manufactures'.[51] The following year the Directors secured an agreement from Fox Talbot to demonstrate the calotype process.[52] The commercial roof studio also opened and operated until 1852.[53]

The demise of the studio marked the real start of mass commercial photography. The following year, 1853, rooms for new photographic courses were constructed and the divergence of entertainment from education began. Gradually the old shows gave way to the new. It is, however, important to note that there is no distinct chronology here. Trapeze acts, musical events, automata, magic shows all ran alongside those more rational entertainments for some time. The programme from the 1860s shows the diversity of instruction and amusements on display and an illustration of a 'spectre drama' from 1863 shows the stage as a scientist's laboratory equipped with telescope, orrery, an open book, and the flasks of the chemist. In 1867 'Leotard or the automaton who or which?' was being exhibited.[54] Lectures on spiritism, 'optical, chemical and mechanical illusion' ran into the late 1870s.[55] However, slowly but surely the old *laissez-faire* approach to education and entertainment was nearing its end.

By 1879 bazaar stalls were in place in the great hall and the Polytechnic seems to have operated as a mix of shopping, entertainments and displays. Thefts were common.[56] A report from the same year suggested that the stalls and theatricals should be abandoned and that the institution should become 'a microcosm of technical art' [and] 'ingenious apparatus whether automaton or of any other kind should be sought out and utilised'.[57] Anatomical and wax exhibits, displays of magic were abandoned in favour of the latest scientific and technical inventions and instruments, and in 1882 the old apparatus was sold, after the Polytechnic had gone bankrupt; it recovered in many respects, but the age of edutainment was over and the Polytechnic was transformed into an educational institution.[58]

There was one last remaining exhibit which blurred the boundaries between education and entertainment, which utilised the science of optics and the art of magic. On February 20, 1896 it was here, at what was by now the Polytechnic Institution, that the first successfully projected moving picture in Britain was shown.[59] If the phantasms were not quite yet of 'the most perfect delineation', then they did 'display all the movements of life'.[60] A longed-for goal had been attained. Natural Magic was about to become Science Fiction.

NOTES

1. *The Times*, 1851, *Polytechnic Scrapbook*, Polytechnic Archive, University of Westminster.

2. It is worth noting here that after 1900 the Lumières' work would turn more towards medical research and production (Auguste) and colour photography (Louis). See Lisa Cartwright, *Screening the Body: Tracing Medicine's Visual Culture*, University of Minnesota Press, 1995, p.1.

3. See Michael Taussig, *Mimesis and Alterity: a Particular History of the Senses*, Routledge, 1993, p. 213.

4. The arm was operated by a man concealed inside. The invention was attributed to Baron von Kampelen. It is probably significant that chess is among the most popular computer games. This invisible girl was attributed to Monsieur Charles. It was a series of spheres linked by tubes to a hidden woman who replied. Both were exhibited at the Polytechnic in the mid-nineteenth century. See also David Brewster, *Letters on Natural Magic*, John Murray and Thomas Tegg, 1834.

5. See Thomas Frost, *Lives of the Conjurers*, Tinsley Brothers, 1876. In the late nineteenth century, the Egyptian Hall in Piccadilly was displaying Psycho, 'the most wonderful automaton ever invented. Psycho's powers are almost unlimited. He plays whist with extraordinary ability; he is a conjurer of marvellous dexterity; and an arithmetician of surprising talent.' At the Polytechnic, a mysterious hand which could write was exhibited: 'the hand reposed on the centre of a table looking like one of Dr. Kahn's wax models', ibid., p. 322.

6. Between 1797 and 1822, for example, there appeared: 1787, Robert Barker's Panorama; 1802, Phantasmagoria; 1806, William Hyde Wollaston's small Camera Lucida; 1807, Edward Orme's *Essay on Transparent Prints and Transparencies in General*, 'panoramas being so much in fashion I should like to recommend a transparent panorama which would produce a striking effect and could not fail to attract by its novelty,' p. 49. This work was printed simultaneously in English and French. It is likely that it was known to Daguerre; 1822, Louis Daguerre's Diorama.

7. See Martin Jay, *Downcast Eyes: the Denigration of Vision in Twentieth Century Thought,* California University Press, 1993, p. 128.

8. See Helmut and Alison Gernheim, *L.J.M. Daguerre: History of the Diorama and the Daguerreotype,* Secker and Warburg, 1856, p. 5.

9. 'The first and most important attempt to develope to the public gaze the microscope on a large scale was Mr. Carpenter of Regent Street who for many years exhibited a solar microscope. (...) The first public exhibition of the oxy-hydrogen microscope was in 1833'. Address, *Microscopic and Structural Record,* Vol. I, 1841. An advert for the Kineorama appeared in *The Athenaeum,* March 13, 1841.

10. The photophone was invented in 1892. See Henry Hopwood, *Living Pictures,* Optical and Photographic Trades Review, 1899, p. 61.

11. ibid., p. 73. This invention was reported in *The Times,* May 28, 1891. A patent was filed in the U.S.A. in August 1891, but not issued. It was not patented in Britain.

12. Barbara Stafford, 'Voyeur or Observer?', *Configurations,* vol. 1, no. 1, 1993, p. 97.

13. See reports of the Daguerreotype process in *Chambers Edinburgh Journal,* March 30, 1839, and *The Athenaeum,* February 2, 1839.

14. Jonathan Crary, *Techniques of the Observer,* M.I.T. Press, 1990, p. 14.

15. Brewster, op. cit., pp. 5 and 157.

16. ibid., pp. 81-2.

17. Frost, op.cit., p. 166.

18. *The Magazine of Science and School of Arts,* April 27, 1839, p. 36.

19. Crary, op. cit., p. 133.

20. Terry Castle, 'Phantasmagoria: Spectral Technology and the Metaphorics of Modern Reverie, *Critical Inquiry,* Autumn 1988, p. 58.

21. Crary, op. cit., p. 133.

22. This was achieved to some extent in the Dircksian Phantasmagoria, and is reported by Henry Dircks, *The Ghost,* E. and F.N. Spon, 1863, p. 52.

23. Taussig, op. cit., p. 198.

24. Walter Benjamin cited in Crary, op. cit., p. 11.

25. Brewster, op. cit., p. 5.

26. Benjamin, 'A Small History of Photography', in *One Way Street and Other Writings,* Verso, 1985, p. 250.

27. Barbara Stafford, *Artful Science: Enlightenment Entertainment and the Eclipse of Visual Education,* M.I.T. Press, 1994, p. 103 (my emphasis).

28. See Richard Altick, *The Shows of London,* Belknap Press, 1978.

29. ibid., p. 170.

30. *The Magazine of Science and School of Arts,* August 24, 1839, pp. 163-4.

31. As late as the 1870s Tussaud's advertisements claimed 'photographs and engravings are colourless and insipid compared to those wondrous waxen figures', *The Standard.* Advertisement, 'London: a Complete Guide to Leading Hotels, Places of Interest', *Amusement,* 1875.

32. ibid., 1872.

33. See *An Address to the Public from the Society for the Suppression of Vice,* 1803, pp. 25-41. This reports the ostensible trade in looking glasses and telescopes masking the selling of indecent prints, watch papers and other articles of that kind. School children were a good market for sales of 'the poisonous trash of the continent'. Anna Aitkin, whose husband kept a print shop at the corner of Castle Street and Leicester Fields, got twelve months hard labour for trading.

34. *Magazine of Science and School of Arts,* May 11, 1839, p. 36.

35. See Richard Gray, *Notes,* Polytechnic Archives, University of Westminster [P176].

36. See Polytechnic Archives, University of Westminster. The original bill is dated December 14, 1837 [R9].

37. See *The Mirror of Literature, Amusement and Instruction,* September 1, 1838.

38. These were made by George Simpson, surgeon at the Westminster Dispensary. Polytechnic Archives, University of Westminster [R45aa/1].

39. The bell at the rival Adelaide Gallery of Practical Science could hold only a mouse. See Altick, op. cit.

40. Polytechnic Archives, University of Westminster [R45aa/1].

41. 'Designed not only for the use of deaf persons, but also conveying intelligence from one house to another... by means of sufficient tubes this chair might be made to convey intelligence from St James's to the House of Lords or even from London to Windsor.' Polytechnic Archives, University of Westminster [R45aa/1]. *The Metropolitan* reported that 'if we can converse over a distance of three-quarters of a mile.... forty miles would be possible provided the requisite tunnels could be constructed', March 1837, pp. 88-9.

42. *The Mirror of Literature, Amusement and Instruction,* September 1, 1838.

43. After the stair collapsed in 1839, the Lecture Hall was doubled in size.

44. *The Magazine of Science and School of Arts* was pleased to report that 'Dissolving Views of Mr Childe and Lectures on Astronomy have replaced the ghastly changing heads and approaching monsters', April 20, 1839.

45. See catalogue for 1844, Polytechnic Archives, University of Westminster [R/44/al].

46. See R67.

47. Polytechnic File (1839-51), Enthoven Collection, Theatre Museum, London.

48. *The Mirror of Literature, Amusement and Instruction,* July 6, 1839, p. 18.

49. September 20, 1839, 'At 3.00 pm, the process of photogenic drawing illustrated', Polytechnic File (1839-51), Enthoven Collection, Theatre Museum, London.

50. *The Athenaeum,* February 2, 1839, p. 814.

51. Dated July 1840, Polytechnic File (1839-51), Enthoven Collection, Theatre Museum, London.

52. This agreement was granted to W.M. Nurse, 'Whereas the said William Henry Fox Talbot has obtained a patent for a new and original invention for improvements in obtaining pictures of Representations of objects and which was sealed on February 8, 1841 for three calendar months for the purpose of experiments and illustrating lectures upon the said invention', Polytechnic Archives, University of Westminster [R41].

53. Richard Beard's studio opened on March 23, 1841. It closed down in 1852 after Beard went bankrupt.

54. Dated February 2, 1867. Polytechnic File, Enthoven Collection, Theatre Museum, London.

55. ibid., dated July 21, 1877.

56. Polytechnic Archives, University of Westminster [R44g].

57. *Report of the Committee of Enquiry,* Polytechnic Archives, University of Westminster [R61].

58. The equipment was bought by the College of Practical Engineering, Muswell Hill. Polytechnic Archives, University of Westminster [R61].

59. This was a few days before shows at the Empire and the Alhambra. Shows ran every hour from 2pm to 10pm.

60. *The Polytechnic Magazine* describes the event tellingly as 'realistic and is, as a matter of fact, an actual photograph', February 26, 1896, Polytechnic Archives, University of Westminster [P176].

2 THE MAGIC LANTERN'S WILD YEARS

Mervyn Heard

Despite a century of development, cinema is still a young upstart compared with the reign of its popular predecessor, the magic lantern show. For almost 300 years, the humble lantern provided pictorial education, amusement and illusion in public halls and theatres and in upper and middle class homes. The movies have spawned literally thousands of books on their theory, practice, personalities and politics, but the magic lantern has received comparatively little attention from historians of the projected picture or indeed of any other branch of the media or popular entertainment.

One of the major reasons for this must surely be the notion of the junk-shop lantern – an old black metal box with a lens for the exhibition of photographs or painted still images on glass. Worse are the *Punch* cartoon connotations of the lantern in performance: the visual aid of the retired missionary, as he or she systematically bores a scattered audience, seated on hard chairs, in a public hall, echoing to the sound of intermittent coughing and squeaky boots.

If we do have another, cosier notion of 'the magic lantern show', it is probably the one about the Dickensian Christmas children's entertainment, with the avuncular, amateur showman delighting a gleeful audience with a colourful version of *Cinderella,* and, maybe, an ingenious mechanical slide or two, like Mr Punch and his growing nose, or the ever popular man-swallowing rats.

Both of these popular conceptions date from the mid to late nineteenth century. The first owes much to the way Victorian photography enthusiasts rejected the lantern after the introduction of the collodion wet-plate process at the Great Exhibition of 1851 enabled their snaps to be fixed on glass. The second arises from the influence on the domestic market of the popularity of the Christmas lantern shows staged by the Pickwickian 'Professor' Pepper and the staff of the Royal Polytechnic Institution in Regent Street, London.

With its unashamedly populist motto 'Science for All', the Royal Polytechnic was soon to become a primary place of resort for the Victorian middle classes and their offspring. Here, inside the impressive Great Hall, visitors could examine a bizarre array of everything from astronomical clocks, steam engines, a glass furnace and a hydrostatic bed to a stuffed pig and 'a wooden bucket carved by a footman in his leisure moments, whilst his family were dining out'. There was also a large tank of water, which allowed sensation-seekers to descend into its murky depths as part of the six-person crew of a three-ton, cast-iron diving bell. In an adjacent lecture theatre displays of popular science and parlour conjuring dressed up as 'natural magic' were presented daily.

However, far and away the most popular attractions were the Poly's breathtaking and ingenious 'dissolving view' entertainments, which featured exquisite, hand-painted slide images executed by and presented by Henry Langdon Childe and his associate, Mr Hill. Each new show was premiered either at Christmas or at Easter-time, and was full of humour. Most were based on traditional stories like *Robinson Crusoe* or *Bluebeard*, and latterly included strong elements of Harlequinade. At other times of the year the the theatre would be given over to more descriptive presentations, such as views of the eruption of Vesuvius or an account of a voyage to the North Pole. All incorporated impressive optical effects and transformations produced by the interplay of up to four massive lanterns, projecting onto a giant screen, beyond which were stationed an army of sound-effect operators.

As an adjunct to performances, the Polytechnic and various other commercial outlets in Regent Street were soon offering child- and adult-size lanterns for home use, together with versions of many of the stories and effects shown. Pepper, Childe and Hill had effectively refurbished the pre-existing image of the lantern show, which dated from the middle of the sixteenth century. They had re-packaged it, to some extent sanitised and 'edified' it, and mass-merchandised some of its more spectacular features in more 'user-friendly' formats, and done so in a manner which the Walt Disney Company would have appreciated.

But in this process they had also expunged, watered down or downgraded some of the wilder, more theatrical techniques which had dominated the period immediately preceding the new age of 'home lantern'. This period had much in common with the age of cinema in its inventiveness and in the dynamism of the professional 'Phantasmagoria' showmen, whose aims were to employ the lantern and custom-built images creatively, powerfully and as part of a fully sensual, multi-media experience.

To understand these aims, we need first to look at the showmen's antecedents and the influences upon them. The origins of the magic lantern are obscure. But current research places its gradual emergence at the beginning of the sixteenth century, with possibly the Netherlands or Denmark as its spiritual home. By the late 1660s and early 1670s the lantern was being widely shown and sold in Europe. In his diary, Samuel Pepys records a visit, in August 1666, from an eminent London optician, Mr Reeves, who demonstrated and sold him a novel 'lanthorn, with pictures in glass, to make strange things appear on a wall'.[1]

Numerous contemporary engravings from the late seventeenth and eighteenth centuries are testimony to the European-led world-wide popularity of the lantern as a simple but effective form of amusement. The most popular pre-1790 images of the lanternist are of itinerant 'gallanty' showmen trudging from place to place with their heavy slide boxes and tin lanterns strapped to their backs. In the summer wayside inns, barns, hired rooms adjacent to the site of public execution and even the open air served as impromptu auditoria. In winter, when the roads were impassable, they would stick to the large towns, performing in private houses, for the families and servants of those who could afford it. It was this practice which was to assist the Polytechnic in marketing the lantern show in the mid 1860s as a traditional Christmas entertainment.

There are, to my knowledge, no detailed accounts of performance by the 'gallanty' showmen earlier than the 1830s, by which time they saw themselves as a dying breed. The images on some of the 12 inch plus 'long slides' which survive from the eighteenth century contain processions of characters and situations which are so esoteric and seemingly unconnected with each other as to be unfathomable. However, what they do demonstrate is the importance of the showman; that these artefacts are merely the raw material upon which the ingenious performer could then build a complete audio-visual scenario, perhaps using music, sound effects or even performing animals. Early illustrations of operators and their assistants show such aspects of showmanship in practice.

In the 1780s and early 1790s two revolutionary developments had taken place. The first was technical: the introduction of the Argand lamp. This had little more to commend it than a cylindrical wick, with a larger and therefore slightly brighter flame. At the same time it did give the optical-illusionist enough extra power to allow further movement behind and away from the screen, and therefore, potentially, far more varied and artful use of the lantern. The second development was a rather theatrical concept, which emanated from a vogue for the Gothic intermixed with an interest in certain scandalous or nefarious 'goings-on'.

Alongside the widespread public knowledge of the lantern, the machine had also been used in a more covert and sinister field of activity, as the conjuring device of 'pseudo-priests', who used it to try to beguile their followers and convince them of their power and influence over the unseen forces. In the mid eighteenth century in particular, there was a sudden upsurge of interest in Rosicrucianism and Freemasonry, and a number of related cults and secret societies began to appear, among them the Martinists, the Illuminati and the cult of Egyptian Masonry. Many made use of hidden lanterns to invoke ghostly images on smoke or to back-project onto paper-thin walls. These conjurers also used 'weather effects', drugs, sound effects, electric shocks, odours, pyrotechnics and even ventriloquism to further disorientate their subjects. The most famous practitioners were Josef Balsamo, also known as Count Cagliostro, and Johann Schropfer, who staged seances in his coffee house in Leipzig and elsewhere in Europe, before shooting himself in a fit of insanity in 1774.

These feats of necromancy were denounced in a series of books in the 1780s which served both as exposés and as primers. In 1785 the German author Friedrich von Schiller commenced publication of his story *The Ghost-Seer* in periodical form. This deals with the activities of a Sicilian conjurer, who employs a hidden lantern and various other effects to fleece his victims. With such material in circulation, it was not surprising that a master showman should eventually materialise with the project of recreating such 'ghost-raising' activity as a form of exposé and 'philosophical' entertainment.

That showman – the first so far as we know – was a mysterious German, who operated under the stage name of Paul Philidor. At least one account suggests that he began presenting his sensational show in Berlin and Vienna around 1789 or 1790. But the first verifiable performance was at no. 31, rue de Richelieu, Paris, in December 1792, in the turbulent Year One of the First Republic. The show was in part a straightforward lantern show offering images of famous European personages, such as the Emperor Josef. But the chief attraction was the *Fantasmagorie*, Philidor's exposé of the techniques of ghost-inducers, which featured an array of favoured phantoms and used techniques I shall discuss later. Its success was no doubt enhanced by the current vogue for the Gothic, as well as by such features as requests for the ghost of your choice 'by prior arrangement'.

Artist's impression of Robertson's *Fantasmagorie*, Paris, c.1798, showing the use of multiple projection, incense burners and other theatrical paraphernalia

The show ran for four months, until April 1793, when it closed down somewhat abruptly. We cannot be sure why, but it seems likely that in the volatile political situation, especially following the execution of Louis XVI in January, Philidor's show was being looked on with suspicion. In any event, Philidor vanished, never to be seen again. It was another showman, a Belgian, Etienne Gaspard Robertson, who was to reach a full realisation of the artistic and creative potential of the *Fantasmagorie*. He premiered his own version in January 1798 at the Pavillon de l'Echiquier in Paris. In March a review describes Robertson's pseudo-scientific manner of presentation, which used a preamble and techniques borrowed from Philidor.

It is perhaps appropriate at this point to highlight some some of the processes which exemplify the 'Phantasmagoria' mode of presentation. As the aim is surreptitious ghost-production, the main images are produced by a system of back-projection, with the technical operators hidden from view. Sometimes the 'screen' is constructed from tangible material, on other occasions smoke is used. Sometimes one lantern is used, sometimes two or more. Lanterns are often moved towards and away from the screen on silent tracks to give the effect of spectres receding or seeming to hurtle straight out into the audience. Another defining aspect of such shows is the style of the painted slide image, which is executed on glass with a solid black background, so as to make the phantom stand out in relief. Projection was not limited to the use of glass images. Opaque objects were also used, and eventually even the projection of live actors. Additional multi-media effects, such as the use of masks, electricity, pyrotechnics, sound effects and physical disorientation were very much down to the abilities of the individual showman.

While he was eager to sustain the persona of the man of science, Robertson's early show included at least one image taken directly from a popular work of Gothic fiction: the vision of the bleeding nun, from Matthew Lewis' popular bodice-ripper, *The Monk*. From the reactions of members of the audience to certain effects there are also indications that in the time-honoured style of most magicians he was also using 'stooges'. In January 1799 Robertson moved to a site offering more atmospheric possibilities – the Cour de Charon, behind the deserted Church and Convent of the Capucines. The position was ideal, since its public approach was via a dimly lit graveyard accommodating the bones of several generations of dead nuns, and it was also handy for passing trade emerging from a nearby dance hall.

It was during this period that Robertson's show flourished. Many of his optical tricks were now set into dramatised vignettes. Scenarios encompassed the mythological as well as literary, classical and biblical subject-matter – such as the appearance of the witches to Macbeth, or Samuel and the spectres made manifest by the ancient priests of

Memphis. But Robertson was plagued by imitators. Within days of his opening at the Capucines two of his former employees were already producing a rival show at his former home, the Echiquier. Establishing patents for his 'Phantascope' did nothing to deter them, for it could be argued that Robertson himself had copied the techniques – from Philidor. Here, as with cinema, protracted arguments over patents dominated the first few years of phantasmagoria activity. These continued until September 1800, in fact, when – with a tribunal finding against Robertson's exclusive right to present the Phantasmagoria – the floodgates were opened. In his own words, 'there was not a quay which did not offer you a little phantom at the end of a dark corridor, at the top of a winding stairway. The lowest amateur of physics, in every region, had his Phantasmagoria. I have found these boxes-on-trolleys, made in Paris, in the depths of Russia and from the frontiers of Siberia to the extremities of Spain.'

The Phantasmagoria had its London debut, in the specially refurbished Lower Hall of the Lyceum Theatre in the Strand in early October 1801. Its presenter, a German showman named Paul de Philipsthal, featured it as the named attraction, although the full show also included exhibitions of various other lantern and 'spirit-related' items and of automata. Details of Philipsthal's career prior to 1801 are as scant as those for those Philidor after 1793, and there is some circumstantial evidence to suggest they were the same person.

The career of the Phantasmagoria in Britain is interesting, not least because it has many features which can be compared with the pattern of the rise of cinema a century later. Like the first films, Philipsthal's show proved an instant hit with London society, and additional daytime performances were put on to cater for the carriage trade. Within weeks a rival exhibition was being advertised at the Royalty Theatre – a short, twenty minute item preceding the normal evening performance. The lessees, Philip Astley, the father of circus and the hippodrome, and his two sons ran a string of theatres, not only in London and the English provinces, but also in Scotland and Ireland and even, significantly, one in the centre of Paris. Their man, a Monsieur St Clair, presented his show at the Royalty for a Christmas season[2] until the end of January[3], when it transferred to Liverpool and thence to Dublin.

In January 1802, Philipsthal attempted to thwart this and future competition by establishing a patent for his famous 'Apparatus for Reflecting Objects'. However, since, like earlier pioneers of the lantern and R.W.Paul, the later British movie pioneer, he was openly selling copies of his apparatus, he was in one respect at least his own worst enemy. At the end of the month, advertisements began to appear for similar devices. Mr Jones, a London optician, marketed an 'optical tube' and claimed to have been selling instruments like Philipsthal's claimed invention 20 years before.[4]

From February 1802 rivalry began in earnest. Famous magicians, like Moritz, who was based at no. 28, Haymarket, began to feature Phantasmagoria presentations as part of their programme, and toured them to smaller provincial theatres. As out of town music halls would in the age of cinema, minor theatres included performances of their own, possibly using commercially available 'kits'. The first such provincial shows were at the Theatres Royal in Bristol and Bath, but within the period 1803-5 such presentations were tried in most accessible large towns with their own theatre. Soon after this the Phantasmagoria, or at least the most sensational aspects of it, was being featured at Bartholomew and other large fairs, as well as in makeshift gaffs. Interestingly, *à propos* the effects of

The twin lantern 'dissolving view' process, as perfected by H.L. Childe in the early 1800s

picture shows on the young, in February 1802 one gaff proprietor, William Grossett, was sent to Bridewell for presenting such a show to an audience of 100 children. The judge considered that the influence of these performances constituted a serious evil.

The fascination with Phantasmagoria probably reached its pitch in 1805, when in January both the Upper and Lower auditoria of the Lyceum were staging competing exhibitions. In the Lower Theatre the famous Drury Lane harlequin, Jack Bologna, offered his *Pantascopia* entertainment, fresh from a brief but successful tour of New England. Upstairs the German team of Schirmer and Scholl sought to upstage Bologna by offering, among many other 'musical, mechanical, aerostatic, acrobatic and optical' treats, their allegedly superior *Ergascopia*, which permitted the ghostly projection of living figures.

Much as the Polytechnic would do later, the Phantasmagoria cultivated its amateurs, and lanterns and slides began to be advertised and sold in greater number. In the early 1800s the lantern to buy for home consumption was the one built to a Phantasmagoria design, in pure black metal, with distinctive, tall chimney, Argand burner, and gliding optical tube to allow for appropriate ghostly manifestations. The most popular images were now also being executed in the Phantasmagoria style, as coloured images on glass but with jet-black surrounds.

Although the Phantasmagoria remained popular until the late 1820s, by about the same time a different process had come into vogue, one which offered possibilities for standardisation and consumer specialisation. During the first decade of the nineteenth century an English theatre designer, Henry Langdon Childe, who reputedly painted slides for Philipsthal's show, had begun to evolve a new form of lantern presentation. Adapting the principles of multiple lantern projection used by people like Robertson, he perfected a dual-lensed system. By slowly shielding one lantern image and simultaneously revealing another – somewhat in the syle of the Diorama – a gentle transformation could be produced. A winter scene could be made to melt into summer. A ruined abbey by day could be darkened and swathed in moonlight. Childe exhibited and perfected this new optical attraction over a period of years, from about 1807 into the late 1820s, but it was really from 1838

The interior of the 'Optical Box' at the at the Polytechnic, with a rear view of two, and a side view of one of its four massive, rail-mounted lanterns

onwards, with the beginning of his long-term residency at the Polytechnic, that 'dissolving views' came to be seen as the epitome of refined visual entertainment.

With the Polytechnic now espousing 'science' rather than pure showmanship, there was a distinct drift away from the concept of magic for its own sake towards a greater fascination with technical revelation. All kinds of ingenious, precision-built slides with cogs, levers and all manner of moving parts were soon demonstrated and merchandised. Even the most beautiful hand-painted slides produced during this period are more remarkable for their technical execution than for artistic flair.

It is largely through this process of rationalisation, followed by greater scientific, educational and propagandist application, that the lantern showman was to end up as the 'lanternist'. In nineteenth century Japan, cut off from Western industrial influences, the magic lantern show developed differently. Instead of standardisation, it retained the intrinsic simplicity of the Phantasmagoria era, when the lantern had first been introduced into that country. It employed multiple projection techniques – up to six lanterns back-projecting individual characters or parts of characters onto fixed, projected 'back-drops'. It is interesting to speculate on how Western lantern projection might have developed if practitioners had been able to continue with the theatrical techniques of the Phantasmagoria show. The technicians' preoccupation with 'persistence of vision' and other simple processes eventually saw the lantern reduced to being merely 'the slave of cinema'. The new visual art form which arose from this was not, perhaps, the one the Phantasmagoria showmen dreamt about.

NOTES

1. Samuel Pepys, *Diary,* vol. 2, p. 309 in the 1953 revised Everyman edition.
2. *The Observer,* December 20, 1801.
3. *The Oracle and Daily Advertiser,* January 28, 1802.
4. *The Morning Chronicle,* February 2, 1802.

Primary Reference Sources

The Magic Lantern Society, *New Optical and Magic Lantern Journal.*

Hermann Hecht, *Pre Cinema History,* Bauker Saur, 1993.

Richard Altick, *The Shows of London,* Belknap Press, 1978.

J.H. Pepper, *The Boy's Playbook of Science,* Routledge, 1881.

Laurent Mannoni, *Le Grand Art de la Lumière et de l'Ombre,* Nathan Université, Paris, 1994.

E.G. Robertson, *Mémoires Récréatifs Scientifiques et Anecdotes,* Paris, 1831-3.

Harry Houdini, *The Unmasking of Robert Houdin,* Routledge, 1909.

3 REALISING THE VISION:
300 Years of Cinematography

David Robinson

The cinema was not invented. Nor was it precisely a process of evolution. Rather it was the realisation of a conception that had been clearly envisioned for centuries before. Edison, Dickson, Demenÿ, Paul, Acres, Armat, Jenkins, the Skladanowskys, the Lumières, the Lathams merely chanced to be the ones privileged to add the last elements to the edifice that had been foreseen and in the making for many generations.

In 1589 Giovan Battista Della Porta, in the chapter of his great work *Magia Naturalis*, which explores the uses of the camera obscura, could describe a definitive cinematographic experience:

> 'Now for a conclusion I will add that, than which nothing can be more pleasant for great men, and Scholars, and ingenious persons to behold; That in a dark Chamber by white sheets objected, one may see as clearly and perspicuously, as if they were before his eyes, Huntings, Banquets, Armies of Enemies, Plays, and all things else that one desireth. Let there be over against that Chamber, where you desire to represent these things, some spacious Plain, where the sun can freely shine; Upon that you shall set Trees in order, also Woods, Mountains, Rivers, and Animals, that are really so, or made by Art, of Wood, or some other matter. You must frame little children in them, as we use to bring them in when Comedies are Acted: and you must counterfeit Stags, Bores, Rhinocerets, Elephants, Lions, and what other creatures you please: Then by degrees they must appear, as coming out of their dens, upon the Plain: The Hunter must come with his hunting Pole, Nets, Arrows, and other necessaries, that may represent huntings; Let there be Horns, Cornets, Trumpets sounded: those that are in the Chamber shall see [upon the sheet] Trees, Animals, Hunters' Faces, and all the rest so plainly, that they cannot tell whether they be true or delusions: Swords drawn will glister in at the hole that they will make people almost afraid. I have often shewed this kind of Spectacle to my friends, who much admired it, and took pleasure to see such a deceit; and I could hardly by natural reasons, and reasons from the Opticks remove them from their opinion, when I had discovered the secret... You shall amend the distance by the magnitude of the Glass.'

This is cinema. Della Porta stages action under the bright light of the sun; he 'photographs' it by means of the lens of the camera obscura;

and at the same time uses the camera as an auditorium, projecting the two-dimensional, luminous image of the original action onto a screen before an audience. He enhances the visual show with sound effects. He assures the focus, amending 'the distance by the magnitude of the Glass'.

The intermediate stages which are characteristic of the cinema as we know it today – a means of permanent recording and reproduction of the image – are still absent; but the notion of the screen experience, of life reproduced as a luminous, moving image, is intact. Della Porta is giving practical directions for realising the timeless imaginings of fable and fairy tale, magic mirrors which show the pictures of other lives and other places.

The camera obscura was already very ancient by the time of Della Porta. The magic lantern only came into use in the 1650s, though Della Porta's description suggests how closely related are these two devices. Both are boxes, greater or smaller; each is fitted with a lens system. One captures within its darkened interior the image of the brightly lit scene outside it; the other, from its brightly lit interior, projects an image onto a screen in a dark surrounding space. In these two magic boxes lies the fundamental technology of the cinema. The camera obscura is the essential element of photography; the technology of the magic lantern remains intact in even the most sophisticated cinema projector.

The magic lantern, as Mervyn Heard's essay relates, started its life in the physic cabinets of scientists and savants, who were dismayed when they saw the device taken up all too soon by showmen and charlatans. We know from eighteenth century iconography that itinerant showmen, often the ingenious peasants of Savoy, travelled Europe with their magic lanterns and hurdy-gurdies, giving shows in barns and village taverns and on lucky nights in the halls of grand houses. We know too that their repertoire already exploited the timeless attractions of popular show business – laughter, fright and the mystical. Today it is not easy for us to conceive the full impact of these luminous images – vague though they must have been, given the feeble light sources and inadequate lenses of the time – upon people who could hardly have known what a picture was. Even in cities, the only representational images with which the humbler and greater part of the population could be familiar were the coloured windows and wall paintings of churches and the signs outside inns and shops. Books were inaccessible to most people, and even then rarely illustrated. Paper and ink were costly: the only place where plain folks' children could draw pictures was in the sand or snow. How astonishing then these vivid representations of life, pictures in light and colour, must have seemed.

Only movement was lacking in the pictures; and from the start there were efforts to supply it. As early as 1659, Christiaan Huygens, the lantern's primogenitor, sketched a series of images for lantern slides, showing a skeleton in different stages of animation, playfully removing its skull. By the end of the seventeenth century lantern showmen were producing illusions of movement in their slides, by overlaying the static painting on glass with a second glass which could be moved by means of levers or ratchets. So, when the image was projected, the sails of a mill could appear to move or a gentleman bow from the waist. Mechanical slides of this kind became more and more elaborate during the nineteenth century. As Mervyn Heard describes, their effects were enhanced by superimposed and 'dissolving' views and the complex effects devised for the phantasmagoria shows of Philidor and Robertson. When motion pictures arrived, at the end of the 19th century, many critics felt they fell short of the glamorous, coloured images of what was now, in a period which took a more rational view of such things, called 'the optical lantern'.

* * *

These effects of movement were achieved by simple mechanical effects. The illusion of movement in the motion picture film depends upon a peculiarity of human perception, called crudely 'the persistence of vision', but which we now know is a complex of optical, chemical and cerebral processes. The simple result of this phenomenon is that we seem to see any image placed before our eyes, for a fraction of a second after the stimulus itself is removed. By extension (the principle of the movies), if a rapid succession of static images, each showing a phase of movement minutely

Joseph Plateau's first Phenakistiscope, 1833

advanced from the one before it, is presented to the eye, our perception blends together the multiple stationary images into one moving picture.

The classical demonstration of the 'persistence of vision', recognised since antiquity, is that a point of light rapidly revolved in the dark-ness appears as a continuous circle of light. Eighteenth cen-tury researchers – Johannes Segner and the Chevalier Patrice d'Arcy – studied this effect to assess the duration of the persis-tent impression.

Studies were resumed in the third decade of the next century. Peter Mark Roget and Michael Faraday recorded the curious optical effects of wheels observed through grills, or through slots arranged around the edge of other turning wheels. In the latter circumstance, Faraday pointed out, the rear wheel appears to be stationary. The series of brief glimpses afforded by the slots gives the impression of a rapid succession of near-static images; and these are linked, by the 'persistence of vision' effect, to give the impression of a continuous view of a static wheel. Faraday found that a more convenient way of demonstrating the phenomenon was simply to revolve the slotted disc in front of a mirror, and observe its reflection through the slots.

The Belgian physicist Joseph Plateau and the Austrian Simon Stampfer recognised that a series of identical images drawn around the edge of the revolving slotted disc observed in this way would also appear to be stationary. From this the obvious step was to make the series of images not identical, but showing successive phases of an action. Now when the disc was revolved and its mirror reflection viewed through the slots, the impression was of a figure in motion.

The device was marketed as a charming and amusing toy, under various names like phenakistiscope or phantoscope. In the late 1860s a more convenient variation was marketed: in the zoetrope the series of images were printed not on discs but on strips, placed inside a revolving drum with slits around the top. This dispensed with the need to view in a mirror and permitted several persons to enjoy the toy at the same time. In 1876 the praxinoscope, patented by the Frenchman Emile Reynaud, dispensed with the slots, and the consequent loss of light, by placing a polygon of mirrors at the centre of a zoetrope-like drum. In this way the rapid succession of images was reflected by the turning mirror faces.

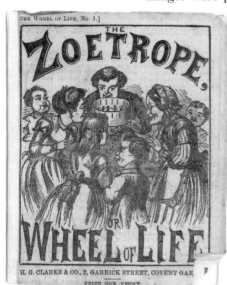

First English publication of
The Zoetrope, 1867

Inevitably there were attempts to combine the moving images of the phenakistiscope and stroboscope with magic lantern projection. In 1843 a practical project for a projecting phenakistiscope was proposed by T.W. Naylor of Newcastle-upon-Tyne. His plan was published in several German scientific journals, and was taken up by an Austrian officer, Franz von Uchatius (1811-1881), who by 1853 was marketing a complex projecting phenakistiscope. In 1871, T. Ross's 'Wheel of Life' incorporated a projecting phenakistiscope into the convenient format of a lantern slide, with a single-slot shutter revolving thirteen times for every revolution of the thirteen-phase picture disc. J.S.Beale's Choreutoscope (1866), another elaborate form of lantern slide, adopted a different approach. Six progressive images were painted on a strip of glass, which was intermittently moved and stopped, to present each image in turn before the lens aperture. The choreutoscope anticipated the cinema projector in its use of a synchronised shutter and a Geneva stop mechanism to achieve an intermittent movement.

The brilliant Emile Reynaud predictably achieved the most perfect solution to the problems of projecting moving images. He adapted his praxinoscope to projection, and went on to develop a spectacular theatrical show he called the Théâtre Optique. All previous persistence of vision motion picture devices had been limited to the brief, cyclical action that could be contained on a disc or the continuous band within a drum. Reynaud had the idea of arranging his images, each hand-painted on transparent material, on a band of unlimited length, wound between two spools, precisely like a motion picture film. Projecting these bands of images, through the medium of the mirror prism, and superimposing them on decors projected by a separate lantern, Reynaud was able to create entire plays. In the last years before the cinema, from 1892 to 1895, the wonderful animated images of Reynaud's *pantomimes lumineuses* at the Musée Grévin were one of the spectacles of Paris.

Hologram, *Arabesque*, by David Pizzanelli, 1989, after Muybridge's original gravure animation series, 1887

* * *

In all these devices which achieved an illusion of moving pictures thanks to the phenomenon of the 'persistence of vision', the images were drawn by hand. The arrival of photography in 1839 inaugurated a new revolution in the perception of representation. Photography was rooted in the earlier of the fundamental magic boxes, the camera obscura. At least since the time of Della Porta, artists had used small, portable cameras as an aid to drawing landscapes, tracing the camera images on translucent paper. This was a laborious process. Experimenters began to look for ways of capturing the camera image automatically. Thomas Wedgwood recognised that the answer lay in the properties of silver salts, which darken on exposure to light; and in 1802, in collaboration with Humphry Davy, outlined a photographic process, concluding that 'Nothing but a method of preventing the unshaded parts of the delineation from being coloured by exposure to the day is wanting, to render the process as useful as it is elegant'. This problem of fixing the image was not satisfactorily solved until 1839 when simultaneously the processes of Louis-Jacques-Mandé Daguerre, continuing work begun by Nicéphore Niépce, and of William Henry Fox Talbot were published. The daguerreotype initially gave more refined results; but the Talbotype (or Calotype), as a negative-positive process, was to be more significant to the future progress of cinematography.

From the 1850s photographs were projected in the magic lantern, and inevitably there were proposals to combine photographic images with the proliferating moving picture toys like the phenakistiscope and zoetrope. The long exposure times required in early photography inhibited early experiments however. Pioneer efforts at projecting moving photographs, like Heyl's Phasmatrope (1870) and Rudge's Phantoscope (circa 1884), depended on painstakingly posing and photographing models for each successive phase of movement.

The introduction of faster and more convenient photographic processes in the late 1870s stimulated photographers to develop means of taking photographs in rapid succession. In 1878 Eadweard Muybridge (1830-1904), commissioned to take 'instantaneous' pictures of horses in motion, devised a system of multiple cameras arranged along a track, with elaborate arrangements of successive shutter releases, to photograph the movement of animals or humans passing in front of them. In France the physiologist Etienne-Jules Marey, challenged by the problem of filming birds in flight, devised a 'photographic gun', which exposed a rapid series of images on an intermittently revolving plate. From this Marey went on to develop other forms of 'chronophotographic' cameras. In 1888 he took a definitive step forward by using flexible paper film rather than plates. Others working energetically and creatively in the same field were Marey's brilliant assistant Georges Demenÿ and, in Germany, Ottomar Anschutz. The chronophotographers, having satisfactorily analysed movement by photography, were in turn attracted to the problems of re-synthesising their images, to recreate motion. This was achieved in a series of devices, more or less based on the phenakistiscope – Muybridge's projecting zoopraxiscope, Anschutz' Electrotachyscope and Demenÿ's Phonoscope.

In the late 1880s all this research and achievement was very much in the air and reported in scientific journals, and could not escape the notice of the world's favourite inventor, Thomas Alva Edison. In February 1888 he met Muybridge when the photographer came to lecture at West Orange, New Jersey, where Edison lived and worked. In October of the same year, Edison deposited a *caveat* with the U.S. patents office, declaring, 'I am experimenting upon an instrument which does for the Eye what the phonograph does for the Ear, which is the recording and reproduction of things in motion . . .'

Edison, as was his wont, assigned an assistant, William Kennedy Laurie Dickson, to develop the idea. Edison provided the facilities, perhaps the impetus, and sometimes the vision; but there is now little doubt that all the experimental and practical work were Dickson's.

The first experiments, begun in 1888, stubbornly persisted with a device based on the mechanism of the phonograph, Edison's favourite invention: but the idea of microphotographs arranged in a spiral around a cylinder was doomed to failure. The breakthrough came with the appearance on the market, late in 1888, of celluloid roll film; and at the same time Edison's meeting with Marey during a visit to Europe in 1889. Dickson's experiments now turned to the use of strips of transparent film; and by 1892 he had achieved the definitive form of a motion picture camera, the kinetograph, and a viewer, the kinetoscope. The kinetoscope was a peepshow, with a continuous looped film that could be viewed only by one person at a time. The film ran continuously: subsequent motion picture devices would rely upon intermittent movement of the film, with each frame momentarily arrested.

Although first publicly demonstrated in 1892, the kinetoscope was not commercialised until April 1894, when the first 'kinetoscope parlor' was opened on Broadway, New York. The name of Edison unfailingly guaranteed publicity; and for a year or two kinetoscope parlors, with the peepshow machines in ranks in converted shops, showing their 40-second films, spread across the world. Robert W.Paul, a scientific instrument maker of Hatton Garden, London, made the happy discovery that Edison had neglected to patent the kinetoscope in England, and successfully embarked on the production of his own model.

In order to keep his customers supplied with films, Paul collaborated with a photographer, Birt Acres, on the production of a motion picture camera, with which, in the early part of 1895, they made the world's first films of news events – the Oxford and Cambridge Boat Race and the Derby.

Other Europeans were also stimulated to develop motion picture cameras in order to supply kinetoscope showmen with new

The Edison Kinetoscope, 1894

films. The brothers Lumière patented their cinématographe on February 13th 1895. Like Henri Joly's apparatus, patented six months later, this was 'reversible' – that is, capable of being used both as a camera and a projector. The race was already on successfully to project the films of the Edison kinetoscope.

The failure of Edison and Dickson themselves to take this step, which now seems so obvious, is not easy to explain. Either it was an uncharacteristic blindness to the ultimate direction and potential of cinema; or we should accept the statement apocryphally credited to Edison:

'We are making these peep show machines and selling a lot of them at a good profit. If we put out a screen machine there will be a use for maybe about ten of them in the whole United States. With that many screen machines you could show the pictures to everyone in the country – and then it would be done. Let's not kill the goose that lays the golden egg.'

Edison could not prevent the inevitable. Dickson himself was involved with two kinetoscope agents, the Latham brothers, in devising a projector, the Pantoptikon, renamed Eidoloscope, which was publicly shown in New York in April and May 1895. Charles Francis Jenkins and Thomas Armat showed their projecting Phantoscope at the Cotton States Exposition in Atlanta in September and October 1895. Finally accepting the fate of the peepshow kinetoscope, Edison was to acquire the rights in this machine which was thereupon boldly renamed and launched in April 1896 as the Edison Vitascope.

In Europe, credit for the first performance of motion pictures before a paying public goes to the brothers Max and Emil Skladanowsky, former magic lanternists, who on November 1, 1895 premiered their Bioscop at the Wintergarten theatre, Berlin. The Skladanowsky films are lively and of excellent quality, but their projection system, alternating frames from two parallel film bands in order to reduce flicker, was too complicated to survive.

Generally the Lumières take credit as founding fathers of the modern motion picture. Their machine was light, neat and versatile, serving as printer as well as camera and projector. In Paris on December 28 they began the first regular daily film projections, in the Salon Indien of the Grand Café, boulevard des Capucines. Backed by their own industrial organisation, they swiftly embarked on a skilful strategy of exploitation, despatching agents across the world, to accomplish the double function of promoting the cinématographe, and photographing exotic locations to enrich the burgeoning catalogue of Lumière films.

Thus the contributions of several centuries were to culminate to bring within everybody's reach the entertainment conceived by Della Porta for great men, and Scholars: 'in a dark Chamber by white sheets objected, one may see as clearly and perspicuously, as if they were before his eyes, Huntings, Banquets, Armies of Enemies, Plays, and all things else that one desireth'.

4 PREMIÈRE ON REGENT STREET

Joost Hunningher

On February 21, 1896 in the Great Hall at the Polytechnic Institution (now the University of Westminster) at 309 Regent Street, London, the first paying audience in Great Britain saw a projected moving picture show. Fifty four people paid one shilling (or if they were 'Poly' members six pence, half a shilling) each to see the Messieurs Auguste and Louis Lumière's film programme on their new invention the Ciné-matographe. This was a bigger audience than for the first commercial showing in Paris on December 28, 1895, when only thirty-two paid one franc each to see the show.

The importance of the 'Poly' event was that in a commercial sense the technology for projecting 'living photographic' images on a screen had arrived here. In sheer market terms, it was the birth of the film industry in Britain. British inventors and manufacturers of equipment responded quickly with other and cheaper machines, more theatre managers included film presentations in their variety shows and, to draw bigger audiences, demanded new programmes. Film makers responded.

The competition quickly became intense; choosing the most suitable equipment may have been as baffling as deciding on computer platforms and programmes today. British pioneers like Birt Acres and R.W. Paul were already working on problems of filming and projection. Acres was developing the Kinetic Lantern and Paul the Theatrograph. Acres, using the Paul-Acres camera, which was the product of their brief collaboration, had filmed the Boat Race and the Derby in Spring 1895.[1]

Acres, Paul and members of the Photography School at the Polytechnic Institution will have been aware of the work of Auguste and Louis Lumière. Their company, the Société Anonyme Antoine Lumière, was a well established photography company set up by their father Antoine in Lyons, producing photosensitive silver nitrate and bromide papers, as well as the 'extra-rapides à Etiquette Bleue' plates and 'Professor Lippman' colour plates. The Lumière film *Sortie d'Usine* shows Lumière employees leaving for their lunch break. The factory gates and number of employees indicate that the brothers were working within a well-capitalised and successful industrial base. Worldwide, only the Eastman Kodak factory in Rochester, New York was a bigger supplier of such photographic products.[2]

Auguste and Louis were in their early thirties and were already well known for their research and innovation into photo-chemistry.[3] In the summer of 1894, they had both seen Edison's Kinetoscope. A local exhibitor had even approached them to make films for the Kinetoscope that would be cheaper than the high prices charged by Edison's agents.[4] The brothers realised immediately that the Kinetoscope was limited to one viewer and set out to design a system for audience viewing. A prototype was developed by Auguste and Charles Moisson.[5] However, it did not work properly and it was Louis, adapting a concept from a sewing machine, who came up with the design for an intermittent mechanism which was able to hold film stationary (for exposure or projection purposes) before advancing it to the next frame at a rate of 15 times per second. By early 1895 'they succeeded in producing and perfecting a combined

GREAT HALL PARLIAMENT

camera, printer and projector for taking, printing and projecting a series of photographs in rapid sequence upon a band of celluloid film. For this invention they were granted a patent in France, no. 245,032 on February 13, 1895 and an English patent, no. 7,187, for the same invention on April 8, 1895.[6] In 1895, The French magazine *La Nature* had run a four-page article[7] on the Cinématographe including detailed technical drawings and illustrations. A précis of this article was carried in a supplement of *The British Journal of Photography*. It ended thus: 'An exhibition was given on July 11 at the offices of the *Revue Générale des Sciences*, at which the evolutions of the cuirassiers, a house on fire, a factory, street scenes, and a dinner party were shown on the screen, and were much admired'.[8]

The Polytechnic Institution, The Great Hall (with 'Parliament' in session) and the Marlborough Room, 1896

MARLBOROUGH ROOM

It is certainly no coincidence that both Paul and Acres decided to show their own machines publicly on February 20 – which was the press night for the Lumière Cinématographe in the Great Hall.[9] The moving picture craze was on. Audiences were curious and by March 9 the Lumière Cinématographe was included in a twenty-minute slot in the variety show at the Empire Theatre, Leicester Square. Paul's Theatrograph opened at the Egyptian Hall variety show in Piccadilly on March 19.

Acres' Kinetic lantern (re-named the Kineopticon) opened at 2 Piccadilly Mansions in Piccadilly Circus on March 21. Other machines like J. Wrench's Cinematograph and William Routledge's Kineoptograph were on the market within months. They met the demand from music halls and theatres of varieties.

The opening stanzas of Mark Oute's poem in the *British Journal of Photography* summarise the competition:

> Such a bustle and a hurry
>   O'er the "living picture" craze,
> Rivals rushing, full of worry
>   In these advertising days.
>
> Each the first, and each the only
>   Each the others wildly chaff
> All of them proclaiming boldly
>   There's the first A-kind-o-graph,
>
> But it is a wonder really
>   How the constant flood of life
> O'er the screen keeps moving freely,
>   Full of action-stir and strife.[10]

SETTING UP IN LONDON

British film pioneers: Birt Acres (top) and R.W. Paul

In the February 19, 1896 edition of the *Polytechnic Magazine* there is an announcement referring to the rental of the Great Hall. 'Last Wednesday (February 12th) we were able to conclude an agreement by which we let out the Great Hall for three months from this evening (...) The Parliament,[11] which has hitherto held its meetings in the Great Hall every Wednesday evening, will in future meet in the Marlborough Room...'[12]

Who concluded this agreement with the Polytechnic Institution? Probably Antoine Lumière, the father of the two brothers. There is a letter from Louis to the Lumières' British agents, Fuerst Brothers, dated February 6, 1896, saying that his father was due to travel to London soon to make arrangements for the Cinématographe.

'We cannot however tell you exactly when he is going, though it will be soon.'[13] Certainly Antoine was at this point 'travelling the length and breadth of Europe to establish a network of Cinématographe franchises in principal cities'.[14] How long Antoine was in London or how often is not clear. However, in a legal action against the Anglo-Continental Company marketing a 'Kinematograph (French Cinematographe)', Antoine swore an affidavit at his London solicitors on March 31, 1896. He states that he is 'temporarily residing at Mathias Hotel, Arundel Street and that 'I am in partnership with my said sons and I am on their behalf at present exhibiting it [the Cinématographe] at the Polytechnic, Regent Street and also at the Empire theatre.'[15]

Certainly Antoine had been in charge of the Paris première on December 28, 1895,[16] and he had also been involved in the decision to put the exhibition of the Cinématographe in Britain under the management of his friend the shadowgraphist and juggler, Félicien Trewey. Trewey had featured in several Lumière films shot in 1895 – *Assiettes tournantes, Chapeaux à Transformation*, and he is the drinking card player on the right in *Une Partie d'E-carté.*

Trewey was a suitable choice for the London launch in that he had

The Polytechnic Institution, 1896

played the Alhambra in London in 1888 'where his act was billed as number six and eight respectively on the programmes for July and September. In the former, he is listed as "Mons. Trewey, The Fantaisiste, Humoristique, in this Shadowgraph Entertainment.""[17] In the autumn of 1895 Trewey was working in New York. Antoine met up with him there and persuaded him to take on the London presentation. Trewey had some practice before London. He returned to Lyons and took some part in the first public showing there on January 25, 1896.[18]

The choice of the Great Hall at the Polytechnic Institution was consistent with the Lumières' cautious marketing approach. There are at least four good reasons why the Polytechnic was chosen. First, it was renowned as a centre for promoting science, technology and education; it called itself 'The Pioneer Institute for Technical Education'. The subjects the Lumières were interested in were well established there. In 1883, under the headship of inventor Howard Farmer, the Institution established the first School of Photography in the world. (The prospectus claimed it was 'The First and uniformly most Successful School of Photography in the World.') Given their interest in photo-chemistry, Antoine Lumière and Howard Farmer must have been aware of each other. The *Polytechnic Magazine* had printed a portrait of and article on Thomas Alva Edison[19] and in January 1896 announced that 'two of Edison's latest inventions are now on exhibition in the Entrance Hall – the Kinetophone which, by a conjunction of photography and the phonograph, enables one to listen to music and watch serpentine dancing at the same time; and the Kinetoscope, by which means apparently living pictures are exhibited; such for instance as a fire scene in which the fireman is shown on duty in a most realistic manner.'[20] Secondly, before 1881, when it was the Royal Polytechnic Institution,[21] the Poly was world-famous for its lantern slide and visual effect entertainments.[22]

THE CINEMATOGRAPHE
M TREWEY APPEARS.

Trewey, *Illustrated Sporting and Dramatic News*, November 28, 1896

In a BBC Radio broadcast in 1948 the pioneer British film-maker Cecil Hepworth said that 'in stable parlance the cinematograph might be described as "by Magic Lantern out of Camera" and the old Poly would certainly have been its birthplace.'[22] We can get a feel of the effectiveness of Polytechnic Lantern Slides from a vivid account written in the 1890s. 'When Mr. Hill[24] had "worked his wicked will" upon his subject, it had grown to a series of no less than sixteen slides – one view and fifteen effects. There are goblins coming out of graves, leaping over tombstones, steaming out of windows, standing on their heads and sinking into the ground.... This series includes one of the best effects ever produced at the Polytechnic, "Sunset on the Lake of Constance." By means of a number of sliding plates, the effect (which includes five slides) of the gradual change of tint on the mountains and water, as the fiery ball slowly sinks, is wonderfully rendered.'[25]

Earlier, in 1869, Charles Dickens had made even an experiment with electricity feel like cinema. 'In the darkened theatre at the Polytechnic, the long flash lights up the room and the audience with the peculiar lurid glare so well known as an effect of brilliant lightning at night, and displays the features of action of every one present. But it is curious to note that, the flash being of instantaneous duration only, it allows no *motion* to be seen. We should think, if guided by our consciousness alone, that the flash lasted an appreciable time; but this would be an error, due to the persistence of the impression on the eye, after the flash itself had ceased. (...) And if the spectators all raise their arms and wave their hands to and fro as quickly as they can, the flash will display the position of the arms, but not the movement of the hands. While the flash lasts, the hand has no time to move, and is consequently seen, as if motionless, in the position in which the flash finds it.'[26]

Matt Raymond, 1924

Thirdly, the large and enthusiastic Polytechnic French Society staged popular events which must have attracted a large following among the London French Community. It organised a 'French Evening of Entertainment' in the Great Hall on June 19, 1895. Nearly 500 people attended and the event was written up in the *Courrier de Londres:* 'Lundi dernier a eu lieu au Polytechnic Institute une soirée entièrement française sous la présidence de M. Marcel Raymond (...) La soirée s'est terminée par *la Marseillaise.*'[27]

Finally, the Polytechnic had two large halls in a central location where hall rentals might have been agreed sympathetically or even on a profit sharing basis.

THE SCREENING

The Press night took place in the Great Hall. The written accounts from publications in February and March are so varied that it is likely that some of the reviews may have been written about later screenings. According to Rittaud-Hutinet, Trewey was the operator on the 20th.[28] Some of the films were too dark, and according to some reviews the projection was inconsistent. To judge by the review in *Photography,* Trewey seems to have had considerable technical problems: 'The exhibition was given to the press in the large hall of the Polytechnic, Regent Street, and after keeping all the representatives of the press, both ladies and gentlemen, cooling their heels for about half an hour, they were admitted. (...) Other pictures include three men playing cards and drinking, but this was far too quick, and the movements were absurdly hurried, this, however, was doubtless due to the apparatus not being quite perfect....one noticeable feature of the show was the very poor illumination of the pictures. (...) Throughout all of the pictures we are bound to say that there was far too much flicker, reminding one altogether of the joggle of the Kinetoscope.'[29]

Trewey's decision to keep the press outside 'cooling their heels' may have covered a last minute attempt to improve the quality of the image. He then seems to have let a 20 year old Polytechnic electrician called Matt Raymond adapt the power supply from 10 amperes to 15 or even 30. He also experimented with the water condenser to concentrate the light from the scissor-pattern arc lamp.[30] The image was considerably improved. Very quickly Trewey recognises Raymond's abilities and 'augmente son salaire et devient son ami' (increases his salary and becomes his friend.)[31] After that 'the only gentleman M. Trewey would trust with the equipment as well as the electrical arrangements was Mr. Matt Raymond. (...) Trewey placed sole reliance upon him for the correct supply of electrical current and proper control of the arc lamp, no small undertaking.'[32]

The Great Hall .

The size of the picture was 6 feet by 4 foot 6 inches and the throw was 60 feet. According to the *Entr'acte*, 'the whole "show" only occupies seventeen minutes, several of which are taken up by the gentleman who acts as a chorus to the play, and furnishes the necessary information anent the pictures and their special features. This role is well and ably performed by Mr. Francis...'[33]

Despite the teething problems, there were some very good reviews. The *Polytechnic Magazine* of February 26, 1896 carried the following: 'The Great Hall has been let for the next three months. Last Thursday it was opened with a special exhibition of a new invention by MM. Auguste and Louis Lumière – The Cinématographe – It is, briefly, living photography, if this term may be used, shown on a screen in the same way as are dissolving views by oxy-hydrogen lantern. The effect is really most wonderful. For instance, a photograph of a railway station is shown, two or three seconds elapse and a train steams into the station and stops, the carriage doors open, the people get out, and there is the usual hurrying and scurrying for a second or two, and then again the train moves off. The whole thing is realistic, and is, as a matter of fact, an actual photograph.'[34]

Later in an interview with a correspondent from *The Bioscope*, Trewey recalled the first showing as 'a memorable performance. The whole of the London Press, as well as every circus, music-hall and theatre manager in London were invited. After the films (...) the screen was drawn up, disclosing on the stage Trewey ready to entertain his guests at a magnificent banquet.'[35] Such a theatrical invitation to a reception seems in keeping with Trewey's sense of playfulness and certainly there is a large stage behind the screen in The Great Hall which makes such a banquet possible.

Barnes uses a long and enthusiastic review by Anna de Bremont in the *St Paul's Magazine*. She claimed that 'a distinctively representative Press and artistic gathering assembled to pass judgment on the new sensation, a judgment which was not only favourable, but enthusiastic. (...) The most lavish in their praises of Messrs. Lumières' marvelous invention were the representative London photographic artists present. Mr Van de Weyde declared it so wonderful that it left him 'breathless' with surprise; whilst Mr Downey pronounced it the most marvellous degree of perfection in the way of photography that the art had theretofore attained.'[36] I can't believe that Anna de Bremont was at the first press screening so panned by the *Photographer* reviewer. While the latter writes about seeing the screening in 'the Larger Hall', de Bremont describes seeing the programme in the Marlborough Hall (also known within the Institution as the Marlborough Room). On December 29, 1896, the *Polytechnic Magazine* issued a frameable memento of the Polytechnic showing both the Great Hall and the smaller Marlborough Room/Hall.

The screenings of the Cinématographe were moved to the Marlborough Hall, but probably not until after the week-end, on Monday, February 24. The commemorative photograph taken at the beginning of the run shows the Cinématographe sign above the entrance to the Great Hall. A sign indicates that the Marlborough Hall is to let.

On Wednesday February 26 the following advertisement appeared in *TheTimes.*'The Cinématographe.Living PHOTOGRAPHS REPRODUCED in movement, life size by means of the Cinématographe of Messrs. A. and L. Lumière, Marlborough-hall, the Polytechnic, Regent Street, Daily (every hour from 2 to 10). Only 54 people came the first day (Friday). Admission 1s.'[37]

We can only speculate as to why the exhibition had moved to the Marlborough Hall. If only 54 people had turned up on February 21 then perhaps the smaller hall would be more suitable and cheaper. Or there may have been an electrical reason. It's possible that the Marlborough Hall provided a stronger current and thus a better light source to solve the 'poor illumination' problem referred to in the *Photography* review. What the change of hall does indicate is how portable the Cinématographe is. It meant that Trewey, with one machine, could organise shows in different venues.

And this is exactly what he did, giving the management of the Empire Theatre of Varieties in Leicester Square a demonstration on February 28 and a 'sneak preview' on March 7. *Entr'acte* had complained that the screening in the Polytechnic was rather grim:

'At the Marlborough Rooms they were given in all nakedness; not so much as a pianoforte accompanied their parade. At the Empire, with musical accessories, they should be much more attractive.'[38] This would suggest there was no musical accompaniment at the Polytechnic. However, according to Robb Lawson in the commemorative programme of 1936, 'the titles were announced by Francis Pochet, who filled up the pauses between each with descriptive speeches, while the operator-electrician, Matt Raymond, changed the reel of film ready for the next picture. A musical accompaniment was provided by a pianist, who supplied simple improvisations based on popular tunes.'[39]

If there was music some of the time or never is another unsolved question. The same is true of the running order of the films, which probably varied quite considerably between days and perhaps even between performances. From the *Entr'acte* account of the sneak preview at the Empire, it is clear that the performances were quite flexible and allowed for encores and even running films like *Fall of a Wall* forwards and then backwards. A Polytechnic Lumière Programme exists which is dated (in a hand-written addition) April 17, 1896. Its order is as follows: 1. The Landing Stage; 2. Boating; 3. Place des Cordeliers

(Lyon); 4. The Biter Bit; 5. Arrival of a Train in a Country Station; 6. Practical Joke on the Gardener; 7. Babies Playing; 8. Fall of a Wall; 9. Trewey's "Under the Hat"; 10. Bathing in the Mediterranean.

This programme consists completely of early French titles and does not yet include any British scenes. Later, Trewey and Raymond also shot London scenes like *Ludgate Circus, Changing of Guards – St. James's Palace*, and *The London Fire Brigade at Southwark*.

Within two years, Lumière cameramen were sent to most corners of Europe, Africa, Asia and the United States. They landed in New York in May 1896. Edison had held his first public projection on a screen at the Kostner and Bials Music Hall that April. However, Edison's "New wonder", the Vitascope, was quickly outdistanced by the Lumière films at Keith Music Hall. Edison's camera, the Kentograph, weighed more than 1,100 pounds. It was impractical for shooting outside away from an electrical power source. Edison filmed in his West Orange Studio, known as the "Black Maria", while Lumière's hand-cranked camera filmed life on the streets.[40] The quality of Lumiere's street life is exactly what Anna de Bremont praised in her review in *St Paul's Magazine*: 'It is the most perfect illusion that has heretofore been attempted in photography (...) Pictures are thrown on a screen through the medium of the 'Cinématographe' with a realism that baffles description. People move about, enter and disappear, gesticulate, laugh, smoke, eat, drink and perform the most ordinary actions with a fidelity to life that leads one to doubt the evidence of one's senses.'[41] Like the screenings in Paris where the Cinématographe 'flourished in two theatres,'[42]

POLYTECHNIC.

LUMIÈRE
CINEMATOGRAPHE

1. The Landing Stage
2. Boating
3. Place des Cordeliers   (Lyon)
4. The Biter Bit
5. **Arrival of a Train in a Country Station**
6. Practical Joke on the Gardener
7. Babies Playing
8. **Fall of a Wall**
9. Trewey's "Under the Hat"
10. **Bathing in the Mediterranean.**

Under the management of Mons. TREWEY

ORIGINALITY not IMITATION.

FRANCIS FOCHET

the Lumière screenings in London became a great success and were financially rewarding to Trewey and the Lumières. The standard financial arrangement with the Lumières was that the Cinématographe plus films were provided for 50% of the box office gross.[43] Another Lumière employee called Paul Lacroix was also in London with responsibilities for the box office.[44] Unfortunately the financial records are lost, but given that in November, 1896 one had to book ten weeks in advance for a seat at the Empire, we can be sure that Trewey and the Lumières made a pretty penny.[45] Later, when Trewey was asked how much money he had made from the London exhibitions, he side stepped the question with, 'I am not a commercial man, but an artist and a philosopher.'[46]

Programme for a matinée performance at the Polytechnic, April 1896

In August, *The Era* reported, 'the attractions of M. Lumière's Cinématographe are endless, and from time to time M. Trewey, who is in charge of this novel exhibition, adds subjects that appeal readily to every class of society. For instance, at the Empire nightly cheers are raised by the excellent representation of a steeplechase. The gallant steeds come along at racing speed towards the footlights, and then pass from the field of view, and the next picture – the finish on the flat – is most exciting.'[47] The Lumière screenings continued at the Empire for 18 months, with regular matinées at the Polytechnic until July, 1896, when Matt Raymond began commercial screenings at Crystal Palace.

Apparently the five months run at the Polytechnic could have ended in disaster. For Trewey claimed that the only near-accident he ever had with the Cinématographe happened in the Marlborough Hall. 'I was sitting in the hall, as usual, very closely watching the screen; suddenly I saw the shadow of flames before me. I am an acrobat, you know, and I can tell you I literally bounded up the stairs to the operating box, where I found my men panic-stricken. Grabbing a wet blanket, I quickly enveloped the machine and films. Five minutes later the show was running as smoothly as before.The spectators never knew how narrowly a fire had been averted.'[48]

As cinema developed, the Cinématographe lost its cutting edge. First, its one round hole perforations meant that Lumière films were not interchangeable with the more widely used Edison Standard and, secondly, the magazine initially made it impossible to take anything longer than a 50 foot length of film. The film craze moved on.

Trewey returned to France and bought a circus. Matt Raymond didn't return to the Poly. He continued in the cinema projection trade installing projectors in the provinces and organising screenings in Belgium, Holland, Germany and France.

The Lumière brothers continued to innovate. Louis designed a wraparound screen 20 feet high and 65 feet in diameter for the 1900 World's Fair in Paris, a camera with a revolving lens which covered 360 degrees. Louis and Auguste continued working on creating a photographic colour process. They experimented with potato flour and dyes and by 1905, they had patented Autochrome. This became so popular that by 1914 the Lumière factory was manufacturing 6000 plates of Autochrome per day. In 1935, Louis invented a stereoscopic 35-millimeter movie camera and filmed another train at the station in La Ciotat.[49] Both continued to research and take out new patents until their deaths. They were honoured for their achievements, but not for accepting decorations from the Vichy government.[50]

By 1936, 20 million people in the UK were going to the 'pictures' every week. In that year the Polytechnic School of Kinematography organised a 40th Anniversary Lumière Celebration. Louis Lumière attended. At a celebration lunch Cecil Hepworth, referring to the 50 foot length of Lumière films, said, 'Half a minute? How much some of us in the trade long that some of the ten thousand footers took less! Your half-minute was a flash of genius.[51] That Friday evening Louis Lumière attended the première in Leicester Square of the Wells-Korda picture *Things to Come*.

NOTES

1. See John Barnes, *The Beginnings of the Cinema in England*, David & Charles, 1976, pp. 26-32. There is controversy over which camera Acres used on those occasions. Barnes, on the basis of a photograph of Acres on location, argues that it was the Paul-Acres camera, although Acres in *The Amateur Photographer*, October 9, 1896, p. 298, claimed to have been the first to have made a portable film camera.

2. Glenn Myrent, 'When The Movies Began and No One Came', *New York Times*, December 29, 1985, pp. 19 & 22.

3. In their lifetimes they took out over 350 patents concerning photographic applications. Figure given by Maurice Trarieux-Lumière, 'Preface', Auguste and Louis Lumière, *Letters*, ed Jacques Rittaud-Hutinet, Faber & Faber, 1995, p. ix.

4. Brian Coe, *Muybridge & The Chronophotographers*, Museum of the Moving Image, 1992, p. 50.

5. Auguste and Louis Lumière, op. cit., p. 311.

6. Will Day, 'The First Public Exhibition of Kinematography', *The Photographic Journal*, October 1924, p. 488.

7. *La Nature, Revue des Sciences et de leurs Applications aux Arts et à l'Industrie*, Masson, Libraire de L'Académie de Médecine, 1895, pp. 215-218. Translation reproduced as Appendix I of Auguste and Louis Lumière, op. cit., pp. 301-302.

8. *The British Journal of Photography*, Supplement, September 6, 1895, p.72. Reproduced in Richard Brown, *The Lumière Cinématographe: the first six Months in England, with an account of Strategy and Price Trends in the early English Film Business*, 1993, p. 17. Copies in the National Film and Television Archive and the Library of the University of Westminster.

9. R.W. Paul showed his Theatrograph at Finsbury Technical College while Birt Acres withdrew from showing his Kinetic Lantern to members of the London and Provincial Photographic Association. In the February 28 edition of *The British Journal of Photography*, p. 138, he apologised for his non-appearance. His machines were 'in the hands of the best London mechanics, but unfortunately they were slow and he was unable to show his latest improvements. He invited all present to a private view in Piccadilly Circus, where he intended to exhibit his machine...'

10. *The British Journal of Photography*, December 4, 1896, p. 93. I am grateful to Stephen Bottomore for showing me this item in his collection of poems about early cinema.

11. The Polytechnic Parliament was a debating society which borrowed its form from Westminster. The Polytechnic Liberals were in power with the Conservatives in the 'role of opposition'. There was an Independent Labour Party with 'their manifesto in favour of Socialism' and a 'new fashioned Radicals' party. All parties had Leaders, Foreign Secretaries and whips, etc., and debated current political issues. For example, in the *Polytechnic Magazine* of January 22, 1896, p. 37, it was announced that 'In our Parliament to-night Dr. Lunn will introduce a motion in favour of putting an end to the Armenian horrors by dethroning the Sultan and dividing Turkey among the Powers of Europe.'

12. The *Polytechnic Magazine*, Wednesday, February 19, 1896, p. 93.

13. Auguste and Louis Lumière, op. cit., p. 116.

14. ibid., note 1.

15. Richard Brown. op. cit., p. 28.

16. Auguste and Louis Lumière, op. cit., p. 84.

17. John Barnes, op. cit., p. 83.

18. See Jacques Rittaud-Hutinet, *Le Cinéma des Origines: les Frères Lumière et Leurs Opérateurs*, Champ Vallon, Lyons, 1985, p. 190. See also Jacques Rittaud-Hutinet, *Les 1000 Premiers Films*, Philippe Sers, Paris, 1990, p. 233.

19. October 10, 1894, p. 190.

20. January 22, 1896, p. 39.

21. It lost the title 'Royal' when it went bankrupt in 1881.

22. See the essays by Roberta McGrath and Mervyn Heard in this volume.

23. 'Lumière and the Early Days of Film-Making', *The Listener,* August 19, 1948, pp. 267-269. This is a shortened version of a broadcast Cecil Hepworth made on the Third Programme, August 3. His recording is in the BBC Archive on long-playing record no. 12116-8.

24. W.R. Hill was a famous optical scene artist who worked on Polytechnic Lantern Shows for 35 years. His partner had been H.L. Childe.

25. Edmund H.Wilke, 'Old Polytechnic Slides', *Magic Lantern Journal,* April 1894, reprinted in eds David Crompton, David Henry, Stephen Herbert, *Magic Images,* The Magic Lantern Society of Great Britain, 1990, p. 89.

26. Charles Dickens, 'Playing With Lightning', *All Year Round,* May 29, 1869, pp. 619-620.

27. The *Polytechnic Magazine,* June 19, 1895, p. 320.

28. Jacques Rittaud-Hutinet, *Le Cinéma des Origines,* p. 199.

29. *Photography,* February 27, 1896, p. 143.

30. Jacques Rittaud-Hutinet, *Le Cinéma des Origines,* p. 199.

31. ibid.

32. Will Day, *The Photographic Journal,* October 1924, p. 492.

33. *Entr'acte,* March 7, 1896, p. 6.

34. *Polytechnic Magazine,* February 26, 1896, p. 107.

35. John Cher, 'Who is the Father of the Trade?', *The Bioscope,* October 17,1912, p.187. With thanks to Stephen Bottomore for showing me this article.

36. *St Paul's Magazine,* March 7, 1896, p. 436, quoted by John Barnes, op. cit., pp. 84-86.

37. *The Times,* February 26, 1896, p. 1.

38. *Entr'acte,* March 7, 1896, p. 6.

39. The Lumière Celebration Commemorative Programme, 1936, p. 15 .

40. Glenn Myrent, op. cit., pp. 19 & 22.

41. *St. Paul's Magazine,* op. cit., and John Barnes, op. cit.

42. Glenn Myrent, op. cit., p. 22.

43. Auguste and Louis Lumière, op.cit., p.107, Letter to the Marquis d'Osmond, January 23, 1896.

44. Auguste and Louis Lumière, op.cit., p.123.

45. *Illustrated Sporting and Dramatic News,* November 28,1896, p.491. With thanks to Stephen Bottomore for showing me this article.

46. John Cher, op. cit., p.187

47. *The Era,* August 1, 1896, p. 16. Note the description of the cut between shots.

48. John Cher, op. cit., p.189

49. Glenn Myrent, op. cit., p. 22.

50. Both brothers accepted Pétain's Francisque decoration. Louis served as a member of his National Council. Auguste's son Henri was an early Resistance fighter.

51. *To-Day's Cinema,* February 21, 1936, p. 3.

5 FRAMEUP

John L. Fell

'The Lumière Cinématographe will begin its fifteenth consecutive week at the Wonderland next week, continuing what was long ago the longest run ever made by any one attraction in this city. People go to see it again and again, for even the familiar views reveal some new feature with each successive exhibition.'[1]

Screen images metamorphosed their shapes and functions. Athanasius Kircher's magic lantern circles reappear in the American Fireman's 'dream balloon' of his wife and child.[2] Other magic lantern throws organised themselves pragmatically, as with the Phantasmagoria. The 'cels' of Reynaud's animated figures were drawn as if on a film strip, square like many newspaper comics, but the Théâtre Optique staged its movements within a painted, rectangular projection.

Early photographs often took their forms cropped after the fact. Daguerre's frame of reference was the rounded camera obscura image, and his portraits were merchandised as ovals, like the collodion process ambrotypes. A variation was an upright rectangle: squared base with an arched top. Stereograph cards carried the same design.

Barque sortant du Port, 1895

Subject matter could dictate composition (columns, statues). When his nudes jumped or bent over, Muybridge composed vertically, horizontally if they walked or if animals ran. Painting and theatre encouraged other sorts of formal self-consciousness. Used as lantern slides, glass plates simulated proscenium entertainment: that is, wider rectangles.[3] Song slides tended toward the rectangular and so did Alexander Black's photoplay *Miss Jerry*. In the famous *New York Herald* drawing of Koster and Bial's Edison performance the screen is elaborately framed. In the famous poster showing an audience engaged by *L'Arroseur arrosé* the screen is edged by theatrical draw curtains; we still part curtains to introduce feature films.

The Lumières' projections roughly measured out in a three-to-four aspect ratio, dimensions common to nineteenth century painting, the so-called Golden Section: $a/b = b/a + b$

The smaller is related to the larger as the larger is to the sum of both, proportions of the postal card or of the Lumières' own Autochrome colour transparencies.

Film borders served a pair of functions. They excluded, and they defined space and movement inside the frame. People and vehicles came and went as if toward or from the wings, but that had been happening in still photography and in Impressionist painting for quite a while. What disappeared seems to have caused little stir.

Like time, offscreen space assumes validity when film segments are joined. Thereafter what's unscened, presumed to maintain continuity with the seen, assumes a different role even in single-shot films. *A Chess Dispute* (R.W. Paul, 1903) makes the point.

Lumière films rarely look artfully composed in the manner of academic still photography. *Niagara Falls* (1896) seems an anomaly, its composition apparently defined by exigencies of camera placement. Otherwise organisation within the frame is functional, like scene-of-the-crime police photos: the corpse in context. Closeups of the photographer's babies excepted, there's lots of 'air'.

Joining surface to space, locales resemble unused sets, like the ominous Paris scenes that Eugène Atget documented, their buildings and streets poised for who knows what occupancy. In the first *mise en scène*, the Lumières cue in performers; and a pair of curtains figuratively parts. Assuming entertainment and neo-realist roles, the amateur players begin to refine audience expectations.

The new idiom stimulated curiosity. Things go by so quickly. Unlike stage action, movement took place anywhere on the screen's illuminated surface. As in a painting, a point of attention escaped gravity. Fortunately the strips were short, and they were reaccessible. Writers describe returning to the repetitious event hoping finally to seize on something they'd not registered at once, perhaps not quite understood, even though the photography seemed to be simply and innocently descriptive (those fluttering leaves). Everything was stubbornly *there:* honest and naïve.

What remained really to understand? A hundred years' perspective informs the question with more complication than clarity. Distanced by time and space, mystery inevitably attends old documents, but photography itself can no longer fall back on its guileless posture.

If we examine something long enough do we discover more? In the 1960s independent film-makers like Andy Warhol and Michael Snow subjected us to interminable single shot films, appearing to enlarge our options for re-examination. In fact, we found that perceptions shifted alarmingly. Watching something overlong we endlessly changed our minds. Rustling in the seats we turned into John Cage accompaniment to the silent images.

Starting as 'trick films', manipulated entertainments re-energised ideological suspicions toward photography. Recall the Godard/Gorin *Letter to Jane* (1972). Remember John Berger's analysis of the dead Che Guevara's photograph.

Forced into testimony, photography's planes stammered, caught among surface truths, self-deceptions that followed from misreadings, and some artists' confidence in the lens's discerning eye. Susan Sontag quotes Nathaniel Hawthorne's *The House of Seven Gables* (1851), where a Salem photographer describes the Daguerreotype, 'While we give it credit only for depicting the merest surface, it actually brings out the secret character with a truth that no painter would ever venture upon, could even he detect it.'[4]

But consider too another deposition, made by one recently 'reading' a Massachusetts daguerreotype which dates from Hawthorne's time:

Barque sortant du Port

'A homely girl with oddly dead eyes, set too far apart and flat as the eyes of a stunned fish in your stagnant bowl – or could she be warming to the verge of a blush and a big-toothed smile? A lopsided face, bigger on her right, a skewed part in the dark horsehair above the high forehead, unmatched eyebrows, a fleshy nose, unpainted, bruised lips, an ample chin and a tall strong neck.'[5]

The daguerreotype's subject is Emily Dickinson, who once wrote

> *I am afraid to own a body –*
> *I am afraid to own a soul –*
> *Profound – precarious property –*
> *Possession, not optional –*[6]

Does photography clothe secrets or do its subjects? When do images lie? When are they trustworthy? When may they be lies that tell the truth?

The Lumière topology is stubborn: bricks, gravel, stucco, cement, snow. Expanses of foreground dominate, distancing us in a world of long shots. Closer in, a table substitutes for ground (*Repas de Bébé*, 1895). In *Une Partie d'Ecarté* (1895) we study the background leaves, but they hardly budge. Pedestrians parallel a train's departure in *Leaving Jerusalem by Railway* (1896). We watch alterations in the ground. Its changes echo the diversity of Jerusalem's cityscape, visible on rises in the background. Reassuring surfaces seem to overcome muteness.

Structures hide more than they reveal, like the felled wall (*Démolition d'un Mur*, 1896) which had obscured trees. The Congressists attending the conference of Photographic Societies in Lyons, disembarking down a gangplank, half-reveal the interior of their vessel (*Arrivée des Congressistes à Neuville-sur-Saône*, 1895). When the factory door opens so that Lumière workers can depart (*Sortie d'Usine*, 1895) we glimpse iron beams and lattice work supporting the building's roof, but we can never see the business's infrastructure. If photographs acknowledge the visible, they refuse to discuss it.

The movement of surfaces may cast shadows, like those on a train platform, or reflections, as with the cars passing (Time of day? Direction? Season? *Arrivée d'un Train en Gare de La Ciotat*, 1895). Combine human and object movement, and fresh possibilities arise, fortuitous *mise en scène*.

On the distant platform at La Ciotat a single figure almost flinches although he's under no danger, then turns to watch the train approach. On the near platform people alternately seek seats and wait on the arrivals of friends and family. Descending, one man glances at the camera without breaking his stride. Unimpressed, he proceeds. A woman lowers her eyes. Preoccupied, most figures pay little mind. A maxim of the North American Leacock-styled cinéma-vérité argued that a protagonist sufficiently absorbed in his own concerns turned oblivious to a camera's presence. Were the Lumières and their camera often invisible because they were unthreateningly unfamiliar?

Some behaviour is stagy, like in *Bataille de Boules de Neige*, (1896). The battlers throw snowballs randomly and finally settle on a questionably convenient bicyclist. Everyone's being told what to do.

In an article titled 'Let there be Lumière'[7], Dai Vaughan paid tribute to *Barque sortant du Port* (1895), a film he had remembered with affection for thirty years and re-viewed periodically. Three men negotiate choppy seas in a rowboat while members of the Lumière family watch events from the vantage of a little nearby pier.

On examination, uncontrolled elements lend a special interest to the film. The boat's departure has an improvised quality because the sea is active, making the trip venturesome. With its bobbing waves the Mediterranean assumes a part. Flat-lighting murky skies cast no shadows. Water dominates the screen, and the men at sea would hold our attention fast except that the jetty's height establishes a second playing space. It's a nice composition. The boat reacts to the waves. The women react to the boat, and we react to both. Like a plaything in *Babies Playing* (1895) and the structured garden in *L'Arroseur arrosé*, the spectators' costumes describe the turn-of-the-century French bourgeoisie.

Outward bound, the oarsmen work against the tide, commanding our sympathy. The women watch, intrigued if not overly interested. One waves briefly to the men. It's all intended to be an amusement for the children. Each woman turns to fuss with a charge's costume or hair. Everyone's gaze is diverted. An adult half-exits from the frame, leaving two children and the other woman. Neither child seems very involved. As the boat shifts course, it's struck broadside by a wave – a big hit, but no-one's watching any more.

Action (the men in the boat) describes character. Reaction (the women) implies motive and suggests narrative. As witnesses, our engagement is encouraged by images which have turned momentarily emblematic: complacent times. Sarajevo was noted for its Moorish architecture, the Marne for good champagne.

NOTES

1. *The Post Express,* Rochester, New York, February 6, 1897, quoted in George C. Pratt, *Spellbound in Darkness,* New York Graphic Society, Greenwich, Connecticut, 1966, pp.15-16.

2. Although Lincoln shows up vertical with unarticulated edges in *Uncle Tom's Cabin.*

3. Newspaper promotion did it too. See ed. Stanley Appelbaum, *Scenes from the Nineteenth Century Stage in Advertising Woodcuts,* Dover, NY, 1977.

4. Susan Sontag, *On Photography,* Farrar, Strauss and Giroux, NY, 1973.

5. Reynolds Price, 'What's in a Picture', *Civilization,* September-October 1995, p. 96.

6. Emily Dickinson, *Complete Poems,* ed. Thomas H. Johnson, Faber & Faber, London, 1970, p. 493.

7. Dai Vaughan, 'Let there be Lumière', in ed. Thomas Elsaesser, *Early Cinema,* BFI 1990, pp. 63-7. Originally published in *Sight and Sound,* Spring 1981.

6 FILMING SCENES IN THE UNITED KINGDOM for the Cinématographe Lumière

John Barnes

One of the wonders of the Cinématographe was the wide range of subjects covered by the Lumière operators. This coverage was worldwide; among the territories visited were Russia, Japan, China, India, Turkey, Egypt, Mexico, South America and the United States, as well as most of the countries of Europe. As far as the British Isles were concerned, the Lumière catalogues list no fewer than 71 scenes.[1]

Probably the first Lumière film to be shot in England was *Entrée du Cinématographe/Entrance to the Cinematograph Exhibition* (no. 250), which showed the outside of the Empire Theatre of Varieties, Leicester Square, where Félicien Trewey was exhibiting the Cinématographe Lumière from a few weeks after its opening at the Polytechnic Institution. Trewey was a famous conjurer and shadowgraphist, a friend of the Lumières and holder of the sole concession for exhibiting the apparatus in Great Britain. During 1896 and until June 1897 the Cinématographe was not available on the open market[2] but was leased out to various exhibitors and restricted to various countries or areas. Since the apparatus was a combined camera, printer and projector, it was a simple matter for exhibitors to take films in the localities in which they operated. Trewey too acted as his own cameraman and probably shot the scene outside the Empire Theatre. It is also likely that he filmed other scenes in the vicinity such as *Danseuses des Rues/London Street Dancers* (no. 249), *Hyde Park* (no. 251), and perhaps other London street scenes too. Conjurers and magicians were very adept at handling the intricate stage machinery required in their acts and the mechanism of the Cinématographe would have presented no problems for an experienced performer like Trewey. Trewey's assistant, the young Englishman Matt Raymond, may well also have taken some of the English views subsequently listed in the official catalogues.

Negatives taken abroad would first be sent to the Lumière factory in Lyons, where they would be developed, printed and vetted for future inclusion in the lists. Perhaps that is why the Lumière films maintained such a high degree of excellence.

When the Cinématographe Lumière was de-restricted in June 1897, several firms in England acted as agents for the Lumière films and apparatus. Among these were Maguire and Baucus (later Warwick

Trading Co.), Philip Wolff, H. Jasper Redfern and Fuerst Brothers. Jules Fuerst of the latter firm became an able cinematographer of news films, and among his most notable achievements were the films he took of Queen Victoria's Diamond Jubilee Procession on June 21, 1897. He is known to have operated a Cinématographe[3] on this occasion and it seems more than likely that some of the Jubilee films listed in the Lumière catalogues were taken by him. As Fuerst Brothers had two cameramen on the route, it is now impossible to tell which scenes were taken by Jules himself.

In the same year the Lumières introduced their Triograph projector.[4] There were two models, Model A for use with regular Lumière films with round perforations and Model B for standard Edison ones. Henceforth, the Lumière films were issued with a choice of Lumière or Edison perforations.[5]

When the Triograph appeared at Gatti's famous music hall in Westminster Bridge Road, the guest of honour was the renowned Alexandre Promio, one of the Lumières' ace cameramen and operators, and for this occasion he ceremoniously operated the new projector himself.[6] Promio had been with the Lumières almost from the start. He introduced the Cinématographe into Spain, where he also took a number of Spanish subjects. He subsequently filmed in Belgium, Sweden, Turkey, Italy, Germany and the United States. It was during a

The London Fire Brigade at Southwark/Londres – Alerte de Pompiers, 1896

visit to Venice in 1896 that he shot the first of his remarkable 'panoramic views', as they were then called, and which we would now more properly refer to as travelling shots. Mounting his camera in a gondola, he took passing shots of the palaces and buildings lining the canals as he glided smoothly by (*Venise, Panorama du grand Canal pris d'un Bateau/Panorama of the Grand Canal taken from a Boat*, no. 295).

Promio's visit to Gatti's music hall therefore did not go unnoticed, since he was now something of a celebrity. During a private performance at Gatti's on October 21, 1897 he introduced a number of English and Irish views,[7] which he had probably photographed himself during his visit. Among the views were a travelling shot of the Mersey and Liverpool Docks photographed from the overhead railway in typical Promio fashion (*Liverpool, Panorama pris du Chemin de Fer électrique*, nos. 704-707).

It is not always easy to attribute a Lumière film to a particular cameraman, but we can be reasonably sure that Trewey, Matt Raymond, Jules Fuerst and Alexandre Promio all took films in the UK which were later shown worldwide and are to be found listed in the Lumière catalogues. Among the British Isles subjects were views of London, Liverpool, Belfast and Dublin. The coverage of Queen Victoria's Diamond Jubilee Procession through the streets of London resulted in a series of nine films (*Fêtes du Jubilé de la Reine d'Angleterre*, nos. 488-496), showing the procession from two different positions along the route.

The early Lumière films were never more than 17 metres (56 feet) long, because this was the total capacity of the Cinématographe Lumière when used as either a camera or a projector. They are the most carefully preserved of all early films. About 1,404 out of a total of some 1,500 films have been rediscovered and restored.[8]

NOTES

1. The Lumière catalogues have been reprinted in the following publications: John Barnes, *The Rise of the Cinema in Great Britain*, Bishopsgate Press, London, 1983; Jacques Rittaud-Hutinet, *Le Cinéma des Origines: les Frères Lumière et leurs Opérateurs* (Champ Vallon, Lyons, 1985) and *Auguste et Louis Lumière: les 1000 premiers Films*, Philippe Sers, Paris, 1990; Georges Sadoul, *Lumière et Méliès*, Lherminier, Paris, 1985.

2   *Amateur Photographer*, November 20, 1896, p. 409.

3.   ibid., July 23, 1897, p. 62.

4.   *The Era*, July 31, 1897, p. 16.

5.   *The Optician*, September 23, 1897, p. 122.

6.   *The Era*, October 23, 1897, p. 18(a).

7.   ibid., p. 19(c).

8.   For a fuller account of the Cinématographe Lumière in the U.K., see John Barnes, *The Beginnings of the Cinema in England*, David & Charles, 1976, revised and enlarged edition forthcoming.

7 MARKETING THE CINÉMATOGRAPHE IN BRITAIN

Richard Brown

There has long been interest in celebrating the anniversaries of commercial film presentation in Britain. Old issues of trade journals such as *The Kinematograph Weekly* and *The Bioscope* disclose that articles – and sometimes features – were specially produced for the 21st, 25th, 30th and 40th birthdays. The 1936 event, based at the 'School of Kinematography' at the Regent Street Polytechnic, was especially elaborate, and included the 'Lumière Celebration' at which M. Louis Lumière was the guest of honour. The formation in 1924 of the Cinema Veterans Society, membership of which was open to anyone who had been in the trade before 1903, was another indication of interest in the early days. Early attempts at recording the past were not antiquarian or academic, and while valuable material was preserved it was often overlaid by a depressingly formulaic pattern of myth-creation. In general, film pioneers active in the 1890s tended to be presented as few in number and existing in picturesquely primitive conditions.

One of the most striking features of the careful re-examination of this period which has taken place in recent years has been the realisation of just how far from the truth this favourite stereotype is. The extremely rapid spread of cinematography both nationally and internationally,[1] the surprisingly large numbers of people taking part, the range and variety of both film and equipment available, and even the amount of capital involved are all factors which indicate that a highly organised, competitive and professionally run business existed in England from the very beginning of film. Certainly no-one with even a superficial knowledge of the subject would now suggest that this was a 'primitive' period. Although research is still at an early stage, more and more evidence is being found of an economic structure within which the business was conducted, and of marketing skills of a level previously unsuspected. It is marketing which provides a particularly appropriate way to examine the progress in Britain of the Lumière Cinématographe, the machine which not only gave the first commercial film performance but which was also widely regarded at the time as representing a level of excellence that rivals tried to emulate.

Traditionally, accounts of the Lumières' involvement with film have stressed the innovatory technical aspects of their invention, and it was not until the early 1980s that this order of priority was first questioned and the suggestion arose that their films were more complex in structure than had previously been suspected.[2] With the recent publication of a selection of the private and business correspondence of Auguste and Louis Lumière, a better understanding is now possible of the commercial strategy they employed to promote the Cinématographe.[3] Originally there seems to have been a difference of opinion between Antoine Lumière and his sons about how best to exploit their invention. In a letter written to his father on October 14, 1895 Louis says that he and his brother have been discussing its marketing and, noting that 'we do not like the prospect of you playing Barnum showing off his magic lantern' he argues for a low cost, low risk approach. He wants to rent the machine out to customers for a fixed daily rate complete with a trained operator, to minimise the Lumière involvement and leave the expenses of hiring a hall and advertising the show to others.[4]

This essentially managerial rather than entrepreneurial approach explains much about the subsequent history of the cinématographe in England. By the time the brothers had taken over the management of the family company, it had already become a large industrial business with interests in many aspects of the photographic trade. Adopting high risk strategies was no longer necessary or appropriate, and the brothers' correspondence shows that throughout the 1890s they invariably considered the possibility of cooperative joint ventures to explore new opportunities, rather than attempting to control everything themselves. Nor was this policy of decentralisation always chosen to avoid capital investment. The imperative was more often to ensure quality and efficiency, and if this could best be achieved by investing in a business run by a known supplier who was reliable and skilful, it was a method preferred to setting up a duplicate in-house operation.

Britain became an important source of supply for raw stock before the Cinématographe itself arrived. Louis Lumière wrote to the company's British agents Fuerst Brothers in November 1895, informing them that a plant was about to be set up at Lyons to manufacture film, but wondering if, before this was done, it might be possible to arrange a licence to maufacture with the Blair Company. This approach, if it was made, came to nothing, and the factory then tried to manufacture ciné film themselves, but encountered severe problems with coating. By January 1896 the Lumières had been forced to return to Blair for their supplies, and Fuerst Brothers were soon ordering an average of ten rolls a week.[5]

The Cinématographe arrived in London in mid-February 1896.[6] It is evident that the English operation represented a compromise between the brothers and their father. The valuable English concession had been given to Félicien Trewey, an old Bohemian friend of Antoine's, who was certainly fond of 'playing Barnum' and is unlikely to have been the brothers' preferred choice. But behind the scenes their influence is apparent in the meticulous care taken over booking strategy, and the careful preparations which were made for recording the daily box-office takings.[7] It seems that the Polytechnic engagement was probably a profit-sharing arrangement.

The press show resulted in a considerable amount of coverage, but early results were modest. The switching of the venue for the Ciné-matographe from the Great Hall to the smaller Marlborough Hall, coupled with a later statement by Trewey, suggests that, overall, the level of business done at the Polytechnic may have been disappointing.[8] According to at least one detailed account, presentational aspects left a lot to be desired, with poor illumination, erratic projection and annoying 'flicker' being especially remarked on.[9] It is important that these early performances are seen in an objective, rather than – as they invariably have been presented in the past – a heroic light, because this emphasises just how necessary it was for the Lumières to have a coordinated marketing policy, capable of sustaining the shows. Despite later enthusiasm, the Cinématographe never sold itself. Indeed, from a contemporary perspective, the 'novelty' aspect was probably not as great as we tend to think it was. At the beginning of 1896, film

Felicien Trewey, probably at about the turn of the century

was neither wholly new nor even particularly successful. Edison's Kinetoscope had arrived in London in October 1894, but less than a year later was commercially finished. Its novelty had not been destroyed by the introduction of projected film; it had just failed to catch on as a permanent attraction. Under the circumstances, what reason was there, at the time, to believe that projected film would fare any better?

Thus it is hardly surprising that a great deal of caution, and even a distinct lack of enthusiasm was shown towards the Cinématographe by variety theatre and music hall managers when Trewey attempted to sell the attraction to them. Indeed, the fact that he was willing to have it included as just one of many competing attractions on a music hall programme suggests a good deal about *his* true feelings. Trewey first approached the Alhambra in Leicester Square, but they turned him down, suggesting that 'the novelty was not considered good enough.'[10] After this inauspicious beginning Trewey next approached the Empire. The Empire management had apparently considered booking Skladanowsky's Bioskop during December 1895 but, for reasons which are not yet clear, did not proceed. Before agreeing to the Cinématographe engagement they insisted on a private demonstration, which was given after the regular evening show had ended on Friday February 28. As they were evidently still not entirely convinced of a favourable audience reaction, an unadvertised sneak preview was held on Saturday afternoon, March 7.

Sandwiched between a Swedish quintette and a troupe of acrobats, the first public presentation of the Cinématographe at the Empire was on the evening of Monday March 9, 1896, at 9:40 pm.[11] Trewey received a large amount – £150 for six performances plus a Saturday afternoon matinée – but it was less than the £30 a night he had wanted.[12] It should not be thought that Trewey's selling problem was unique. The British film-maker Robert William Paul met an equally unenthusiastic reaction. A demonstration he arranged for the management of the Palace in Shaftesbury Avenue failed to impress and led to outright rejection. 'Not regarded with sufficient favour to justify the

The Empire Theatre, Leicester Square, September 1896

management in securing it,' wrote *The Entr'acte*. The following day Paul gave another demonstration, this time to the Alhambra, who were by now anxious to find something which could compete with the Cinématographe, but not so anxious that they were prepared to pay Paul more than £66 per week, less than half the amount Trewey was receiving.[13] A history of problems with registration and the fact that Paul could only offer old kinetoscope films since he had not yet developed a camera must have been significant factors. The response was the same at the Egyptian Hall in Piccadilly where David Devant, the resident conjuror, had the greatest difficulty in persuading J.N. Maskelyne of the potential of film exhibition, finally having to pay for a Paul machine himself and accepting unfavourable terms from the theatre before he was able to show it.[14]

Eventual success did of course come for the Cinématographe at the Empire, but success brought further problems. The Lumière brothers had decided, before the London show opened, that they would not make the Cinématographe or the films available for sale in England for a year, and they had announced this to the photographic press.[15] Denied the genuine article, the less scrupulous were quick to imply that their own shows had some connection with the real thing, and a large number of exhibitors began using the name, often with the adoption of the French final 'e'. R.W. Paul led this 'me too' trend with his 'Animatographe' and, just in case anyone missed the unsubtle hint, followed it with an advertisement for his newly opened show at Olympia which included the line: 'similar to the show at the Empire'.[16]

But although he was using the Cinématographe in this way for his own advantage, Paul nonetheless sought to differentiate his product from other British machines. 'Beware of imitations and infringements now being offered, and falsely purporting to be of French origin,' he warned his customers in April 1896 – a disingenuous lead quickly followed by one of his rivals, Fred Duval, who was warning his own customers a month later to 'Beware of spurious machines purporting to be French'.[17] John Henry Rigg of Leeds and Ernest Othon Kumberg, a French Phonograph infringer[18] based in London, went one stage further, announcing in *The English Mechanic* for March 13 that they were 'Sale Agents' for the 'French Cinematograph' (sic). 'On view daily at the Polytechnic and the Empire, Makes £30 every day, A rapid fortune for exhibitors...' promised the advertisement, but it was doubtless Rigg and Kumberg who hoped to make the 'rapid fortune' since it transpired in due course that they had been asking the enormous sum of £120 for the machine from unsuspecting would-be exhibitors. Faced with this situation, the Lumières proved willing to defend their rights and succeeded in obtaining a permanent injunction and costs against Rigg and Kumberg, in what is believed to be the first legal case involving cinematography in England.[19]

Further evidence of the pre-planned and structured marketing policy adopted by the Lumières in England can be traced in the provincial schedule of the Cinématographe. Some time in April Trewey signed contracts with both the Moss and Thornton and Stoll theatre owners – the largest and most prestigious circuits of the time.[20] This agreement gave the Cinématographe immediate access to nationwide coverage via key first-run theatres, reinforcing its 'premium' image. Since the films could not be seen at any other show, the Cinématographe could always be promoted as both 'special' and 'genuine'. Regional advertising for it frequently emphasised a message of product differentiation, typically warning: 'Beware of Imitations'. (It followed, of course, that *everything* was an 'imitation' and, by implication, all English machines inferior.) Indeed, by the middle of 1896, the situation was somewhat farcical, with virtually everyone associated with cinematography warning someone else to beware of imitations.

A pattern of carefully staged repeat visits was implemented in the British regions during 1896, with the Cinématographe appearing at Cardiff five times, at Swansea four times, and at Birmingham, Newcastle-upon-Tyne and Edinburgh three times each.[21] Moreover, this was safe, predictable and profitable business of the kind originally envisaged by the brothers, with the theatre owner taking responsibility for advertising costs and promotion and the Lumières receiving a guaranteed flat-rate fee rather than a percentage of the box-office take. The experience when the show played in Manchester suggests that the brothers were right to minimise the risks. Due to the lack of either a Moss and Thornton or Stoll theatre in that city, Trewey booked the Lesser Free Trade Hall for four weeks, and tested the Cinémato-graphe's appeal to the limit by presenting it unsupported by a variety programme and in direct opposition to the established theatres in the town. Once again, considerable care and forward planning is evident. Madame Trewey was in charge, with a lecturer, Harry Vernon, and his assistant, Hutton. A press show was held on Saturday afternoon, May 16, and for this 'seance', as it was termed, specially printed invitation cards were distributed. Advertising as usual stressed that the show was 'The Original' and warned of imitations.

But weekly reports in the *Music Hall* make clear that despite this care the show was not successful. Searching for causes, the reporter suggests a lack of posters outside the building, and in a criticism of the price level adds, 'I regret very much that one of the weeks of exhibition the charge was not reduced to sixpence.'[22] Manchester certainly lacked the large affluent population that London's West End could provide, but it is likely that the real problem was related to perception of value rather than simply price level. From a contemporary perspective – especially a poorer regional one – a 15 to 20 minute presentation, of which only about ten minutes actually consisted of films, must have appeared very expensive and of doubtful value when compared with a varied, three-hour music hall programme. The Manchester experience provides graphic proof that a film exhibitor in 1896 – even one with a premium image like the Cinématographe – could not rely on novelty alone to bring automatic success. Sensitivity to presentational and demographic factors was already essential.

The final stage of the Lumière strategy in Britain began in May 1897 when both the Cinématographe and the films were offered for unrestricted sale. Once again, the company pulled back from a direct involvement in the selling operation, preferring instead to appoint Fuerst Brothers to handle sales of the equipment, and reaching a non-exclusive agreement with Maguire and Baucus for the sale of the films in both Britain and the United States. In over two years the Lumières had introduced no significant improvements to the original Cinématographe, and not only was it now outdated technically, but the 'unique' system of round hole perforations was completely anachronistic. If the company had expected that market monopoly could be achieved by this method, their hopes must have died by the middle of 1896. It is certainly possible that market developments in Britain may have moved faster than the brothers had expected, and without doubt the decision to withold their equipment helped to destroy its ultimate chance of success by stimulating other makers to produce their own cameras and projectors.

Can this be said to represent a clear failure of their marketing strategy? Certainly, if the traditional way of viewing the history of cinematography as a technically-driven linear development is followed. But the problem with such a model is that it is not well suited to accommodating strategic rather than logical or derivative developments.

Moreover, all the evidence points to the Lumière operation being esentially strategic, with product development subordinated to commercial objectives. In any case, ordinary experience suggests that a company run by the same management simply does not move from being brilliantly original and innovative in one year to reactionary and obtuse only two years later.

Clearly an assessment of whether the Lumière marketing plan was a failure or a success can only be attempted if the evolution, and particularly the structure, of the British film market during 1896 and the first half of 1897 is examined in considerable detail. This can best be done by looking at price behaviour during this period for the equipment manufacture, film exhibition and film production areas. A preliminary attempt has been made at this, using data gathered from advertisements placed in *The Era* by a wide range of companies during this period. The findings can be very briefly summarised.[23] The overall picture which emerges is one of very early maturity, market segmentation, sector specialisation, and different sector characteristics created by different economic imperatives. Both equipment-making and film exhibition suffered from rapid and severe price falls during 1896, reducing their profitability, although not their potential, since they were both still expanding. In the first case the main reason appears to be the lack of a British 'master' patent capable of maintaining a monopolistic structure; and in the second case problems were increasingly related to low levels of market entry cost, leading to overcrowding. But during the same period the film production sector behaves quite differently, with trade prices for film remaining unchanged from June 1895 to June 1897. As increased demand fed through from the growing exhibition sector, the filmmaker was able to add volume to undiminished margins. The maintenance of price levels in an otherwise highly volatile market suggests that some kind of price-fixing or immature oligopoly was involved.

By May 1897 it must have been clear to anyone analysing the market that film production represented the area of highest profit. Perceptive businessmen like the Lumières would certainly have been familiar with British market trends. It is clear that their policy of 'wait and see' with regard to the Cinématographe was justified by market conditions. Even if they had supplied the machine in large numbers during 1896 – at the inevitable cost of large capital investment, distribution expense and so on – there is no reason to think that the entrenched oligopoly of U.K. manufacturers would have acted differently from how they did. Prices would still have been forced down to such an extent that volume importing into Britain would have been very unlikely to be profitable. But by waiting, and by keeping to a pre-determined time schedule, the Lumières were able to assess mid-1897 market conditions and forward requirements, and react accordingly without then having to dismantle an expensive structure.[24] To concentrate on film production from 1897 was the right decision. The achievement of the Lumières as filmmakers is justly celebrated, but their commercial strategy also demonstrates creativity, and needs to be understood if a balanced picture of their work is to be achieved.

NOTES

1. The most comprehensive review is Deac Rossell, 'A Chronology of Cinema, 1889-1896', *Film History*, vol. 7 no. 2, Summer 1995, pp. 115-236.

2. Alan Williams, 'The Lumière Organisation and "Documentary Realism"', in ed. John L. Fell, *Film Before Griffith*, University of California Press, 1983, pp. 153-161. In Williams' opinion, ' the Lumières do have a clear position in film history, but it seems likely that this is best defined in financial and organisational terms, rather than technological ones' (p. 154). See also Marshall Deutelbaum, 'Structural Patterning in the Lumière Films', pp. 299-310 in the same volume.

3. Auguste and Louis Lumière, *Letters*, ed. Jacques Rittaud-Hutinet, Faber & Faber, 1995.

4. ibid., pp. 27-28.

5. ibid., pp. 47-48, 100, 110, 116 and 119-120. The Blair Company had supplied the film which was used by Birt Acres in March 1895 to take the first successful British films.

6. According to the 1936 Commemorative Programme, the Lumières had been invited to the Polytechnic by Quintin Hogg. To my knowledge there is no contemporary evidence to confirm this.

7. Auguste and Louis Lumière, op. cit., Letter to Paul Lacroix, February 17, 1896, p. 123.

8. Advertisement for the Cinématographe, *The Times*, Wednesday February 26 to Friday February 28, 1896, p. 1. See also John Cher, 'Who is the Father of the Trade? Interview with M. Trewey', *The Bioscope*, October 17, 1912, p. 187. The book recording income at the Polytechnic for the early part of 1896 is missing from an otherwise complete set of ledgers preserved at the University of Westminster Library. The loss probably occurred many years ago.

9. 'The Cinématographe', *Photography*, February 27, 1896, p. 143.

10. *Entr'acte*, March 28, 1896, p. 5.

11. For the possible Skladanowsky booking, see 'Was Lumière first? New Claim to Priority' (Letter from E.A. Pickering), *Today's Cinema*, March 13, 1936, p. 1. The private demonstration given on February 28 is noted in the *Entr'acte*, March 7, 1896, p. 6. The 'sneak preview', ibid., March 14, 1896, p. 4. Advance advertising for the Empire began in the *Times* for Monday March 2, 1896, and the first 'official' performance at the Empire is advertised in the *Times* of Monday March 9, 1896.

12. *Entr'acte*, March 7, 1896, p. 6, and March 14, 1896, p. 4.

13. ibid., March 28, 1896, p. 5. *The Era*, February 28, 1898, pp. 19.

14. See David Devant, *My Magic Life*, quoted in John Barnes, *The Beginnings of the Cinema in England*, David & Charles, 1976, pp. 119-120.

15. *British Journal of Photography* (Supplement), March 6, 1896, p. 17. Orders were in fact being taken by November 1896 (*Amateur Photographer*, November 20, 1896, 'Lumière's Cinematograph', Letter from Fuerst Bros). Delivery, announced for May 1897, kept to the original schedule.

16. Used for the first time in a *Times* advertisement for Olympia, March 26, 1896, p. 1.

17. *The Era*, April 16, 1896, p. 24, and May 2, 1896, p. 25.

18. A Phonograph infringer was someone who exhibited a Phonograph without permission from the Edison Bell Company, which owned the rights.

19. Affidavit of Antoine Lumière, Chancery Case L.696, March 31, 1896. PRO. J4.5205/593. The affidavit is transcribed in full in Richard Brown, *The Lumière Cinématographe: the first six Months in England, with an account of Strategy and Price Trends in the early English Film Business*, 1993. Copies in the National Film and Television Archive and the Library of the University of Westminster.

20. Nominally separate, but in fact closely linked both financially and managerially.

21. Information from John Barnes, *The Cinématographe in the United Kingdom*, Archives of the Barnes Museum of Cinematography, St Ives, 1994, p. 19.

22. *Music Hall and Showman*, June 12, 1896, p. 18.

23. For the full account, see Brown, op. cit., pp. 5-15.

24. The Lumières introduced their 'Model B' projector or 'Triograph' in July 1897. It was designed to take standard Edison perforations, but did not have the success in England of the original Cinématographe. See John Barnes, *The Rise of the Cinema in Great Britain*, Bishopsgate Press, 1983, pp. 124-130. Lumière films with round perforations were still available in England as late as September 1899.

© Richard Brown 1995

8 EVIDENCE OF EDITING IN THE LUMIÈRE FILMS

André Gaudreault

The prospect of the centenary celebrations of the cinema has given rise to a series of initiatives in France, among which the project of making an inventory of the Lumière films is probably one of the most interesting.[1] It has led to the establishment of real 'workshops' to investigate and research into the corpus of Lumière films, unjustly neglected till today.[2] The work has gone so far so fast that I think it is obvious that our knowledge of these films has already made a big leap forward. This will allow researchers to make new and stimulating contributions quite different, one hopes, from the traditional droning-on the Lumière output usually inspires. For my part I shall at least attempt to do so in the present article, which is the second piece of published work to come out of the research programme I began in September, 1993, with a view to the Centenary year.[3]

I think this programme has produced interesting results in so far as it has confirmed a relatively 'daring' working hypothesis (in which I only partly believed) and has led me to different readings of both the period literature about the films (catalogues, leaflets for users, etc.) and the films themselves. The hypothesis is more or less the same as the one I formulated some 15 years ago about the Méliès films,[4] when I tried to challenge some of the main traditional clichés, but this time it is applied to the Lumière films. Méliès, it was said, had had nothing at all to do with editing. Through postulating the falsity of this idea, I finally came to a conception of Méliès' works which was completely different from that of the traditional cinema historians, and concluded by showing how he had, basically, been 'one of the first to think of cinema in terms of continuity'.[5]

I thus embarked on the present study with the following presupposition: there must surely be, at the very least, some evidence of editing in the Lumière films, films which are basically so little known. I thought it would certainly be interesting to examine the Lumière films from this angle and to make an inventory of the various instances of some kind of editing. I have not been disappointed: the reality of editing in the Lumière films has literally *jumped out at me*. I already suspected, of course, that I was going to find many examples of *virtual editing* in films recounting the journey or the coronation of some dignitary or another, but I had not imagined that the examples I would be listing would be as varied and recurrent as they turned out to be.[6]

In fact, the Lumière films contain very many cuts, and I am inclined to believe that the famous idea of 'continuous shooting without editing', supposed to be characteristic of this kind of filming, was really only a myth, pure and simple. Of course, there still is a very large number of films which were shot in one take, but to go on peddling the idea that the Lumière films were all shot in continuous takes would be pointlessly to conceal the many divergent practices in the films, which basically form a system, as I shall try to show. But before going any further I must go back to the very conception of the Lumière Cinématographe as a *device*, because as far as editing and certainly shooting were concerned it was the apparatus itself which basically dictated part of their attitudes to the first film-makers.

For the Cinématographe, as a device (like any device for that matter) is a device which constrains, precisely because of the rules which are intrinsic to it.[7] The constraint was caused both by the apparatus itself, which was designed to be driven by the crank handle (thereby reducing the possibility of attaching a larger magazine) and by the 'compulsory' 17 metre footage restriction. The base the apparatus stood on, which prevented any sideways movement, and the fixed height imposed by this base (probably not adjustable at first) were further limitations. In fact the first Lumière cameramen should be seen as somewhat captive participants in a system imposed on them, and the various innovations they made considered so many 'transgressions', conscious or otherwise, of the norms established in advance by the people who had made the final adjustments to the apparatus (or, better, the device).

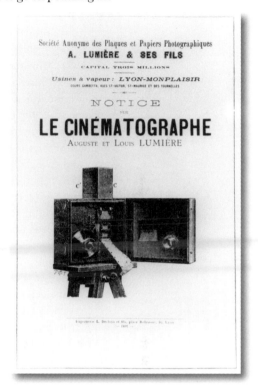

Explanatory leaflet for the
Cinématographe, 1897

The Lumière Cinématographe was a device adjusted to ensure the strictly continuous shooting of successive images of a single event seen from a single and unique point of view (*single-viewpointedness*, as I have proposed calling this process)[8], and, what's more, it was a fixed point of view. It was not designed to produce a composite assembly of various shots of the same or different subjects (for which I have suggested the corresponding term, *multi-viewpointedness*). The idea of single-viewpointedness is very significant in its own right, because it conveys the fundamental system of the Cinématographe, and does so even if moving from single-viewpointedness to multi-viewpointedness is still relatively simple. Transcending the relative fixity of single-viewpointedness was a simple matter too.

Indeed, all that was necessary to subvert fixed single-viewpointed-ness into variable single-viewpointedness was to put the camera on a moving object (like Promio's famous gondola in Venice). And, for instance, all that was necessary to 'invent' the 30° continuity shot, which represented a minimal form of multi-viewpointedness (in this case a sequence of *two* different points of view of the same subject) was a bit of spontaneous reaction during live filming, which is what happened to the cameraman shooting the film titled *Loubet aux courses* (no. 1031). This film is actually composed of two filmed segments, juxtaposed (probably without splicing) for the simple reason that the cameraman was forced to react to the early departure out of shot of the subject of his film, President Loubet himself. The film shows us Loubet and his entourage moving from left to right near the dais. At the moment when the President leaves the frame (to the right), the cameraman makes a slight, abrupt movement to the right, which results in a hasty whip pan lasting three or four frames. Almost at the same moment, he interrupts the shooting for the time it takes to reposition his camera after having turned it round through about 25 or 30°, and then finally resumes shooting to follow the rest of the events, after an ellipsis of only a few seconds. Thus the film demonstrates a rare example, for the time, of continuity through a *nearly* straightforward cut (we mustn't forget the few frames of the whip pan) between two different shots with adjacent camera angles. This represented an 'editing' process carried out in the camera, without cement or scissors, which made two series of relatively different images follow each other.

The Lumière films harbour numerous examples of similar *'unintentional' moments* of editing, even if the idea of multi-viewpointedness as such was not really important to the Lumières. Indeed, for them (as for all the people involved in the world of film-making before the turn of the century) a film (or a 'view') represented in principle a single scene (or as they also said at the time, a single 'tableau') even if, all through their catalogue of film views, one can feel the hidden presence of editing running just beneath the surface. In fact, the catalogue is full of examples of what could be considered 'virtual editing' but which probably turned into real editing when the films needed to be screened. As an example, let us take the series titled *Voyage de Monsieur le Président de la République en Russie*,[9] which is composed of the fourteen following films:

606 Arrival of the President in St. Petersburg.
607 The President reviewing the Guard of Honour.
608 Parade of the Guard of Honour.
609 Arrival of the President and the Tsar at Peterhof.
610 The Rest of the Parade marching past Admiral Avelan.
611 Russian officers attached to the President and Journalists.
612 Review at Krasnoye-Selo: Charge of the Empress's Hussars.

613 Review at Krasnoye-Selo: Artillery.

614 Review at Krasnoye-Selo: Cossacks.

615 Review at Krasnoye-Selo: Defence Artillery.

616 Review at Krasnoye-Selo: Grenadiers.

617 Review at Krasnoye-Selo: Infantry.

618 Review at Krasnoye-Selo: Attendants.

619 Panorama of the Peterhof line.

It is obvious that the very idea of editing is contained implicitly in this simple ordering of titles. One may even imagine, without too much risk of error, that the list follows the chronological order of the way things happened (and if this is not the case, it certainly follows another logic of 'editing'). This collection of 'views' is nothing more nor less than a genuine *multi-viewpoint* report, even if its multi-viewpointedness had stayed at the implied level and no one ever had the idea of presenting the fourteen strips side by side. The simple 'lining-up', piece by piece, of the various components of this series for the purpose of projecting them is an activity related to editing, and one which produces in the spectator an effect similar to editing (the only notable difference being the interval between the shots).

To begin with, indeed, another limitation of the Lumière apparatus was that it did not allow more than one 'view' to be screened at a time. In other words, *after each 'view' had been screened*, the projectionist had to *load a new film* in the apparatus. Each programme was thus composed of a systematic alternation of periods of projection and periods of waiting. But a time came (which is still difficult to date precisely) when the procedure changed to continuous projection of several strips (with or without leaders, with or without a pause between them, I can't say), if only to avoid the tedious job of loading about 100 views a day. In the end the Lumières marketed a device 'allow(ing) the projection of very long strips of film',[10] the Carpentier-Lumière projector (date of invention still unknown),[11] which in one of its versions could 'hold four hundred metres or more of film'.[12] There can be no doubt that as soon as it became available the Carpentier-Lumière projector allowed several of its users to think in terms of editing and thus favoured the establishment of the multi-viewpoint film.

We should remember that it was rather a long time before the concept of the film as a multi-viewpoint whole was recognised. In this respect, 1902 was the year of transition. In fact, it was during this year that the proportion of multi-viewpoint films began to exceed the number of single-viewpoint ones. Thus the Lumière brothers produced more definitely multi-viewpoint films after a certain date (which remains to be clarified but is probably not before 1902 on the basis of my present knowledge), particularly in the titles numbered 2001 to 2023. These films, all listed under the label of 'phantasmagorical views'[13] are fictional works whose narrative ambitions are much greater than in the Lumières' usual work. One can realise this just by reading the explanatory leaflet published in the catalogue. Thus, to give only two examples:

2001 *Le Château hanté*

A Magician conjures up the apparition of an old witch whom he sends to bring him a young girl; he commands the girl to lure a young traveller to the castle. Upon arrival, the traveller finds himself confronted by all sorts of unpleasant surprises: chairs which give way beneath him, the appearance of a ghost that he tries to fight and which disappears, etc. Finally, the ghost is transformed into a young girl whom the young man courts, but at the moment when he comes near her, he finds nothing more than a skeleton. Furious, he seizes a stick to strike the skeleton and draws back in surprise on seeing the skeleton turn into the Magician, who takes hold of the traveller and makes him disappear in a swirl of smoke.

2016 *L'Estafette*

A dragoon is assigned by an officer to carry a dispatch. He sets off, and after passing an Alsatian farm where the inhabitants come out to welcome him, he continues on his way along the edge of a wood and is ambushed by some German soldiers who chase after him and wound him. A wild race ensues between the injured man and his enemies, but after fantastic efforts, exhausted, dying, the messenger manages to complete his mission, and his pursuers fall in turn into a French ambush. They are taken prisoner while the messenger, carried by two soldiers, is brought before the high command. As he dies, he himself hands over the letter he was entrusted with. The general pins his own cross on the chest of the soldier killed in action.[14]

We can deduce from reading the explanatory notes that a good number of these films have multiple viewpoints. This seems evident in the case of *L'Estafette*, at least, which recounts the wanderings of a soldier entrusted with a dangerous mission. As for *Le Château hanté*, it is made in a single shot, at least on one level: unity of viewpoint is indeed maintained all through the film. But all the same, the film has a great deal to do with editing. In fact, it is a Méliès-type film, which contains, for each of its various instances (about ten) of the famous trick transformation effect achieved by stopping the camera, a remarkable number of 'cuts' of the same type as those found in the works of Méliès. However, this time the difference is that the 'editing' seems to have been carried out only at the shooting stage (in other words, in the camera).[15] Thus, what Jacques Malthête de Méliès said in 1981 doesn't seem to apply here:

This effect [stopping the camera] is [in Méliès] always associated with a splice. (...) I know of no exception to this rule. Every appearance, disappearance or substitution was certainly carried out in the shooting, but then edited in the laboratory on the negative for one simple reason: this effect (...) does not work if the rhythm is broken. The mechanism of the camera was such that you couldn't stop on the last image of the 'before effect' shot while the set or the characters were changed, and then start up again on the first image of the 'after effect' shot without getting a significant variation in rhythm.[16]

It was probably the specific mechanism of the Lumière Cinématographe (as opposed to the camera used by Méliès) which allowed the Lumières in most cases to get away with stopping the camera without subsequent editing work (whereas Méliès always had to). The mechanism of the device from Lyons must have actually been very smooth, because of its lightness and the relatively good engineering which went into it, and this enabled 'flawless' camera stops.[17]

Despite this, the Lumière brothers' multi-viewpointedness, when it appears, always seems more or less accidental. Let us take the rather precocious case of one of the rare examples of editing evident in the catalogues, the films numbered 1230, 1231 and 1232, which are presented as follows:

1230   Nice: Panorama on the Beaulieu to Monaco railway line. I.
1231   Nice: Panorama on the Beaulieu to Monaco railway line. II.
1232   Nice: Panorama on the Beaulieu to Monaco railway line. III.
(These last three views can be *added* together).[18]

This shows that the temptation of editing could be very strong as early as 1898 (which is the presumed date of the shooting of these films). But not strong enough to over-rule that essential parameter of the single-viewpointedness system, the famous *autonomy of the shot,* which was reflected particularly strongly in the commercial practices of the production companies. As with the practice, widespread until 1906 (as much, and perhaps even more, in the United States as in France), of selling films *shot by shot,* the corollary of which was the importance of the exhibitor's role in organising the sequence of films to be screened. Not only was it the exhibitor who decided the order and number of films to be screened during each of the sessions that he organised, thus exercising clear 'editorial control', but he also chose how many shots to buy from such and such a film recently shot by the studios, and thus became the principal agent of editing, or at least the one who had the last word. This was the truth, and it was announced as such in the catalogues of the time, particularly for the *Passion Plays,* but also for several other films which came onto the market in

Auguste Lumière tests the 'ultra-rapide' photographic emulsion

the early years of the establishment of the multi-viewpoint system (between 1902 and 1905).

Moreover, in *Panorama on the Beaulieu to Monaco Line*, there may also be straightforward reasons of commercial strategy which explain the relative 'lethargy' of the producers. In fact, in a later edition of the catalogue (the one quoted above and believed to date from 1907), the three *Panorama* strips were still sold individually. It is only on the level of what the catalogue writes about them that a development in the direction of editing-mindedness can be felt. The comment now reads (and note the word in italics): 'These three views, which are consecutive and can be *joined*, were taken at one of the most picturesque places on the Riviera'.[19] Thus, in the editing it recommends for the films, the producing authority moves from the notion of *addition* ('added') to that of *continuity* ('joined'), but without actually going ahead and joining them up itself.

The commercial strategy which prevented the Lumières or their agents from proceeding themselves to the editing of the three *Panorama* strips may be due to the fact that, with a few rare exceptions, *all the titles* offered in the Lumière catalogues were *the same length* (the famous 17 metres)[20] and *the same price*.[21] So each 17-metre view has its own entry with a number and title (with or without a description). The only exceptions are as follows:

No.765, *Danse serpentine*, whose price is specified as slightly higher than the standard price;[22]

No.1045, *Les Petits Lutteurs* (whose length is specified as 13 metres, or four metres less than the uniform length);[23]

the series *Le Cake-Walk au Nouveau-Cirque* (nos. 1350 to 1354), which shows black dancers and whose prices vary from 42 to 49 francs (the lengths vary between 21 and 25 metres);[24]

the *Vues fantasmagoriques (Scènes de Genre et à Transformations*, mentioned above, which are all probably longer than 17 metres[25] and which vary in price (specified for each of them in the catalogue).[26]

In the other catalogue I have available (known as the 1901 catalogue), which contains all the views from no. 1 to no. 1299 (thereby excluding the *Vues fantasmagoriques* as well as the *Cake-Walk au Nouveau-Cirque* series), no special price is indicated for No. 765, *Danse Serpentine*.[27] The Lumières were probably willing at that time to 'let it go' for the standard price of 40 francs instead of the 43 francs they would demand later. However, they made up for this from a financial point of view with No. 1045, *Les Petits Lutteurs*, which in spite of the four 'missing' metres (the 1901 catalogue agrees with this) was still sold at 40 francs. Thus, it can be said that *all the views* of the 1901 catalogue are at the uniform price of 40 francs and that apart from two exceptions, all conform to the *uniform length* of 17 metres.

This uniformity was precisely one of the parameters of the Cinématographe, and it should be concluded that the constraints it exerted functioned like a yoke which had the effect of pointing production in one given direction. An example of this can be found in films 1104 to 1106, which are described in the 1901 catalogue as follows:[28]

1104   *La poupée*, act I – Choeur des Prêtres
1105   *La poupée*, act II – Le Curé et les mannequins
1106   La poupée, act III – La poupée

Given the different parameters of the analysis I have just made of the Lumière catalogue, how could we possibly entertain the idea that this sort of division into 'acts' has anything whatever to with the demands of dramaturgy? No, the formal division of these films is certainly a legacy of what could be called the *metric yoke* specific to the Lumière brothers.

NOTES

1. The aim of this project (now practically completed) was 'to collect, by means of research undertaken, with the help of foreign collaborators, all over the world, and make an inventory of [the Lumière films as a heritage], in order to analyse, carefully identify and restore the recovered films, and finally to show them widely but respectfully(...), thanks to the help of the Lumière Brothers Association(...), the Cinémathèque Française, the Lumière Institute, the Musée du Cinéma de Lyon and the Film Archive of the Centre National du Cinéma.' (Michelle Aubert, Curator of the Film Archive of the Centre National du Cinéma, Letter to the author of the present article, December 28 (predestined date!), 1994.

2. For my part, I was lucky enough to visit two of these 'workshops'. The main one was at the Film Archive of the Centre National du Cinéma, where the team was made up of Anne Gautier, Jean-Marc Lamotte, Nathalie Leplongeon and Robert Poupard, under the direction of Michelle Aubert. But I also visited the one at the Université de Lyon II, where Antoine Morin and Laurent Lorriot worked under the direction of Jacques Rittaud-Hutinet. I was able to benefit from the invaluable collaboration of the members of both teams, and it is thanks to their vast knowledge of the body of

Lumière films that my research made such rapid progress. I am most grateful to them and to Laurent Mannoni for his help all through my work.

3. The first was a lecture entitled 'Le montage dans la production Lumière: essai de typologie', given at the Université Louis Lumière (Lyon II) in November 1993. The present text was the basis for a paper given to the *Cinéma: Acte et Présence* Symposium at the Musée de la Civilisation in Quebec in April 1995. I spoke about some other findings of this programme at the Lyons Lumière Conference in June 1995. The present article will appear in French in a book titled *Du Montage dans le Cinéma des premiers Temps*, which will be published in 1996 by Nuit Blanche, Quebec and Payot, Lausanne. The work on editing in the Lumière films is part of a wider-ranging research programme on the beginnings and development of editing which I embarked on several years ago.

4. In a paper at the Symposium on Méliès which took place in 1981 at Cerisy-la-Salle, France. See '"Théâtralité" et "Narrativité" dans l'oeuvre de Georges Méliès', in ed. M. Malthête-Méliès, *Méliès et la Naissance du Spectacle Cinématographique*, Klinksieck, Paris, 1984, pp. 199-219. The paper first appeared in Spanish as 'Teatralidad y narratividad en la obra de Georges Méliès', *Georges Méliès*, Filmoteca de la U.N.A.M., Film Collection no. 4, Mexico, December 1982, pp. 81-100.

5. ibid., p. 216.

6. Nor was I prepared for the shock of discovering, in the course of my research on the Lumière films, a specific incidence of editing in the strips made for the Zoetrope. I have written about this in my paper for the Lyons Lumière Conference, June 1995 (papers due to be published during 1996).

7. However, the Cinématographe was not as constraining as, shall we say, keeping within the same family of devices, the 'automatic photo booth', whose formula, applicable to and generally applied by all of them, can be interpreted as follows: 'You will enter the booth and sit on a seat facing a glass pane. You will then get a series of four flashes going off in your face at regular intervals. Upon leaving the booth, you will collect a strip of four photographs which show you in closeup. These photographs will be arranged one above the other and will show the four successive poses you happened to adopt at the moment of the four successive flashes.' Who would have thought, for instance, of standing up between the first and second flashes (thereby presenting his torso to the glass), then of climbing up on the seat before the third flash (showing the lower part of the body) and, for the fourth flash, completing the whole mise en scène by holding up his boots to give the illusion that they are attached to the legs seen in the third pose? This would swap *temporal sequence* for a composite *spatial contiguity*, in which the set of four photographs no longer shows the same face in four successive poses, but rather four contiguous parts of the same body: head and shoulders in the first photograph, torso in the second, legs in the next and feet in the last. Who would have thought of that? To be honest, I must say that I know at least one person who had fun subverting the device of the automatic photo booth in this way, so thanks to Raynald Gaudreault for telling me about his personal experience of this.

8. See my book *Du littéraire au filmique, Système du récit*, Meridiens Klinksieck, Paris/Presses de l'Université Laval, Quebec, 1988, p. 19.

9. At least, in the *Catalogue général des vues positives*, undated but published no earlier than 1901. In the *Catalogue des vues pour Cinématographe* (also undated, but the Film Archive of the Centre National du Cinéma has established that it was published in 1907), the same series has a slightly different title: *Voyage de M. le Président Félix Faure en Russie*.

10. Quotation taken from the (undated) pamphlet *'Cinématographes A. et L. Lumière et Matériel pour Projections animées'*, p. 3, in the Collection of Laurent Mannoni.

11. Laurent Mannoni writes me as follows: 'The exact dating of the Carpentier-Lumière projector presents a problem, strangely enough. Everyone says 1898. I'm not at all sure. It may be then, but (after very detailed checks) there is no patent for the Carpentier-Lumière projector. (...) I really hope to solve this puzzle.' Letter of November 13, 1993.

12. *'Cinématographes A. et L. Lumière et Matériel pour Projections animées'*, p.16.

13. Even if some of them, strangely, have absolutely no connection with phantasmagoria – see *L'Estafette* below. The sub-title of the category should be noted: *'Genre and Transformation Scenes'* (*Catalogue des vues pour Cinématographe*, op. cit., p. 15).

14. ibid., pp. 15 and 18.

15. I shall have to wait to be more sure of this, as unfortunately I have still not been able to get access to the orginal strip of 35mm film.

16. Letter of May 1, 1981, quoted in my article '"Théâtralité" et "Narrativité" dans l'oeuvre de Georges Méliès', op. cit., p. 216.

17. Anne Gautier and Jean-Marc Lamotte, two of the contributors to the above-mentioned inventory project, tell me that some of the stop camera effects in the Lumière films which do not show cuts on the negative do in fact show them on the projected prints. I have not yet been able to se the prints myself, but should like to take this opportunity of expressing my deepest appreciation to Anne Gautier and Jean-Marc Lamotte, who have kindly provided me with a great deal of information about the Lumière films, which they have been in daily contact with for almost two years. They have become real living catalogues, and they're pleasant to 'read' and 'consult' too!

18. *Catalogue général des vues positives,* p. 46 (my emphasis).

19. *Catalogue des vues pour Cinématographe,* p. 44 (my emphasis again).

20. Thus in the 1907 catalogue, p. 61: 'Unless otherwise stated, the length of the views is between 16 and 17 metres'.

21. 'Price of each view... 40 francs', ibid.

22. 43 francs instead of the usual 40 francs, ibid., p. 38.

23. ibid., p 9. As there is no specific mention of price, we can assume that the film was still on sale at 40 francs.

24. ibid., p. 40.

25. This still has to be confirmed in a later stage of the present research. The only data I have available now are the approximate running times of two films of the category: *Le Chateau hanté* (no. 2001), one minute 55 seconds, and *Le Prestidigitateur au Café* (no. 2004), two minutes 40 seconds. In any case we can see that these two films are much longer than the 'regulation' length of 17 metres (whose running time is equivalent to about 50 seconds).

26. This is the same as for the Cake-Walk series and the *Danse Serpentine.* The 14 phantasmagorical views were sold in a price range going from 40 (no. 2002, *Une Farce de Gavroche* and no. 2023, *Le Moustique récalcitrant)* to 130 francs (no. 2016, *L'Estafette).* The variation in prices is probably not only due to the differences in length. The production costs of each film may perhaps have been recovered through the sale price (these were works of fiction, which may have implied widely varying expenses on each). In any case, this is what is suggested by the little calculation I have indulged in on the basis of the only data I have available at the moment. Thus *Le Château hanté,* which was sold at 55 francs, would work out at 28.70 francs a minute, whereas *Le Prestidigitateur au Café,* sold at 105 francs, works out at 37.50 francs a minute. However, we need to check a few more things before we can get to the bottom of this situation.

27. op. cit., p. 29.

28. ibid., p. 42.

9 BACK TO LUMIÈRE, OR THE DREAM OF AN ESSENCE: Some Untimely Considerations about a French Myth

Roland Cosandey

A STATEMENT

I doubt whether even a protracted anniversary like the one we are now experiencing with cinema can ever be a time for thoughtful reconsideration rather than just a chance to celebrate. At best the occasion can be used as a means of passing on ideas. I do not want to cast a shadow over the University of Westminster's Festival in particular, nor harm the reputation of all the conferences which have mushroomed in the past two years at such hallucinating speed. They all have their logic and their good reasons, even if the main incentive is probably the chance of getting finance because it really is a celebration – and not, for example, of restoring some dubious pile of decaying prints, or publishing a national filmography, or establishing a catalogue, or setting up a team to do long-term research, or anything else you would like to get money for in normal circumstances.

As a member of the International Domitor Brotherhood, I must say that neither research nor researchers can live on anniversaries. It is in the longer run that things develop and are perceived as developing. Some fields have already been more affected by change than others (early cinema as a 'new concept', for instance), some are emerging, others are at a standstill.[1]

Unlike Méliès (with studies by Frazer, Costa, Hammond),[2] Emile Cohl (Don Crafton),[3] or even the silent period of French cinema in general (Abel, of course, but also a new generation of historians around the French periodical *1895*),[4] the Lumière domain, that unique kingdom in filmland, seems to remain not only a private French hunting-ground, but also a territory which still needs mapping. What kinds of map? Nothing less than a critical edition of the Lumière catalogues published between 1897 and 1907, an analytical filmography, and a bibliography. And in general terms, to make my point clear, it needs something called history.[5]

Some of the points I shall discuss here can be taken as more or less explicit responses to my genuine astonishment at such a situation, which seems particularly striking when one remembers how significant the Lumière legacy is.

ABOUT WORDS

Recalling the long process of composing the call for papers for the Lumière Conference which took place in Lyons in June 1995 leads me to some general thoughts about naming and about what lies beneath or behind what can seem to be mere choices of words.

The main hold-up (among others) was about the distinction to be drawn between 'Cinématographe' and 'cinématographe', that is between a fairly easily identifiable machine, *the* Lumière Cinématographe, and a common utterance, cinématographe, which spread very quickly over the French-speaking world as the name of any film camera or projector or even film show, like the word 'bioscope' in English or Dutch.

Neither the Lumière patent of February 13, 1895, nor its addenda identify the device by this name. These texts use a particular descriptive sentence: 'machine servant à l'obtention et à la vision des épreuves chronophotographiques' (machine used in taking and viewing chronophotographic prints).

In fact the neologism was introduced by Léon Guillaume Bouly and was used as 'Le Cinématographe' or 'Le Cinématographe Léon Bouly' to describe his own chronophotographical machine in two patents dated February 1992 (the 12th) and December 1893 (the 23rd). The patents were not renewed, because Bouly did not pay the renewal fees, and the word became public property.[6]

Nonetheless, the name was attributed to the Lumières as soon as the first reviews of their presentations were published, between March and August 1895. And the Lumières themselves used the word quite often in their correspondence, where they talk of 'our "Cinématographe"', usually putting the name in inverted commas.[7]

CINÉMATOGRAPHE, LE

A look at the main French dictionaries tells us how deeply rooted the annexation, or the confusion, is. The *Dictionnaire alphabétique et analogique de la Langue française,* better known as the Grand Robert (1966), gives only 1895 as the year of first use, which we know is wrong not only thanks to film historians such as Coissac (*Histoire du Cinématographe,* 1925), but also from the testimony of a linguist like Giraud (1958).

The *Grand Larousse de la Langue française en sept volumes* (1971) goes a bit further: 'mot créé en 1895 par les inventeurs, les frères Lumière' (word created in 1895 by the inventors, the Lumière brothers), although several other entries dealing with cinema vocabulary do quote Giraud!

Under the heading 'cinéma' (first usage 1900, stated via Giraud), the Larousse produces a linguistic example of its use, which is not just a formal phrase since it states that 'Les frères Lumière sont les inventeurs du cinéma' (the Lumière brothers are the inventors of the cinema).

Although its title page tells the user, not without affectation, that the work has been 'reviewed and improved by learned revisers', the more recent *Dictionnaire historique de la Langue française* (edited by Alain Rey, 1992), is very misleading, at least under this heading.

The Cinématographe, illustration from its Manual, 1897

Under 'Cinématographe' we read 'mot composé par les frères Lumière (1892, comme nom propre)' – word devised by the Lumière brothers (in 1892, as a proper noun) – and then that 'Le mot désigne l'appareil inventé par les frères Lumière pour reproduire le mouvement par une suite de photographies' (the word designates the apparatus invented by the Lumière brothers to reproduce movement through a series of photographs).

This is certainly not the most accurate description of the thing itself, but after all the dictionary is dealing with linguistic forms, not with objects of reference. So it continues with a linguistic commentary on the word by pointing to the fact that 'la forme abrégée *cinéma* est immédiate (1893), ce qui montre la popularisation rapide du procédé (phènomène analogue pour métropolitain-métro)' – the abbreviated form *cinema* is immediate (1893), which shows how quickly the procedure becomes popular (an analogous phenomenon occurs with metropolitan [underground train]-metro).

There's no discipline like historical linguistics! In this case, Giraud would again have been a very helpful source, however arguable some of his other judgments may be.

' NO! EMPHATICALLY NO!'

Back to the call for papers I mentioned above: the distinction between 'Cinématographe' and 'cinematograph' is not merely formal, for the Appearance of the first Lumière films (or, to put it more accurately) the first Appearance of the Lumière films anywhere) is not the same thing as the first films ever projected anywhere.

The idea that it is, however, is widely accepted because of another strong belief: as the Lumières are considered the true and sole 'inventors' of cinema, the first projected screenings could only be Lumière ones. The shift is easily made by anyone who can't understand the point that Hopwood made, stressing it as early as 1899: 'No! There is not, there never was, an inventor of the Living Picture.'[8]

The quotation is used as the opening motto in Laurent Mannoni's book *Le grand Art de la Lumière et de l'Ombre – Archéologie du Cinéma*, which is one of the most interesting reassessments of the development of the 'invention' ever published in France, at least since Deslandes et Richard's *Histoire comparée du Cinéma* (1968). The Lumière achievement is described in the last chapter, which Mannoni titles 'Les Ouvriers de la Onzième Heure' (The Eleventh Hour Workers) – a provocative reading in the French context.

ABSOLUTE MEANS ABSOLUTE

The notion of 'The Invention' is attached to the Lumières like a genesis out of nowhere, or cunningly dissected down to its minutest details in order to demonstrate that their way was the only one faithful to or programmed by the stamp of an essence of cinematography.[9]

And even the Lumière Cinématographe's method of distribution is considered as an absolute beginning, a total innovation or a long-planned, thoroughly worked-out marketing strategy. Without any positive evidence, the Lumière sons (at the time they were still sons, legally) are supposed, in the last months of 1895, to have developed 'une stratégie d'expansion mondiale' (a world strategy for expansion) and even to have 'anticipé[e] *aussi* sur un dispositif de production-distribution' (and also established the foundations for a production-distribution system).[10]

In fact the most recent published source, one of the few available about the Lumières, the several hundred letters from or to Auguste or Louis edited by Rittaud-Hutinet, shows how slowly the process of commercialisation went, and how dependent it was on a complex context which was largely out of their control.[11]

In Germany, for instance, according to the most up-to-date information we have, a situation obtained which the blind spot of the tradition has ignored. It was not the Lumières who chose a concessionary for the German empire, but the would-be concessionary, Ludwig Stollwerck, who chose the Lumière Cinématographe after having carefully weighed up his options between deals with Edison, Demenÿ, Birt Acres and finally the Lumières. This is not to say that the latter did not have convincing arguments, the main one being that their machine was a 'good little earner', a fact which derived from the compactness of the device and maybe also from the quality of its by-product, the views. But even the question of quality is very arguable; there are many testimonies which emphasise the unsteadiness of the projection and its disturbing, flickering effect, as well as its acknowledged high photographic quality.[12]

SOFTWARE/HARDWARE

By-products, those famous film strips! How come? We need to emphasise another strange thing – at least strange to us, who are so accustomed to the notion of the Lumière films as the essence of cinema. Neither Stollwerck, in his enthusiastic decision to sign a contract with the Lumière subcontractors, nor the Lumières themselves, seem to have expressed any interest in the strips stronger than technical reverence and concern they should be looked after physically.

This is not to dismiss the Lumière production as rubbish or as secondary to the machine whose abilities it had to demonstrate, nor to forget the very well studied range of its subject matter, but rather to bring out a problem which has never been discussed seriously : what was the aesthetic status of a Lumière or a non-Lumière cinematographic image of, let's say, symbolically, 1896? Could it have any?

Could the silence or the unawareness we have alluded to be related to the absence of any aesthetic status – however Proustian or impressionist or deeply faithful to the innate expression of realism in the French cinema we may find them today?

The answer is probably not far away. I suspect that a look at the state of the discussion about photography at the time, and its relation with the wider aesthetic struggle about naturalism would provide some clues.

The fact that the two sons (soon to become the brothers we are familiar with) did once publish a small practical treatise for their customers leads some critics to speak of vision and deep aesthetic awareness. Whereas what we find in the treatise is common or garden advice about asymmetric composition being more dynamic and less boring than centred image construction.[13]

AUTHORSHIP OR AUTEURISM?

In the same perspective, the attribution of authorship, which, in the case of the Lumière repertoire, is a very tricky part of a highly legitimate enquiry into the work's identity, has led to the making of an 'auteur' out of the most symbolically rewarding cameraman or operator ever to handle a camera, Louis Lumière himself, who unlike Edison can be visualised in the action of cranking, not just in the action of sitting at his desk, thinking hard.

The tradition worked out two definitions. The older one constructed less an opposition, more a complementary couple: the Inventor (Louis Lumière) and the Magician (Georges Méliès).[14]

Two famous series of monographs, which contributed to the consolidation of the auteur topos in France, *Cinéastes d'aujourd'hui* (published by Seghers) and *Anthologie du Cinéma* (L'Avant-Scène du Cinéma), included Louis Lumière in their collections, the first by Georges Sadoul (1964), the second by Vincent Pinel (1974).

The French myth of a French film primacy condensed *ab ovo* in the Lumières' work seen as essentially realist is expressed in many ways and has by no means been forgotten, although its form has shifted slightly from sheer nationalism to a more subtle and non-organic cultural claim.

SINCE WHEN?

One may ask: since when? When did this shift happen? We know that the invention of Méliès as the father of cinema has a birth date, the year 1929, when the famous Méliès Gala put him in the pantheon for ever.[15]

We know that the designation of Emile Cohl as the father of the cartoon began in the late teens and reached a triumphant conclusion during the 1930s (just when Disney, thanks to the *Silly Symphonies*, was being widely acclaimed in France). But what about the father of these fathers?

Jacques Aumont is certainly right to emphasise the importance of the Lumière retrospective organised by Henri Langlois at the Palais de Chaillot, Paris, in January 1966. He describes the event as 'perhaps the moment when the transformation of the Lumière myth becomes visible, the moment when the inventor becomes a film-maker'. Through the magnificent visual qualities of the Views, restored and shown as a unique revelation, the idea of cinema as the assumption of reality (and of France as the rightful place of such an expression) was incarnated in a body of work identified by one name, that of Louis.[16]

The notion of Lumière as an artist, an auteur, here makes its closest connection with an ontological conception: Louis Lumière is being credited with the skill, the creative power or the intuition to reveal at one stroke the true essence of cinema or to reveal to the cinema its true essence. About the centenary, for instance, we've been able to read statements like this: 'If this celebration has to maintain any one definite position, it's this: with Lumière "Cinema really is Cinema".

The Lumière pathway through the century of cinema exists. It leads to Rossellini and Godard, to Straub and Kiarostami.'[17]

THE ALL-THERE-FROM-THE-BEGINNING THEORY

One of the most famous illustrated film descriptions is probably Sadoul's analysis of *L'Arrivée d'un Train en Gare de La Ciotat*. The film is presented in a series of four frames, and Sadoul comments on this break-down by observing that every scale of shot is to be found in the film, from the most extreme LS to the biggest CU. Approached in this way, how could the film appear anything but completely inaugural? By dismembering the spatio-temporal unity of this view, the 'analysis' produces a strange, self-confirming object. Of course it doesn't present it as the first film ever made, but in trying to reveal the presence of a supposed variation of scale of shots and of a sort of editing, it designates a good portion of the elements which would later define cinema as a specific language.[18]

Moving us on from teleology to totalisation, the next example is not as unusual in critical discourse as one might think when 'on looking into it' one tries to reckon out all the possible consequences of the position:

> '..in a few months, the Lumière brothers, with extravagant ease, had anticipated a century of cinema of which nobody at the time could have had the least idea... On looking into it, moreover, we can find the most modern of our films in their work too...
> Cowboys, soldiers, ghosts, comedy, it's all there. Without forgetting the aesthetic arsenal of almost the whole of classic cinema which was to follow: *Assiettes tournantes* could have been shot by Méliès and *Mauvaises Herbes* by Griffith. We think of Ford when we see *Nègres dansant dans la Rue,* of Ozu *(Repas de Famille),* of Chaplin *(Douche après le Bain).* There's some Sternberg in *Colleurs d'Affiches,* some Renoir in *Danseuses des Rues.* As for Eisenstein or Walsh, they're there already, in *Procession à Séville* and *Escrime au Sabre japonais* respectively.'

Written by film critic Louis Skorecki, the piece is not, as it might seem, a tribute to 100 Years of Cinema by the College of Pataphysics,[19] but a section of an article which appeared in the Parisian daily *Libération* on March 11, 1993. I am borrowing it from one of the most recent books on the Lumières, *Le Roman des Lumière,* edited by Bernard Chardère, where the jewel is displayed in the last chapter, 'Plaidoyer pour un Créateur' (Plea for a Creator), and introduced by a non-indifferent sub-title, 'L'Avant-garde Lumière' (the Lumière Avant-garde).[20]

MONUMENTS

There is a monument in Lyons which says the same thing in heavy stone, in a style Skorecki, Chardère and any sensible passer-by would probably reject because of its pompousness. It crowns the staircase of the Monplaisir-Lumière underground station. On one side of the square, Antoine Lumière, father to the would-be brothers, built one of his sumptuous *fin-de-siècle* villas, which is now occupied by the Lumière Institute.

Auguste and Louis Lumière, circa 1915

The monument looks like a huge horizontal strip of film. A carved text identifies the subjects: 'Auguste Lumière biologiste 1862-1954 / Louis Lumière physicien 1864-1948 / Inventeurs du Cinématographe' (Inventors of the Cinématographe), and qualifies them as 'Bienfaiteurs de l'Humanité' (Benefactors of Humanity). The humanitarian good deeds alluded to are illustrated along the strip, and surprisingly they are strictly cinematographic: 'Les premiers Films, les grands Reportages, les grandes Mises en Scène, les Films scientifiques' (the first Films, reporting, great productions, science films)...[21]

Nearby there is a street with a detailed name-plate: '8ème Arrt. / Rue du Premier-Film / Auguste et Louis Lumière / 1894' (sic. 8th District, First Film Street, Auguste and Louis Lumière 1894). Everyone knows that the first Lumière film ever screened showed the workers of the Lumière factory leaving the plant. *Sortie d'Usine*, or *Sortie des Usines Lumière* or *Sortie des Ateliers de l'Usine Lumière à Lyon* (the Lumière titles are less titles in the modern manner than descriptions of subject matter) was projected by itself on March 22, 1895, then on April 17, and again on June 10, this time with seven other film strips.

In the French tradition it is not just the first Lumière film ever shot or projected onto a screen, it is the first film ever made, and since there is a street-name stating this primacy, the fact must be officially true. Today we know three versions of this self-promotional film. This gives us convincing evidence about shooting strategy, but also, rather ironically, provides further nourishment for the myth of absolute primacy. *Le Monde*, for instance. recently published an article about the 'discovery', identification and restoration of the three prints, under the title 'Le Premier-né du septième Art' (the seventh Art's First-born),

March 19/20, 1995. The fact that one of the versions was shot before the other two leads the writer to consider *La Sortie des Usines Lumière à Lyon* more emphatically the first film than ever.[22]

SOME REASONS

I will not try to analyse the reasons for the complex situation I have tried to sketch. The emphases may change from one Lumière celebration to another, but nonetheless some things are constant. One of them is probably the need to overcome a feeling of inferiority, to express a hankering after preeminence, France having once been the leading world nation in the field of cinema. Lumière is France and France lost the economic contest sometime during the teens. The recognition asked for is either recognition of the 'invention' as being French, or of a naturalistic essence of cinema belonging intrinsically to the genius of France proper. Interestingly enough, both claims are of a cultural nature.

The idea that the art of cinema is above all French has been around since the 1920s and is still around. The self-image at stake in the recent European debate about film quotas and the tough negotiations with the American film business are the latest evidence of this kind of feeling, this time expanded to a transnational level. Isn't it symptomatic that the proceedings of the Rencontres cinématographiques de Beaune of 1992 were published under the ambiguous title *Sunlight ou... Lumière: le Cinéma européen,* where 'Sunlight' suggests American hegemony – but what about Lumière?

Cinema seems to be considered as France's generous gift to the world – the model being Arago and the Daguerreotype process offered to the world by the French government on August 19, 1839. In 1996, France will donate – to those countries where one hundred years ago the Lumière cameramen went to shoot – a print of 'their' films. And to the nations which were not, at the time, granted such a visit the Mother of the Arts[23] will give a print of the programme of the first public (Lumière Cinématographe) film screening, the ten 'Views' shown in Paris on December 28, 1895.

CONDITIONS ARE WHAT THEY ARE

To some extent conditions favour the image of the Lumières as absolute originators. A great lack of evidence helps the legend appear true, although the mere possession of evidence is not usually enough to reopen a historical debate. What is needed then to play that kind of role in helping us understand the history of the Lumière Cinématographe?

The possibility of comparison is materially close to non-existent. The Lumière prints are an extraordinary exception just by the nature of their massive existence as an archive. No other body of homogeneous work, even from later periods during the first 13 years of silent cinema, has been preserved on such a scale; nearly all the 1,425 or 1,426 views catalogued from 1897 to 1907 in the published catalogues still survive today. The survival of a representative sample was known about since the 1940s, and the films have been seen since the 1960s. For nearly half a century these Lumière films have shaped our picture of the very early landscape of cinema in rather an exclusive fashion, either directly, or indirectly through many documentaries of different kinds.[24]

The theoretical decision to privilege projection as a sign of specificity distinguishes between the ways of viewing film in a radical manner, eliminating the films produced for the Kinetoscope because it is not a projected image.

Some features of contemporary audience reaction have been picked out selectively, the ones which support the idea that the cinematographic image had the impact of an absolute novelty, and that the Lumières' slogan, 'la vie prise sur le vif' (instant life), was the beginning of a programme without precedent.

A still very protective attitude towards the secondary sources does not help in the formulation of hypotheses or the promotion of research in the field. The private correspondence of the cameramen is still not available in its original form, and one has to be satisfied with very unsatisfactory edited fragments. The famous file of copies of the commercial correspondence during the crucial period from October 1895 to February 1896 was obviously consulted by Sadoul in the 1940s, and known thereafter as an important but untraceable source. Well, it reappeared last year in Lyons, but the file, called 'Le Cahier Lefrancq' after its owner, Max Lefrancq, Louis Lumière's grandson, is still of the 'No Trespassing' kind.

One also has to take into account a certain indifference among researchers, which could be the result of tantalising obstructiveness and the monopolisation of data known to exist, but it may also come from the notion of a field which is non-problematic because everything seems to be settled already.

What should begin now is general recognition that there are questions to be asked about this part of film history and its cult of heroes. Apart from a few historians – Deslandes, Pinel, Mannoni – most of the work about the Lumières has tended to ascertain rather than to question, to organise its picture around frozen certitudes rather than to introduce the part of disbelief which may lead to sound problematics, to real research perspectives.

This indifference may also be considered as the damaging result of a poor historical tradition, at least in the domain of film. Be that as it may, one may wonder why nobody has yet made the trip to Roubaix, where the Archives nationales keep their 'Entreprises' – that is, Companies – section. Any French student working on a B.A. dissertation, any American scholar with a generous grant from his Humanities department (but be careful in summer: French archives have strange opening hours) would find all the annual reports of the Etablissements Lumière from 1892 to 1901. If this information does not provide a scoop in the next two or three years I shall, alas, have to consider my grim observations as confirmed.

LIGHTS ON!

Let's go back to the Lumière Conference held at the Université Lumière (Lyon 2). Although it did not satisfy my own (exaggerated) expectations, I have to recognise that the meeting managed to demonstrate one crucial measure of progress: it is possible nowadays, in France, and even in Lyons, to talk about the Lumières without being a 'Lumièriste'. (A certain resistance to the conference among young French researchers certainly expressed their suspicion that such a shift was inconceivable, and that the conference would turn into a pilgrimage.) But actually none of the papers I was able to hear clashed directly with the critical (or polemical, if you prefer) framework I have developed here. Even more excitingly, some contributions took the first steps towards objective approaches to some of the most myth-laden aspects of the Lumières' career, like their integration in the bourgeois society of Lyon or the two brothers' persistent struggle for official recognition of their worthiness, from one anniversary to another of the so thoroughly French invention of the cinématographe.[25]

But my call for these issues to be problematised is still very relevant. What the conference could not achieve was on the one hand to open up access to the secondary sources mentioned above, and on the other to overcome convincingly the fragmentation of a field still occupied by local research projects blind to the question of a more general historiographical framework.[26]

I want to end on a cheerful note, by saying that the most important step foward has in fact been taken. Today, nearly 98% of the Lumière films which figure in the catalogues published between 1897 and 1907 are preserved, restored and accessible, thanks to the work done by the French national film archive, the Film Archive of the Centre National du Cinéma. And the next step will soon be taken too: the long-awaited publication of a critical Lumière filmography.

One can only hope that such instruments will have their effects on the study of this very early part of film history.

NOTES

1. The latest Domitor bibliography is a convenient place to examine some of these configurations. See ed Elena Dagrada, *International Bibliography on Early Cinema*, Domitor, Madison, Wisconsin, 1995.

2. John Frazer, *Artificially Arranged Scenes – the Films of Georges Méliès*, G.K. Hall, Boston, 1979. Antonio Costa, *Georges Méliès – La Morale del Giocatolo*, Il Formichiere, Milan, 1980; 2nd edn, Clueb, Bologna, 1989. Paul Hammond, *Marvellous Méliès*, Gordon Fraser, 1974.

3. Donald Crafton, *Emile Cohl, Caricature and Film*, Princeton University Press, 1990.

4. Richard Abel, *The Ciné goes to Town – French Cinema 1896-1914*, California University Press, 1994. Eds Thierry Lefebvre, Laurent Mannoni, *L'Année 1913 en France*, Association française de Recherche sur l'Histoire du Cinéma, Paris, 1993. Ed Thierry Lefebvre, *Images du réel – la Non-fiction en France (1890-1930)*, Paris, 1995 (1895, no. 18).

5. In the most recent French Lumière publications another phenomenon may be observed, which is very revealing of the poor state of things, at least as far as single-author books are concerned. What is intended by the publishers (and sometimes by the authors themselves) to look new turns out to be nothing of the sort, the Bernard Chardère case being the most obvious, the novelised Lumière biography by Jacques Rittaud-Hutinet, written, as one of his reviewers pointed out, in the manner of Barbara Cartland, the most farcical.

6. See Jean Giraud, *Le Lexique Français du Cinéma des Origines à 1930*, à compte d'auteur (private publication), Paris, 1958, and Laurent Mannoni, *Le grand Art de la Lumière et de l'Ombre*, Nathan, Paris, 1994.

7. One should add that the first letter we know of which uses the word comes rather late in the dense chronology of the first Lumière screenings during 1895. It is dated October 4. So what about earlier? The letter is to be found in Auguste and Louis Lumière, *Letters*, ed Jacques Rittaud-Hutinet, Faber & Faber, 1995, p.23.

8. Henry V. Hopwood, *Living Pictures*, The Optician and Photographic Trades Review, London, 1899, p. 226. See also Stephen Herbert, *When the Movies began... – a Chronology of the World's film Production and film Shows before May 1896*, The Projection Box, London, 1994.

9. See Didier Caron, 'L'In(ter)vention Lumière', *Cinémathèque*, Paris, no. 5, printemps 1994, pp. 104-116.

10. See Auguste et Louis Lumière, *Correspondances*, ed Jacques Rittaud-Hutinet, Cahiers du Cinéma, Paris, 1994, p. 69, note 2. The English edition – Auguste and Louis Lumière, *Letters*, ed Jacques Rittaud-Hutinet, Faber & Faber, 1995 – omits this note about the strategy for world expansion, but the letter to Carpentier of November 25, 1895 which prompted it can be found on pp. 50-51. The reference to the production-distribution system *is* in the English edition, on p. 36.

11. See Auguste et Louis Lumière, op. cit. For discussion of the book's methodological failure and editorial flaws, see my account in *Cinémathèque*, Paris, no. 7, printemps 1995, pp. 133-138.

12. See eds Roland Cosandey and Martin Loiperdinger, 'L'Introduction du Cinématographe en Allemagne – de la Case Demenÿ à la Case Lumière: Stollwerck, Lavanchy-Clarke et al., 1892-1896', Archives, Toulouse, Perpignan, no. 51, November 1992.

13. Auguste et Louis Lumière, 'La Photographie Oeuvre d'Art' (Photography as a Work of Art). I do not know if this was the title of the original treatise. The fragment appears in Bernard Chardère, *Lumières sur Lumière*, Lumière Institute, Presses universitaires de Lyon, 1987, pp. 100-105. The text is said to be part of ed. Henri Gautier, *Les Appareils et leur Usage*, Bibliothèque scientifique des Ecoles et des Familles, quoted without further information. Barthélémy Amengual takes the Lumière advice as a kind of aesthetic manifesto. See 'Lumière, c'est le Réalisme...' in *Lumière, le Cinéma*, Lumière Institute, Lyons, 1993, pp 56-63. See in the same publication an implicit refutation of such a statement by François Albera, 'L'Entrée du Cinématographe dans le Champ artistique', pp. 72-77.

14. This is best illustrated by the two books jointly provided by Maurice Bessy and Lo Duca, *Louis Lumière, Inventeur*, Prisma, Paris, 1948 and *Georges Méliès, Mage*, Prisma, Paris, 1945.

15. See Roland Cosandey, 'Georges Méliès as l'inescamotable Escamoteur – a Study in Recognition / L'inescamotable escamoteur ovvero Méliès come Discorso', in ed Paolo Cherchi Usai, *A Trip to the Movies – Georges Méliès, Filmmaker and Magician (1861-1938)/Lo Schermo incantato – Georges Méliès (1861-1938)*, International Museum of Photography at George Eastman House,

Rochester, New York/Edizioni Biblioteca dell'Immagine, Le Giornate del Cinema muto, Pordenone, 1991, pp. 55-111.

16. '...peut-être le moment où se lit exactement la transformation du mythe Lumière, où l'inventeur devient cinéaste' (perhaps the moment in which the transformation of the Lumière myth, when the inventor becomes a film-maker, can be read exactly), Jacques Aumont, *L'Oeil interminable – Cinéma et Peinture*, Séguier, Paris, 1989, p. 15. See the whole of the chapter 'Lumière, "dernier peintre impressioniste"', pp. 13-36. From our point of view, the main unsolved (and central) question in Aumont's brilliant argument is: what entity is he naming when he uses the Louis Lumière patronymic?

17. Bernard Chardère, Thierry Frémaux, 'La petite Planète Lumière', La Lettre du premier Siècle du Cinéma, no. 7, *Supplément à la Lettre d'Information du Ministère de la Culture at de la Francophonie*, no. 380, December 8, 1994, pp. 2-7. See also Barthélémy Amengual, 'Lumière, c'est le réalisme...' in *Lumière, le Cinéma*, Lumière Institute, Lyons, 1992, pp. 56-63. 'The Lumière pathway' is not just a form of words, it is also an interpretative tool. The expression is used as the title to the penultimate section of *Lumière!*, an anthology of 79 Lumière films selected by the Lumière Institute, Lyons, 1995. The section includes the following six views: *Vue prise d'une Baleinière en marche, Bicycliste, La Bataille de Neige, Puits de Pétrole à Bakou, Lancement d'un Navire* and *Indochine: le Village de Namo, Panorama pris d'une Chaise à Porteur*.

18. Georges Sadoul, *Histoire générale du Cinéma – 1. L'Invention du Cinéma 1832-1897*, Denoël, Paris, 2nd revised and enlarged edn, 1973, p. 300. This particular view carries a heavy burden: the legend of its sensational effect on an audience supposed to be completely taken in by photographic verisimilitude (the public is said to have been scared of being wiped out by the steroscopic moving train) leads to the belief that it must have been one of the first screened. But actually no such subject was shown in the ten promotional Lumière screenings between March and December, 1895, nor was it shown at the Salon Indien opening in Paris on December 28.

19. The College of Pataphysics flourished in the period after the Second World War. Based on some of the precepts of Alfred Jarry, it offered parodic accounts of rhetorical and scientific languages. Its best known representatives were the writers Raymond Queneau and Boris Vian.

20. Bernard Chardère, *Le Roman des Lumière*, Gallimard, Paris, 1995, p. 453. The book is a vaguely updated reprint of *Lumières sur Lumière*, op. cit.

21. 'Monument erected by the Lumière Committee, R. Charpentier President, H. Deleau General Secretary', the work was completed thanks to the generosity of a cooperative association presided by Napoléon Bullukian. It was the work of the sculptors P. and M. Lapanerey and the architect Hubert Fournier. It was installed on September 30, 1962.

22 The three versions can be seen in the third episode of Martina Müller's German television series *Kino vor 100 Jahren – Cinématographe Lumière*, Westdeutscher Rundfunk (WDR), 1995.

23. The phrase 'mother of the arts' originates in the poem *Les Regrets* by the 16th century French writer Joachim du Bellay (Editor's note).

24. Deslandes has already made a point about this: 'Par ailleurs, il nous semble indispensable de comparer les films Lumière aux innombrables films de plein air, "réalistes", tournés à la même époque en France et dans d'autres pays, avant de présenter ce "réalisme" [qui serait propre aux vues Lumière opposées par Sadoul aux films du Kinétoscope] comme une caractéristique essentielle des films Lumière et la raison essentielle de leur succès.' (Moreover, it seems indispensable to us to compare the Lumière films with the countless other outdoor, "realist" films shot in the same period, in France and in other countries, before presenting this "realism" [supposedly specific to the Lumière views that Sadoul opposed to the Kinetoscope films] as an essential characteristic of the Lumière films and the main reason for their success.) See Deslandes et Richard, op. cit., vol 2, p. 270.

25. The proceedings may not be published as soon as one would wish. But the renewal can be observed in other publications as well. See for instance François de la Bretèque, 'Les Films Lumière: des Témoins de la Fin de siècle? Pour une Historiographie du Cinéma Lumière', *Les Cahiers de la Cinémathèque* (Perpignan), no. 62, March 1995, pp. 7-16.

26. See the Lumière conference call for papers in *1895*, no. 15, December 1993, pp. 135-136, and some developments mentioned in my review of the Lumière *Correspondances in Cinémathèque*, op. cit.

PART
TWO

EARLY

CINEMA–

THEN AND

NOW

10 THE DIFFUSE BEAM: Cinema and Change

Simon Popple

The arrival of cinema, in common with many of the new phenomena unleashed at the close of the nineteenth century, immediately excited public imagination. The possibilities for its employment seemed endless, from a base adjunct to music hall and sideshow performances to an almost noble aid to the surgeon, scientist and historian alike. There were of course as many prophetic declarations in its favour as there were cautionary and dismissive sentiments.

'Last night I was in the kingdom of the shadows
If you only knew how strange it is to be there. It is a world without sound, without colour. Everything there – the earth, the trees, the people, the water, and the air – is dipped in monotonous grey. Grey rays of the sun cross the grey sky, grey eyes in grey faces, and the leaves of the trees are ashen grey. It is not life but its shadow, it is not motion but its soundless spectre.'[1]

Maxim Gorky was not wholly convinced about the qualities of cinema, and fearful of the uses to which it would be put by unscrupulous operators, but grudgingly concluded that 'It is not exactly piquant but quite edifying.'[1] He, like some of cinema's fiercest critics, could not help but be momentarily entranced by the sheer novelty of moving images, despite the many imperfections.

However, once the initial novelty of the first few months of its introduction began to wane, cinematographers faced a dilemma. Could the cinema survive in its present form, or, like many entertainments before, would it merely fade from prominence once something more exciting arrived on the scene? The simultaneous introduction of Rontgen or X-rays in 1896 as a popular entertainment is a case in point. This new 'invisible photography', pioneered by Wilhelm Rontgen, proved a massive draw as a form of entertainment in the early months of 1896, at the exact moment cinema was commercially launched in Britain. The public revelled in demonstrations of this magic art which allowed them to look inside their own bodies, and going to the X-rays was as popular as going to visit animated picture shows. Yet by the end of the year they had all but disappeared from public exhibition. The same fate had already befallen Thomas Edison's Kinetoscope. Would cinema be next?

In fact it was the Rontgen Ray which disappeared hastily from the entertainment arena, finding its real applications in medicine and science. But cinema demonstrated a massive potential as a basic recording tool; a facility to document and preserve virtually every facet of daily life, and go beyond into worlds both unfamiliar and unimagined. Whilst audiences were initially attracted by the sheer replication of movement, this comprehension was augmented by a transport of delights. Influenced by the new novel by H.G. Wells, *The Time Machine*, the early film pioneer Robert William Paul was inspired to employ the new medium of cinema in the creation of a Time Machine:

> 'He had been reading the weird romance *The Time Machine*, and it had suggested an entertainment to him, of which animated photographs formed an essential part. In a room capable of accommodating some hundred people, he would arrange seats to which a slight motion could be given. He would plunge the apartment into Cimmerian darkness, and introduce a wailing wind. Although the audience actually moved but a few inches, the sensation would be of travelling through space. From time to time the journey would be combined with panoramic effects. Fantastic scenes of future ages would first be shown. Then the audience would set forth upon its homeward journey. The conductor would regretfully intimate that he had over-shot the mark, and travelled into the past – cue for another series of pictures. Mr Paul had for a long time been at work on this scheme, and had discussed it here and there.'[3]

Although never realised, Paul's scheme demonstrated a desire to take the cinema beyond the immediate bounds of its early exhibition, into new contexts and circumstances. Later that year, in July 1896, Paul was also proposing to the British Museum that it establish a National Film Archive to preserve a record of British society, ostensibly from his own films. Unfortunately for us his kind offer and suggestion were declined.

Others shared Paul's conviction that there was more to the cinema than its initial role as a vicarious entertainment. In 1898 the Polish Lumière cameraman Boleslaw Matuszewski issued what was effectively the first film manifesto, *Une Nouvelle Source de l'Histoire*, in which he outlined the possibility of establishing an archive of historical film. He published a further title, *La Photographie Animée*, which contained a number of suggestions for the use of the cinema in the service of science and education as well as entertainment. Indeed, it was Matuszewski who had pioneered the filming of surgery in Warsaw that very same year. These surgical films were soon commonplace and offered marvellous training facilities for surgeons.[4]

The scientific application of the cinema proved extremely popular, as both public and professional audiences were drawn to the subjects of these films. In cinema's first full year its scientific potential was recognised:

'The Kinematograph having literally at its birth been dragged into the service of the omnipotent music hall (much in a similar way to that in which the poor x-rays are now being trotted out at every bazaar) as a novel and interesting form of entertainment (which it undoubtedly is), its scientific value is likely to be obscured, if not temporarily lost – a misfortune which every earnest worker in science should, I think, do his utmost to avert.(...) I scarcely know of any problem in science where movement of any kind is concerned in which the Kinematograph will not be helpful and oftentimes a powerful assistant. When King Roderick first visited the necromantic tower of Toledo – or at least so runs the legendary history – he beheld on the linen cloth taken by him from the coffer the painted figures of men on horseback of fierce demeanour; anon the picture became animated, and there at length appeared depicted upon its magic surface a great field of battle with Christians and Moslems engaged in deadly conflict, accompanied with the clash of arms, the baying of trumpets, the neighing of horses. Can the imagination conceive that which the mind of science cannot execute? Of a Truth;

   The Photographic art is ever able
   To endow with truth mere fable.'[5]

Advertisement for the
Unseen World series,
Urban-Warwick catalogue,
1903

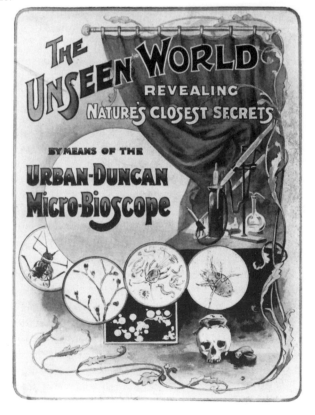

These applications were further augmented by the pioneering use of microscopic and slow motion time-lapse photography, and several firms began to specialise in the production of scientific and natural history films. One individual in particular, Charles Urban, pioneered the introduction of scientific films with the popular *Unseen World* series in 1903.

Another application of the cinema was the capturing of what were generally regarded as 'Actualities', or news and documentary subjects. The camera covered public and sporting events, wars and civil disturbance, ethnographic, topographical and industrial subjects. In an era when foreign travel was still the privilege of the rich, or a necessity of war, and when the majority of the population had been no further than the seaside, one can only guess at the impact these images must have had. For the first time cinema-goers had the opportunity to visualise people and places they had only seen in static, graphic and photographic representations. People became familiar with royal and state events, and subjects like the Derby and the Boat Race, boxing matches and F.A.Cup proved extremely popular. Initially these actuality and news films were shown alongside the staple diet of cinema fare, features, comedies and melodramas. But it was not long before specialised news cinemas began to appear. The first in Britain, the Daily Bioscope, opened opposite Liverpool Street Station in London on May 23 1906.[6] This was closely followed by the birth of the news-reel, and the launch of the *Topical Budget* in 1911. Physical horizons were further expanded by films of exploration, mountaineering and big game hunting, such as Cherry Kearton's films of Theodore Roosevelt's African expedition of 1908. But perhaps more than any other film of this type it was Herbert Ponting's films of the ill-fated Scott Antarctic expedition of 1911 which produced some of the most stunning and strangely alien images the British public had seen. While exposure to subjects from distant places and remote habitats was making the world a smaller place for cinema's audience, there was also a curious, almost antithetical process taking place.

One of the earliest, and most reproduced films was *Sortie d'Usine,* the 1895 Lumière film of their workers leaving the Lumière factory. The Lumières filmed their own workers on many occasions and screened the efforts to the enthusiastic workforce. Whether these reactions were motivated by delight at the process of the cinema, or more the result of seeing themselves represented, is a matter of debate. Film exhibitors often emulated this popular practice when they moved to a new town, inviting the locals to be filmed and then to visit a screening to see themselves. Recognition was a frequent and widely reported occurrence:

'SNAPSHOTS

"Hello Bill!" – When showing animated pictures it is said to be no unusual thing for a girl to cry out "Dad!" on seeing the figure of her father, who is perhaps a soldier in South Africa, walking on the screen, whilst old pals of soldiers can barely resist the impulse to call out to their pictures in the old terms, "Hello, Bill!"

A Pathetic Incident – A pathetic incident recently occurred in the St James's Hall, Manchester. Messrs. Edison were showing some scenes of the Whit Monday Sunday School processions in Manchester. Suddenly a woman's voice in the audience was heard to proclaim hysterically, "There's my Annie!" And it was, but alas! in the interval between the photograph being taken and the day on which the poor mother saw the picture the child had been killed. To the mother the illusion was too real but too transient, and for the time being she simply saw her little one walking serenely behind the banner of her Sunday School in the most natural way imaginable. After this incident hundreds of people from the neighbourhood in which the little girl lived came to see the almost living image of their departed friend.'[7]

So as well as offering up whole new worlds and experiences cinema was also directly focused on the individual. People saw themselves and the rest of humankind represented on the very screen before them. Their own lives, occupations and circumstances were called into question by this new medium, and comparisons were not always favourable. Cinema's ability to depict real people and situations had repercussions in its fictional representation. It was characterised as a medium suited for detection and identification. Stories about people recognising missing relatives, or people caught in compromising situations by the camera became the standard plots of fictional stories about the cinema.

'TELL-TALE PHOTOGRAPH

Wife's Deception Discovered At Cinematograph Show. . . . .

A man named Julien Boistard presented himself at the police station of Petit-Montrouge on Monday to give himself up for the murder of his wife. He had shot her with a revolver as the result of a quarrel, which arose in a curious way. Boistard had been to see a cinematograph display in the Rue de la Gaîté, and among the pictures was one representing the Rheims aviation week. On the films he recognised his wife, making merry at the buffet. His wife, who was by his side, also recognised the tell-tale picture and fainted, whilst the wronged husband cried out his woes to the audience. He had believed his wife to be spending a holiday with some relations, while he was doing his military service. The performance was suspended, the lady taken to a chemist's and brought round. Then the couple went home, and the quarrel ensued. Fortunately for all concerned, the angry husband's aim was bad and he had not hit his wife at all. She had merely fainted again. He was set at liberty by the commissary on the understanding that the quarrel should be made up.'[8]

Rudyard Kipling provided one such example in his 1904 short story *Mrs Bathgate*, and the poet Guillaume Apollinaire produced a macabre short story about the commissioning of a snuff movie. Like the bugs that the camera exposed to the public through the lens of the microscope, cinema's audience was itself only so many microbes on a rather large piece of rotten cheese.

Because of the cinema's potential to represent recognisable and identifiable images and patterns of behaviour it seemed destined to draw a swift series of responses from those in authority. It was rather surprising then that the first example of direct government intervention in the industry was the Cinematograph Act of 1909 which sought to legislate for the safety of cinema patrons. Even stranger was the failure of government to legislate in the area of censorship. The British Board of Film Censors emerged in 1912 as a voluntary organisation to which film makers could submit their works for classification, and began classification in 1913. On this evidence it was almost as if the cinema was dismissed as an unimportant sideshow for more than the first decade of its existence. This could not be further from the truth. The arrival of the cinema in the theatres, music halls and fairgrounds of Britain unleashed a wave of moral panics and calls for legislation. Cinema was blamed for everything from promiscuity and juvenile delinquency to white slavery and the spread of disease, much as theatre and music hall had been earlier. In a survey carried out by the National Council Of Public Morals in 1917, schoolchildren were questioned on the potential evils of the cinema by Dr Marie Stopes:

Advertisement for lantern slide to be projected between screenings, from a trade paper, circa 1905

Have you seen any picture which you thought at the time was bad to see? – No, but I saw a picture once which I thought was vulgar. It was called "_____."

Supposing you went into a picture house and you met a fairy at the door who told you could see any picture you liked, what kind would you like to see? – I should like to see a picture about a circus.

What sort of picture would you like best? – I should like a good drama, but not a love drama. A nice drama like *Little Miss Nobody*, which I thought was very nice.

Why don't you like love dramas? – There is too much fooling about in them, and there is always hatred between two men and two women.

You don't like to see two men hating each other? – Well, it is a lot of silliness. I do not think it would happen in real life.

You never got any disease at the cinema? – No, but once I got scarlet fever, but not in a cinema.

Did you ever get anything? – No, I did not catch my disease there.[9]

Many of the more sensational claims had their basis in real events and cases, but through the magnifying lens of the popular press they provided ample ammunition for those interested in imposing control upon the cinema. For example, the early sites within which the first moving pictures were exhibited, the music hall penny gaff and fairground, were often insanitary and little more than death traps.

Even after the advent of fully regulated permanent cinema, management handbooks offered advice on disinfecting the auditoria with the audience in occupation!

When Members of Parliament did examine issues relating to these problems they invariably failed to find sufficient evidence to back up some of the wilder accusations levelled at the cinema.

'A Patron of the Mutoscope

We are as interested as the most puritanically minded M.P. could wish in the suppression of all photographs of an indecent or suggestive character. It is a misfortune that so beautiful an art should allow for such degradation, and it behoves all photographers to do what they can to see that such a stigma shall not attach to their calling or hobby. At the same time, it is doubtful whether public interest and private morality is served by undue exaggeration which only too often accompanies the attempts of the misguided but well meaning enthusiasts to suppress everything which a too prurient mind can savour in any way of suggestiveness.'[10]

Where legislation was forthcoming, in the areas of safety, and later, protection of the fledgling industry, there was very real evidence that action was needed.

One of the defining events in the early history of the cinema was the Paris Charity Bazaar Fire of May 4, 1897 when 121 people died as a result of a fire started by an ether lamp in a cinematograph demonstration. The event was doubly notable because of the social status of many of those who perished, and the event was widely covered in the society press. The fact that fires and explosions were a common feature of existing magic lantern entertainments which shared the same lighting technology was neither here nor there. The eventual legislation imposed through the 1909 Cinematograph Act gave local councils the responsibility for licensing all premises for exhibition of films, and many prosecutions under the act followed.

The cinema elicited rather more than just a legislative response from those in authority. Legislation, in the form of the 1909 Act, merely controlled the physical domain of the cinema, but the social, moral and political challenges offered by the films in terms of their subject matter were, and still are, contentious. Many early commentators, both in the popular press and from clear institutional perspectives, such as those of the judiciary or the church, began to articulate

Trade advertisement, circa 1913

reservations about the social consequences of the cinema. A clear pattern of issues begins to emerge from the moment of the arrival of commercial cinema in 1896. Vested interests within British society regarded the cinema with deep suspicion, if not downright hostility. It was often regarded as a diversionary and potentially inflammatory entertainment, open to a myriad of abuses.

These debates centred around the issues of social conformity, crime, political unrest and public morality. It was often felt that exposure to unsuitable subjects threatened the very fabric of late Victorian and Edwardian society, and that the sense of escapism experienced by cinema goers, the vast majority of them working class, could lead to resentment and discontent. Glimpses of other worlds, however fleeting, were not always healthy. The symbols of authority, the monarchy and armed forces were a constant feature of early cinema presentations, Queen Victoria's Diamond Jubilee of 1897 proving extremely popular. Military reviews were another constant feature, as well as the yearly series of society events such as Ascot and the Henley Regatta. But so were films which mocked authority, poked fun at such figures as the police or clergy and showed alternative lifestyles, although from a fiercely moralising perspective. They were hardly likely to provoke mutinous uprisings, but their very presence heralded something altogether new, a growing tendency towards a rejection of the values of class and duty.

A leading issue of the day was women's suffrage, and a whole genre of suffragette cinema ensued. We are all probably familiar with the images of Emily Davidson throwing herself under the King's horse, but a whole series of usually anti-suffragette films were made, nearly all of them comedies. Perhaps the earliest was Bamforth's 1900 film *Women's Rights* in which two women have their skirts nailed to a fence whilst discussing women's issues. These films became a regular feature in the years directly preceding the First World War, revelling in titles such as *A Suffragette In Spite of Herself, How They Got The Vote, The Elusive Mrs Pinkhurst*, and *Selina's Flight For Freedom.*

One in particular, Clarendon's 1913 film *Milling The Militants*, contains all the common themes, but at least this particular suffragette has the last laugh:

'MILLING THE MILITANTS
The spouse of a suffragette has a sad experience after dreaming dreams of suppressing his better half – Brown is blessed with a large wife and a small family, whom he is left to look after while his better half goes forth armed with a hammer to smash, burn and plunder. Brown falls asleep and dreams that he is Prime Minister and making laws to suppress the militants. Brown is gloating over a recalcitrant female when he is awakened, and his wife is upsetting a pail of water over him, at the same time scolding him

for sleeping and neglecting his duties. His courage fails him, and the late ' Prime Minister' begs for mercy on his knees.' [11]

Other films tackled social issues such as working conditions. For instance, Kineto's 1910 film *Day in the Life of a Coalminer*, filmed in the Wigan Coalfields, drew clear parallels between the hard physical nature of the coalminers' work, and the luxury of those who relied on their toil.

The manipulation of cinema for political ends was to become an art following the First World War, but already its persuasive power was more than apparent. Institutions, including the Church and Parliament, [12] were keen to make use of the propaganda potential of the medium,and even more generally cinema was applied to the task of influencing popular opinion, often too successfully for its own good:

'A FILM OF THE DECREPIT HORSE TRAFFIC
The Royal Society for the Prevention of Cruelty to Animals has enlisted the Cinematograph on behalf of the Bill dealing with the decrepit horse traffic. It may be said at once that the pictures as shown privately yesterday are never likely to be displayed before the general public, for, deeply impressive as they are, no censor would pass them for general exhibition, and no cinematograph theatre manager would put them into an ordinary programme. The earlier pictures show the arrival of the animals and their weary progress through the streets, and to these, pathetic as they are, no objection could be taken. But in the closing stages, by way of an argument in favour of a humane killer, the film shows a primitive method of slaughtering the unfortunate beasts by driving a knife into the chest. As the blood surges out the animal's death struggles are seen with repulsive realism. The society itself admits that these pictures cannot be shown in public, however vividly they prove the need for some improvement of existing conditions.'[13]

The relationship between the cinema and crime was another constant theme in this formative period. In many ways it was a double edged sword, seen both as a means of inciting crime, and at the same time as a means of showing its consequences, and even as a means of apprehension. Court cases involving juveniles influenced by films towards criminal behaviour were commonplace, and their punishment usually included prohibition from local cinemas.[14] Yet the vast majority of these films showed the degradation and penalties of a life of crime. For instance, the Mottershaws' 1903 film *A Daring Daylight Burglary* showed the chase and capture of a burglar, and an article in *The World's Fair* in April 1912 outlined several occasions when the cinema had acted as an agency for the apprehension of criminals.[15]

That the cinema grew and prospered from this formative period was undeniably due to its sheer adaptability and the inventiveness of its many advocates. The extreme diversity of film's application outside the context of the commercial cinema, in the fields of science, education, as a detective medium and as a social and historical document, must shift our emphasis away from the traditional historiographic concerns with film as pure entertainment. Many responses elicited by cinema refer to the novelty and heightened sense of spectacle it offered its audience. Yet the single most significant response concerned the realism with which film represented its subjects. Film intruded into the lives of its Victorian and Edwardian spectators in a way that no other medium of the 1890s could. Photography had had a similar kind of impact in the 1840s, ultimately increasing the range and constituency of the reproduced image. It had accelerated the transfer of visual information and assumed many roles later adopted by cinema. Photography again dominated other representational forms because of its perceived capacity to represent images with the highest sense of pictorial realism. Above all else it altered the perception of the physical world, shifting the traditional boundaries between art and science, blurring the distinctions between instruction and entertainment. Cinema further automated this ongoing process, surpassing the power of the photographic image, with the added perception of motion.

NOTES

1. Maxim Gorky, Review of the Lumière programme at the Novgorod Fair, *Nizhegorodski Listok*, July 4, 1896.

2. ibid.

3. An Interview with Robert William Paul, *The Era*, April 25, 1896.

4. 'The Cinematograph in Surgery', *Chambers Journal*, August 26, 1899, p. 621.

5. V.E. Johnson M.A., 'The Kinematograph from a Scientific Point of View', *Photography*, December 10, 1896.

6. I am indebted to Richard Brown for this information.

7. *The Photographic Chronicle*, August 1, 1901, p. 61.

8. *The World's Fair*, October 2, 1909.

9. Report of the National Council Of Public Morals, 1917.

10. *British Journal Of Photography*, August 15, 1901.

11. *Kinematograph Weekly*, June 19, 1913.

12. There was a long running series of articles in the *Field Officer*, e.g. October 1906, extolling the virtues of the cinema in the service of religion.

13. *The Times*, February 27, 1914, p. 6.

14. 'Boys Bound Over Not To Enter Picture Theatres', *The Times*, February 13, 1914, p. 8.

15. 'The Cinema Detective', *The World's Fair*, April 13, 1912.

This chapter draws on material from the forthcoming publication *In The Kingdom of Shadows* by Colin Harding and Simon Popple, Cygnus Arts, 1996.

11 SPORT AND THE FIRST FILMS

Luke McKernan

Moving picture film was an invention of the late nineteenth century for which we can cite a few significant names: Edison, Dickson, Marey, Lumière. Cinema, however, is an altogether wider phenomenon and its inventors are many more in number. Among them we must name the entrepreneurs, the enthusiasts, the subjects of those first films, and the first audiences. The invention of cinema was a collective activity by a broad selection of late Victorian society, the first people to leave their mark to future generations on moving picture film.

Among Victorian films some of the most significant are sports films, for apart from their popularity at the time and the interest that they generate now, sport and sportsmen played a leading role in the invention of cinema. Indeed one may even go so far as to say that the mere mechanical construction of a film projector has been overestimated, and that it was boxing that created cinema. Cinema was ultimately the creation of its audience, and many among that first audience were not interested in films per se; they were interested in sports.

Before films were even shown to an audience, sport was central to their development. The notion of combining motion pictures with the realism of photography has its origin in the experiments of Eadweard Muybridge, described in outline in David Robinson's essay. Muybridge's commission was from Californian businessman Leland Stanford, who wanted to solve the age old conundrum of whether a horse's legs were ever all off the ground during a gallop. Muybridge's experiments proved conclusively that a horse's feet did in fact all leave the ground at certain points. Thus this embryonic form of motion photography came into being through a problem of chief interest to the horse racing community, though the results became of great importance to scientists, biologists and artists.

Muybridge continued his sequence photographs with sponsorship from the University of Pennsylvania, where during the mid-1880s he photographed sequences of hundreds of subjects, some animals, but mostly human, many of them athletes, with results which seem as much to show off the athletic form as an object of attraction in itself as to be a serious scientific study of motion.

Muybridge's experiments in sequence photography created a huge impact and were a direct influence on the science of chronophotography developed at Station Physiologique, Paris by Etienne-Jules Marey and Georges Demenÿ. Many of Marey's subjects were also human athletes, in fact often Demenÿ himself, whose background was in gymnastics and who was an important figure in the promotion of physical education in France, writing several text books on gymnastics and physical exercise with ideas which were widely adopted. Cinema therefore began with the study of motion, making the movement of both horse and man an object of scientific interest and a spectacle in itself. The sporting figure anatomised lies at the heart of motion picture experiment from the very beginning.

Part of *One Stride in Ten Phases*, photographic sequence by Eadweard Muybridge, 1887.
The horse's name was Clinton, the length of his stride 2.7 metres, its time approximately 0.52 of a second

We know how the studies of Muybridge and Marey in turn provided inspiration for Thomas Edison. But Edison's (and Dickson's) Kinetoscope was not a machine designed with scientific study in mind. A peepshow device, it was always aimed at the commercial market, and chose its first film subjects accordingly. The two deciding factors in selecting subjects for the Kinetoscope were their commercial potential and the restrictions of Edison's Black Maria studio at West Orange. The subjects that came to be chosen were entertainers and sportsmen. The very first experimental subjects of 1892 were in fact gymnasts in the Marey mould, but this was while the Kinetoscope was still being developed. Once the machine was ready to be presented to the public, popular subjects had been selected, as is shown by the line-up of film titles at the first public Kinetoscope show in April 1894: *Sandow, Horse Shoeing, Barber Shop, Bertoldi (Mouth Support), Wrestling, Bertoldi (Table Contortion), Blacksmiths, Highland Dance, Trapeze* and *Roosters*.

Eugen Sandow, star of that first film show, was a German body-builder and promoter of physical health of world renown. He successfully combined a serious promotion of physical fitness with commercial display, appeared in various theatres, and had been frequently photographed before being invited to appear before Edison's Kinetograph camera. Sandow is remarkable in early film history for having been not only a star of the world's first commercial film presentation, but also at both the first commercial presentation of projected film in Europe (Max Skladanowsky's show at the Berlin Wintergarten, November 1, 1895) and the public debut of the prestigious Biograph projector in Pittsburgh on September 14, 1896. In his Edison and Biograph films Sandow struck body-building poses; for Max Skladanowsky he wrestled briefly with one Grainer.[1] Sandow represented the changeover from film as a medium of scientific study to a medium of entertainment. But the next stage – moving from studies of athleticism to athletic display – was the record of a sporting event itself. No subject was more suitable for the camera or more significant in the development of cinema than boxing.

Some athletic and boxing displays had been included among the earliest Edison experiments[2] but the first recognisable sporting event on film was the Leonard-Cushing fight recorded in the studio in June

1894. The inspiration behind this film was the Kinetoscope Exhibition Company, one of three Edison Kinetoscope concessionaries set up in the summer of 1894, formed by the brothers Gray and Otway Latham, Samuel Tilden and Enoch Rector. Their interest was in boxing and in using the Kinetoscope as a means of exhibiting fights.

Mike Leonard and Jack Cushing, two minor prize fighters, fought six rounds in the Black Maria. Each round lasted a minute, with a seven-minute interruption between rounds while the film was changed. Eventual customers attending a Kinetoscope parlour would pay to view each round in a separate machine before learning of the result in the sixth (publicity made sure that the result was a secret, a secret that remains since the film does not survive in its complete form).

The Leonard-Cushing fight opened in New York in August 1894, with great success, and the Kinetoscope Exhibition Company raised the stakes the following month by securing the world champion Jim Corbett to be filmed fighting Peter Courtney. Again six rounds were filmed, with a knockout (by Corbett) prearranged for the sixth round.

In fact Corbett was a highly significant figure in the history of boxing, one whose professional approach and conduct inside and outside the ring did much to elevate the status of the sport, which then existed in a semi-criminal state. Prize fighting was officially banned in the U.S.A., though this was enforced to somewhat varying degrees state by state. It is indicative of the narrow (male) target audience that the first Kinetoscope exhibitors were aiming to attract. Dancers, acrobats, body-builders and boxers – the Edison Kinetoscope was hardly gearing itself toward a broad or family audience.[3]

Despite their success with their Kinetoscope boxing films, the Lathams were frustrated at the limitations of the machine – in screen size and more particularly in the solo audience that it could attract, and in common with other inventors around the world at this period, began to experiment with showing Kinetoscope pictures on a screen. They poached Dickson and another Edison employee, Eugène Lauste, to work for them from December 1894, and by February 1895 their first test film was ready. Following a press showing in April, on May 4 the Lathams gave their first commercial film, a boxing match between 'Young Griffo' (a renowned fighter of the period) and 'Battling' Charles Barnett, filmed on the roof of Madison Square Gardens. The signifi-

The Leonard-Cushing Fight,
Edison, 1894

cant addition of a loop to the film (the 'Latham loop') allowed far more film to pass through the camera without tearing, allowing continuous filming for eight minutes instead of the one minute separate rounds previously. The film was presented on May 20,1895 at 156 Broadway, New York, the world's first commercial presentation of projected film; in effect, the birth of cinema.

The Lathams' Eidoloscope projector, 'little more than a Kinetoscope with an arc lamp behind it',[4] produced a small, indistinct image, and although they toured with the machine for several months and filmed other subjects, including a wrestling match, it was an inadequate device which did little to create a true idea of cinema or to attract people outside the narrow sporting audience defined above.[5] That breakthrough came through the work of the Lumière brothers in France. Their machine did not address itself to a specialised audience (sports or otherwise), but to the world – literally, as they rapidly sought to exploit it all over the globe by means of touring operators. But the Lumières, despite their main interest in actuality, seldom recorded news or sports events. They were more interested in the scenic view than the truly immediate or meaningful public event. Although some public, international events like the coronation of Czar Nicholas II or Queen Victoria's Diamond Jubilee were covered, few genuine sporting events ended up in the Lumière catalogue.[6]

To return to boxing, Jim Corbett earned five thousand dollars for making the Courtney film, and it is important to note the large sums of money involved, as there was very little money in boxing alone at this period, and Corbett for instance was making such fortune as he could from his appearances in the theatre. His opponent in the 1897 world heavyweight championship bout, Bob Fitzsimmons, similarly derived a comfortable income from portraying himself in touring stage shows, and it was the ten thousand dollars put up for their bout that saw the start of huge sums being put into prize fights by the moving picture industry.

Fitzsimmons, originally from Cornwall but raised in New Zealand, had defeated Peter Maher, briefly Corbett's successor when the latter conceded his title on February 21, 1896 (a bout that Enoch Rector had attempted to film, but the weather defeated him and it was all over in one round anyway). This earned Fitzsimmons the right to challenge Corbett on March 17, 1897 at Carson City, Nevada (the first state to legalise prize fighting). Enoch Rector, now operating separately from the Lathams, had devised a unique 63mm format to ensure exclusive use of the resultant film, and took a huge 11,000 feet of film using three cameras positioned next to each other and used in sequence. Rector's extremely advantageous central camera position shows how much the fight was staged with the eventual film, and the money that it would bring, in mind. The static epic which emerged was converted into a programme (with commentary and gaps for reel changes) which lasted almost two hours, thrilling boxing audiences despite its apparent visual tedium. This was especially so because the camera had recorded the controversial blow to the stomach by which Fitzsimmons defeated Corbett in the fourteenth round. The world's first feature-length film was a boxing match.

But the sports film, which had played a significant part in the growth of moving pictures, was to develop elsewhere, notably in America and Britain. In America the boxing film continued to flourish and to be present at key stages in the growth of American cinema. The Jim Jeffries-Tom Sharkey fight on November 3, 1899 became the first live event to be filmed by artificial light, as employed by the American Mutoscope and Biograph Company. The great commercial value of such sports films was shown by the purchase of the exclusive filming rights, organised by William Brady (Corbett's business manager and a future film producer of renown). This was to become an enduring trend, and two other trends were also established: the pirating of illicit footage (Albert Smith of the Vitagraph company took advantage of Biograph's arc lights to take his own unofficial film), and the filming of recreated fights, a speciality of producer Siegmund Lubin, who offered 'facsimile' versions of Corbett-Fitzsimmons, Jeffries-Sharkey and other popular bouts. Many audiences across the country were hoodwinked into thinking they were buying tickets to see the real thing. In the early American boxing film we can see the very birth of American cinema – realism and drama, newsfilm and fakery, commercialism, populism, professionalism, two protagonists battling within the perfect staging, the ring.

In Britain, though American boxing matches were popular, British fighters did not have the same box office draw, and other sports proved more appealing to British audiences. The first British film-makers were Birt Acres (cameraman) and Robert William Paul (producer of rogue Kinetoscopes) who met in February 1895 and by March had produced their first test film, showing their mutual acquaintance Henry Short coming out of Acres' house dressed in cricket whites – to show up better on film, however, and not as an expression of a sporting interest. Their first commercial film was taken on March 30 1895, and showed the Oxford and Cambridge boat race. Given the tiny image of the Kinetoscope, this was a surprising choice – Edison Kinetoscope titles had been very largely individuals filmed in a studio, and boxing matches were not the least suitable for filming because they could be contained within a studio setting. The film does not survive, so we cannot judge how it would have looked, but clearly Acres and Paul were as interested in recording sporting actuality as in creating a finished product ideally suited to the available means of exhibition. The actuality was pre-eminent, the expression only secondary, an abiding theme in British film-making, and illustrated by Acres and Paul's further films (produced together and subsequently solo), notably the Derby of 1895, filmed in three scenes by Acres on May 27, 1895, showing the course being cleared, the pre-race gallop, and the finish with crowds pouring onto the course afterwards. Again the results could hardly have looked at their best in a Kinetoscope, and it seems not improbable that Acres and Paul were looking ahead to potential film projection, as others were doing simultaneously in France, Germany and the USA, and which Acres was to achieve by the end of 1895, Paul soon after.

The pair split up acrimoniously in July 1895. Acres, after some prestigious success early in 1896, soon went into decline as a producer, lacking the commercial nous of his former partner. He retained his interest in actuality film, and particularly sporting film, however, filming football matches, the 1896 Derby and the legendary British boxer Jem Mace (a former champion and later trainer who discovered Bob Fitzsimmons), 65 years old and still fighting. But for Paul as a solo producer the 1896 Derby was to be a personal triumph and an event of considerable significance for the nascent British film industry. On June 3, 1896 Paul and his assistants journeyed down to Epsom, positioning their single camera on a cart close by the finish on the right (looking up the course) with a view just over the crowd's heads as the horses approached. This single shot record, though unremarkable to modern eyes, caused a sensation – not for its filmic qualities, but for the actuality that it had witnessed and the

The Sensation of the Nineteenth Century !

THE

KINEMATOGRAPHE

Is a marvellous development of instantaneous photography. By means of a powerful Electric Machine figures instinct with life and actuality pass before the eye a screen. These pictures are photographed at the rate of a thousand a minute, and represent every motion of real life with marvellous fidelity.

This wonderful scientific novelty is now attracting crowded and enthusiastic audiences in both London and Paris.

Further developments are being made daily by the Celebrated English Artist—

BIRT ACRES, Esq.,

Whose Studies of Animated Photographs have never been equalled.

The Mechanical and Electrical arrangements under the Management of Mr. A. JONES.

PLEASE ADDRESS—

T. M. HOWARD,

319, HOE STREET, WALTHAMSTOW.

Publicity for Birt Acres, 1896

circumstances of its exhibition. Paul's team rushed the exposed film back to London from Epsom with all speed, and in a remarkable feat for the period had the processed film on the screen at the Alhambra and Canterbury music halls within 24 hours.

The expectant audience were already thrilled by the news – the Derby had been won by the favourite Persimmon, owned by the Prince of Wales, and the Derby was in any case no mere sporting event but a national obsession. Scenes of wild excitement (not really evident from Paul's film) had occurred on the course following the victory, and when the film of the finish was shown to the theatre audience with the news still buzzing in their ears, the result was electrifying, triggering the same outburst of patriotic enthusiasm as people wildly cheered the film and the orchestra played *God Bless the Prince of Wales.* They demanded that it be shown again and again. As no other film had done before (but as many would do later) Paul's 1896 Derby film created emotion through its triumph over time. Yesterday became today. Several of the first witnesses of cinema commented on its potential to revive the past, to preserve something of present life for posterity, but the Derby film went further in collapsing time altogether. It was not a record of the race by the sporting standards to come, but in its moment, and in its particular circumstances, it proved the perfect emblem of the event.

The horse racing film could not long remain as a single shot of the finish, and within a few years increasingly larger camera teams were being employed by the emergent newsfilm companies to produce a more comprehensive record, though with the same hectic race to get film of the major events to the cinemas in the shortest time possible. Like boxing, horse racing proved particularly appropriate to cinema, not this time for its setting, but for its predictable dramatic structure and its comparative brevity, using up little expensive film stock. Other sports proved more resistant to the early film producers. Association football in Britain was entering a period of phenomenal popularity with massive crowds attending matches, but the camera with its initial 50 to 100 foot capacity could not begin to produce even an emblematic record of such an event. The climax of a horse race was obvious and constant – but football did not rise to a climax in that way and the few goals could not be predicted.

Nevertheless some simple records of football matches were produced, the first in 1896 by Robert Paul, the next in 1897 by the Lumières, whose simply titled *Football* is one of the British-produced titles in the Lumière catalogue, and Brighton's G.A. Smith. The earliest surviving film of an actual professional game, Blackburn Rovers versus West Bromwich, was taken by the Welsh-based Arthur Cheetham in 1898. Cheetham placed his camera directly behind the goal and recorded some four minutes, showing each half: the action far in the distance, figures in grey stripes engaged in a vague sporting struggle. Yorkshire cameraman Jasper Redfern became a specialist in recording local football (and cricket) matches, and there was probably more hope of attracting the interest of a partisan audience for such a local event. But by 1899 the Warwick Trading Company were filming the F. A. Cup final, and the catalogue description of their (lost) record of the match between Sheffield United and Derby County shows that advanced, multi-shot filming was underway: 'The Sheffield United and officials entering the field; Mid-field play; Sheffield obtains a corner, showing goal play, scrimmage and goal kick; Derby County's only goal, showing other goal, enthusiasm of the vast audience, goal keeper busy'.[7] R.W. Paul's two films of the 1901 F.A. Cup Final replay (between Tottenham Hotspur and Sheffield United) do survive and show a similar liveliness, the beginnings of a satisfying sporting record and drama rather than an animated photograph. As the dramatic film was developing and finding a form for itself, so too the non-fiction film, and within this the sporting film, was taking shape and finding its cinematic nature.

Cricket, a game taking place over days rather than hours, naturally defied the first film-makers. Instead they concentrated on the personalities and their style of play. The legendary W. G. Grace, whose hundredth century was scored in cinema's founding year of 1895, was a popular subject as a famous public figure, it being sufficient for audiences just to see the great man in motion, for example the Prestwich Manfacturing Company's *Dr Grace's Jubilee Procession* (1898). But cricket films generally came to mean batsmen demonstrating strokes, usually in the nets, as exemplified by the first known (certainly the earliest surviving) cricket film, that taken by Henry Walter Barnett of Ranjitsinhji practising in the nets at the Sydney Cricket Ground in December 1897, one of four films taken by Barnett of the England-Australia test series of 1897-98. Ranjitsinhji is seen in similar practice alongside Grace in James Williamson's *Cricket*, filmed at Hastings in 1901. Again, catalogue descriptions of lost films indicate that some coverage of a cricket match in progress was nevertheless attempted very early on, with Warwick showing views of the England v Australia final test match of 1899.[8]

But the problems of dramatising a full football or cricket match on film were not solved to any degree until the 1920s by the then well-established newsreel companies, when large camera teams, greater camera capacity, and a greater idea of judicious camera position to capture the drama inherent in the games was realised and recorded. Horse racing films reached maturity far earlier, and before 1910 extensive records were being made by large camera teams of the Derby and the Grand National which were annual film highlights in Britain. Other sports filmed to some degree or other in Britain by 1900 were golf, cycling, polo, cycle polo, water polo, wrestling, gymnastics, and of course the perennial favourite, the Oxford and Cambridge boat race. In America, college sports – baseball, American football, athletics – were naturally popular and filmed faithfully by Biograph in particular, who also produced an extensive record of the 1899 America's Cup yachting race. Wherever sports flourished, the sports film did too.

Cinema was the invention of its audience. Without that audience film would have remained a tool of scientific discovery; through the wishes of that audience films came to depict certain subjects in certain well-defined ways. Spectacle, drama and realism were the defining attributes of cinema, and sport could ably supply all of these. Moreover, the desire to create sports films with ever greater realism created the building blocks of American cinema: the move from peepshow to screen projection, from short film to extended film, and from that to a full evening's entertainment. All, it could be argued, came through boxing. In Britain, the Derby of 1896 stamped

Spectators afloat at the Oxford and Cambridge Boat Race, filmed by Birt Acres in 1895

film as a definably British product, capable of showing British triumphs, and showed the way to speedy newsreel work and ever greater skill in the depiction of sports on film.

But more than helping to define cinematic form, sports films very simply let people see sport. Many in the Victorian era knew of boxing and its most celebrated protagonists, but very few had ever seen a fight before films could show one. Cinema widened people's view of the world, and certainly their view of the sporting world. It was the beginning of sport as a worldwide popular phenomenon, something that went hand in hand with the rise of film through the twentieth century. Look today at Corbett, Cushing, Grace and Persimmon and we see the birth of twins: motion pictures and mass appeal sport.[9]

NOTES

1. Sandow's interest in the cinema went still further; in 1897 he made a patent application – British patent 17,565 – for a stereoscopic film system, impractical, but nevertheless one more facet of a remarkable man.

2. In his catalogue of Edison production, Charles Musser lists for 1891 *Men Boxing*, for 1892 *Man on Parallel Bars, Boxing, Fencing and Wrestling*, and for 1894 *Athlete with Wand, Amateur Gymnast, Men on Parallel Bars, Boxing Match, Wrestling Match and Boxing*, all made prior to the Leonard-Cushing fight. Charles Musser, *Before the Rapid Firing Kinetograph: Edison Motion Pictures, a Filmography with Documentation, 1890-1900*, Cineteca del Friuli/Giornate del cinema muto, Pordenone, 1996).

3. The publicity behind the Corbett-Courtney fight and film resulted in Edison himself being called before a grand jury investigation, where he blatantly but judiciously denied all knowledge of such activities.

4. eds. Stephen Herbert and Luke McKernan, *Who's Who of Victorian Cinema: A Worldwide Survey*, BFI, 1996, p. 77.

5. George Pratt's essay, 'Firsting the Firsts', in ed Marshall Deutelbaum, *'Image' on the Art and Evolution of the Film*, Dover, New York, 1979 details the travels and fortunes of the Eidoloscope.

6. An example is the 1896 Melbourne Cup horse race in Australia (catalogue nos. 418-423).

7. Warwick Trading Company 1899 catalogue, nos. 5158-5162.

8. The earliest cricket films are discussed further in Barry Anthony, 'Earliest Cricket on Film', *Wisden Cricket Monthly*, December 1993, pp. 32-33.

9. That other creation of the sporting fervour of the 1890s, the modern Olympic Games of 1896, was not filmed. Film may just possibly have been taken of the 1900 and 1904 contests, but the unofficial games in Greece of 1906 were definitely filmed, and the 1908 official Games in London saw the start of proper Olympic coverage. See Taylor Downing, *Olympia*, BFI Film Classics, 1992, pp. 12-13.

12 THE TREATS OF TRICKERY

Michael Chanan

Film, from the very start, was an art of both realism and illusion, veracity and deception, transparency and trickery – in short, a highy paradoxical medium. This is even true of the work of Louis Lumière, widely regarded as the father of filmic realism. The early film show was seen by many as a magical act in itself, a piece of magic which was sometimes presented by magicians on the stage, whose more traditional acts would also be filmed and turned into subjects on the screen. Soon, these subjects would be re-enacted using filmic tricks like interrupted action and superimposition, which also gave rise to new magical effects.

The first explicitly magical films are usually attributed to Méliès, theatrical illusionist and owner of the Robert Houdin Theatre in Paris. The story of how he hit upon the idea of the camera tricks which his films employed is well known: one day, according to the legend he fostered himself, he was filming in the Place de l'Opéra in Paris when the film in his camera jammed. He fiddled with the machine to get it going again and continued filming. When he projected the film he discovered that an omnibus was suddenly and magically transformed into a hearse. Thus, by accident, was born a crucial discovery, namely, that film doesn't just reproduce the profilmic scene, it can also be manipulated to present as apparently equally genuine the unexpected, the unlikely, and the completely impossible. Substitution by stopping the camera and replacing an element in the scene in front of it is known as stop-frame technique. The visual effect is a magical transformation.

There is no reason why it could not have happened that way, and every reason to suppose that it might well have done so, not only in Méliès's case but also others, for ever since Archimedes we have known about the role of the happy accident in the process of invention and discovery. At the same time, however, such techniques were often derived from the adaptation to film of photographic practices used in magic lantern entertainments. In England, the principal protagonists in the development of trick effects were the members of the 'Brighton School'. In 1897, one of them, G.A. Smith, patented a method of double exposure – though the technique was common photographic knowledge – and began to make trick films like *Photographing a Ghost*:

> Photographing a Ghost... causes astonishment and roars of laughter. Scene: A Photographer's Studio. Two men enter with a large box labelled 'ghost'. The photographer scarcely relishes the

order, but eventually opens the box, when a striking ghost of a 'swell' steps out. The ghost is perfectly transparent so that the furniture, etc., can be seen through his 'body'. After a good deal of amusing business with the ghost, which keeps disappearing and reappearing, the photographer attacks it with a chair. The attack is amusingly fruitless, but the ghost finally collapses through the floor. A clean, sharp, and perfect film (Smith's catalogue description).

Voyage dans la Lune/Trip to the Moon, Georges Méliès, 1902

Soon came films in which inanimate objects would suddenly become animated. In one remarkable example of the genre, a British film distributed in the U.S. in 1904 called *An Animated Picture Studio,* the scene shows a young woman dancing for a camera and then sitting on the photographer's knee. The photograph of her dance appears within a picture frame standing on an easel in the centre of the scene, and comes alive. When the dancer protests and throws the picture on the floor, the shattered image continues to dance. (The dancer in the film is thought to be Isadora Duncan, says Ian Christie, adding that this 'makes an already intriguing little allegory even more poignant.')[1] Metaphors for the dangerous magic of the film camera, the mastery of the trick effects on which these films depended, was extensively pursued.

Some theorists have suggested that fascination with 'trick' devices in the early days of cinema may be equivalent to a fascination with *trompe l'oeil* effects, or with anamorphic distortion, both of which occurred in painting in the period following the invention of artificial perspective.[2] Photographers, however, who engaged in comparable practices, were liable to arouse suspicions, as if guilty of some kind of transgression. Just before the turn of the century, a new monthly pictorial called the *Harmsworth Magazine* carried an article entitled 'PHOTOGRAPHIC LIES. With Remarkable Photos, proving the uselessness of the Camera as a Witness'. A photograph, the article warned, 'is absolutely inadmissible as evidence of anything, unless it is proved conclusively that it was in nowise faked after being taken. The faking can be carried on almost to any extent. In fact, nothing is impossible to the clever knight of the camera.' After illustrating and explaining photographs of ghosts, of the same man in two positions, and such-like, the author reassures the reader: 'we doubt if photographers, amateur or otherwise, were ever guilty of using their knowledge of fakes for any purpose other than that of amusement, and that indeed was our idea in shedding light on this comparatively unknown subject.'

But with moving pictures the scope for entertaining deception is hugely augmented, and film makers begin to exercise new forms of mendacity. Early film was not so much a system of representation as a medium of visual reproduction – which is by no means the same thing. It was not yet an elaborated artistic language, but a diverse set of fragmentary codes. And as the elements of these codes first appeared, in necessarily piecemeal fashion, the intensified sense of photographic authenticity also brought with it the seeds of greater and more intense fabrication.

A strong case can be made, independently of any theoretical definition of the properties of illusion, for the role of trickery in upsetting the assumptions of normal vision and established habits of perception. For while reality was given by the camera, illusion was produced by the screen. The screen itself, and not merely the images on it, was felt to be alive, animated in a metaphorical as well as a literal sense. Early film makers quickly learned to use trick effects both in order to intensify these sensations and to raise a laugh. Among the earliest examples is the comic scene which pokes fun at people who are taken in by the magic of the screen, like a Biograph film of 1902 called *Uncle Josh at the Moving Picture Show;* where, according to the catalogue a 'country bumpkin...becomes so overwhelmed by watching his first motion picture from a stage box that he tears down the screen in his enthusiasm to help the heroine of one of the films'.

But early cinema did far more than play on its own strangeness in this naively self-reflexive way. Its powers of animation became a metaphor which lent itself to the process of technological innovation of which it was itself a product. This is the symbolic content of a great range of films that present us with the panoply of scientific and technological marvels of the times, from X-rays to automobiles, usually going awry. In this way film seems to become the medium of the emerging technological age *par excellence*, both its literal and its symbolic embodiment. Its images encompassed every other invention of the day, not just picturing them in action but in scenarios that express both wonder and fascination, and the need to exorcise fear and suspicion.

Films about motor cars, for example, were legion. R.W. Paul made a film entitled *On a Runaway Motor Car Through Piccadilly Circus* (1897), which showed the view from a car 'speeding' through the streets, photographed according to the catalogue description in some kind of accelerated motion (the film itself is lost). The effect was probably achieved by steady under-cranking of the camera. No great act of imagination was needed to know the impression under-cranking produces on the screen: that it speeds up the action. (Just as over-cranking slows it down.) This would have been obvious to all operators of hand-cranked cameras.

Another example of a trick-effect motor car film is James Williamson's *An Interesting Story* (1905), where the multi-shot format of the short narrative elaborates a running gag. A man is so engrossed in the book he is reading that he has his breakfast, prepares to go out and leaves the house with his eyes continuously glued to the pages. Oblivious to the world, he gets run over by a motor vehicle, and is flattened to the thinness of a sheet. Two passing cyclists stop and pump him up again with their bicycle pumps. The whole thing is done by stop-frame technique, just like Méliès's magic transformation.

A more sober form of appropriation of the camera for science is found in the different kind of film launched by Urban in 1903, under the name of 'Unseen World': the scientific subject filmed through a microscope, with individual titles such as *Birth of a Crystal*, *Cheese Mites*, *Circulation of Blood in the Frog's Foot* and *Anatomy of the Water Flea*. (Cecil Hepworth immediately produced a parody, *The Unclean World*, in which a scientist inspects his food through a microscope and discovers two large insects; two hands appear in the frame and pick them up, revealing them to be clockwork toys. Here too early cinema reveals one of its most characteristic traits: a penchant for self-satire.) The technique of microscopic filming produces a double magnification, first through the microscope and then the projector, which appears to reveal an entirely new spatial dimension. A similar discovery in the dimension of time takes place through time-lapse photography, originally known as 'speed magnification'. This is simply the logical extension of the stop-frame technique employed by the trick-film makers, where instead of stopping once and starting again, the frames are photographed one by one. Since this is also the basis of animation, it not surprising that animation films appear around the same time.

There was another mode where trick techniques were used in a more exploitative fashion – trickery in the disreputable sense. The big early producers like Lumière, Pathé and Urban, established networks of cameramen around the world, and prototype 'news footage' continually flowed in. But whenever, for whatever reason, cameramen were unable to film the real thing, they resorted to fakery. Williamson filmed *Attack on a China Mission* in the garden of a rented house in Hove in 1900, and later staged scenes from the Boer War on a local golf course. Albert Smith, returning in 1898 from Cuba to New York during the Cuban-Spanish-American War, boasted that he had taken footage of the Battle of Santiago Bay when he hadn't, so he faked it, using models and cigarette smoke. It was a hit, and the public did not apparently suspect its real nature. Smith refers to the episode in his autobiography as the birth of 'special effects'.[3] Not surprisingly, when he then went to South Africa, he felt no compunction about dressing up British soldiers as Boers and passing it off as footage of the Boers in action. Nor was he the only one to claim he had filmed what he hadn't. The film business from the start recognised as enterprise every kind of exploitation of people's imagination within its means.

In many respects, given the intense suggestibility of the medium, this is not difficult to understand. But it ought to forewarn us against discussions of the nature of realism and truth in the cinema, or the veracity of the image, which fail to take account on the one hand, of the poor fit between truth as concept and as image, and on the other, the dialectical antitheses of these qualities; the illusion and deception of the signifier. This difficulty, nowadays associated with ideas of postmodernism, is not unique to the visual culture of the late twentieth century. The problem of the simulacrum and the simulation of the image was born with photography and enormously extended by film, whose appearance rode roughshod over all existing aesthetic categories. There is only a thin line (perhaps one should call it a fuzzy one) between the discovery and exploitation of 'special effects' in scientific films (like time lapse and magnification); the use of similar techniques (especially stop frame and reverse motion) in trick films which belong to the realms of humour, magic and fantasy; and the deception of the fake actuality.

According to the orthodox accounts, trick films, which make impossible things happen, were a favourite genre of early cinema. This is true, but by itself an insufficient and misleading account of the matter. Even if one added, 'as if there were a compulsion to see how far you could go,' there is more than that to it. For the trick film is not simply a genre, but a mode which enters into other genres as well. The comic exploration of trick devices, the special effects of the scientific film, and the 'cheating' which went on in the early topicals, are inevitable concomitants of the same process. The motivation varies – the pursuit of magic, illusion and fanstasy, the seizure and penetration of physical reality, the re-enactment of human drama – but all were equally pertinent, indeed crucial, to the articulation of the capabilities of the medium, including especially its capacity to reshape space and time. In a nutshell, the trick is in the recombination of images. In fine, it is precisely in the transgressive nature of trick film technique that we discover the node that links the realism and the illusion, the deception and the veracity of cinematic art.

NOTES

1. Ian Christie, *The Last Machine – Early Cinema and the Birth of the Modern World*, BBC/BFI, 1994, p. 127.

2. Anamorphic distortion is the painting of an object in such a way that it only appears correct – that is, undistorted – from a specific position other than the normal frontal position for viewing a painting. An example can be found in Holbein's *The Ambassadors* in the National Gallery, London, where a skull is painted anamorphically and only appears undistorted when the painting is approached obliquely from below while mounting a staircase.

3. For a full account of the episode, see Michael Chanan, *The Cuban Image – Cinema and Cultural Politics in Cuba*, BFI, 1985, p.24ff.

This essay draws on material in the author's *The Dream That Kicks – the Prehistory and Early Years of Cinema in Britain*. Second Edition, Routledge, 1996.

13 THE ROLE OF THE INTERTITLE IN FILM EXHIBITION, 1904-1910

Martin Sopocy

The concept of the exhibition aid is an important one for reconstructing the history of early film. It can be defined as any on-site intervention in the film experience, exterior to the film itself, whose intention is to make it more intelligible as narrative or to enhance its effect as entertainment or its clarity as document. Its relation to film imagery is exactly that of a caption to a photograph. It identifies, it explains. It elaborates on the image. It gives background information or points out what is significant though not immediately apparent.

In a 1978 essay this writer presented evidence that the assumption of James Williamson's earliest films was that, while they were showing, a narrator or lecturer would explain or amplify their images.[1] The narrator concept was subsequently found to have a variety of implications for early cinema exhibitions, not just in Britain but also in the United States, Japan, indeed almost everywhere films were shown in the earliest years. André Gaudreault, Germain Lacasse, Jean Châteauvert and others have contributed extensive documentation on its use in Quebec,[2] and Charles Musser in an article first printed in *Framework* enlarged the concept by showing that, besides the lecture, such related strategies as the printed programme, the intertitle, sound effects and even actors speaking dialogue behind the screen were used as exhibition aids in the film show's early years.[3] To these can be added the fairground barker's spiel, which *primed* the audience by explaining in advance the images it would see inside the tent; and the musical accompaniment – when, that is, it was used as non-verbal comment or to create a context of mood for the images. Essential to the concept is that an exhibition aid is never part of a film's release print. Thus both an on-site title-slide flashed on the screen and music played by an on-site pianist during the show qualify as exhibition aids. But intertitles or sound-tracks consisting of music or (for that matter) sound effects or spoken dialogue, by being part of the release print, do not. *Then* they help to specify its makers' intentions toward it as a film experience. The on-site lecture, as distinct from a voice-over narration, is an exhibition aid because, not being present in the film's release print, it is subject to a fairly wide range of variation, variation which may or may not conform to the film-makers' intentions.

Less understood than the aid of lecturing, and far more problematic, has been the process which led to the introduction of intertitles into the negatives of film narratives, and the role of that process in the rise of the movie theatre. There are of course several well known instances of early intertitled narratives (Méliès' *Voyage dans la Lune*, 1902, to name one of several of his films which have them, and Porter's *Uncle Tom's Cabin*, 1903, to name another), but they appear to have been exceptions to the general practice of their time. An especially interesting instance of early intertitling is James Williamson's (also exceptional) *A Reservist Before and After the War*, released in Britain in December 1902. That the pair of intertitles in this film were present in its original release prints is evident from its original advertised length of 290 feet, which closely conforms to the 286-foot length of the print in the National Film and Television Archive (my own measurement of it is closer to 287 feet, but I have concluded that Williamson, despite disclaimers to the contrary – and presumably to simplify his bookkeeping – most often advertised and sold his films in lengths raised to the next multiple of five, and this could well account for the discrepancy of from three to four feet we find in this instance; the print I saw in the NFTVA appeared to have lost no footage). In contrast to the intertitles of Méliès and Porter, which function as chapter-headings, identifying the moving tableaux which immediately follow them, Williamson's titling in this film is striking and precocious. In the first instance, it heralds a sudden change of mood in the action of a scene, and in the second it is used to indicate the passing of time. These titles succeed in making the film self-sufficient as a showpiece – that is, unreliant for its dramatic effect on any on-site aid, and on that account cheaper and easier to show. The more self-sufficient the film, in fact, the more salesworthy, and the more widely it could be distributed. It is interesting therefore that this obviously successful experiment was, if the evidence of Williamson's extant films is an indication, never repeated by him. We must ask ourselves why, and the answer certainly bears on the universal assumption of the earliest days of the commercial film that it was the exhibitor's prerogative to decide on the means he would use to convert the films he bought from manufacturers into proper shows. The exhibitor insisted on his role as showman, and resented the intrusion of the film-maker into what he considered his act. This assumption governed the American film market no less than it did the British, though its consequence was slightly different for each.

To my knowledge the first writer to observe that 1904 was the year in which titles began to appear in significant numbers in film narratives was Kemp Niver, who, after years of working with the paper prints – those rolls of paper contact prints from negatives that the largest American companies submitted to the Copyright office to establish rights of authorship during the early years of the film business – mentions it in *The First Twenty Years*.[4] In 1978 this finding was corroborated by a group of archivists and scholars working under the aegis of FIAF (the Fédération Internationale des Archives du Film) using different data, namely some 600 extant prints of French, British, American and German films made prior to 1907. The FIAF group found that till 1904 intertitling in film narratives was, though not unknown, atypical of trade practice. For instance, of the sixty-three 1903 films viewed by the group, only two (one French, one German) were found to contain at least one intertitle. But in 1904, out of an even smaller sample of 32 films, 15 were found to contain one or more: that is, almost half of them. I think we must take this to imply a growing market for self-sufficient films, and that it denotes the rise of the motion picture theatre – or nickelodeon, as it was called in the United States – meaning by the term a venue independent of on-site aids, except usually the one of music.

This revolution in film exhibition seems to have rested on the chase films, chiefly British, of 1903 and afterwards, and the discovery, chiefly American, that they, together with Méliès' stage-framed films and certain 'action' anecdotes, made self-sufficient film exhibition possible.[5] This in a sense forced into being film exchanges, or renting agencies, to serve as middlemen between exhibitors and manufacturers. There is an abundance of evidence, however, that the nickelodeon phenomenon did not grow to the size of a boom until 1906, when in the United States nickelodeons were suddenly everywhere.

But if we agree that the relative absence of intertitles in pre-1904 film prints implies a degree of reliance on on-site aids, and agree further that the introduction of intertitles on a large scale in 1904 denotes the rise of nickelodeon exhibition (plus, incidentally, a photoplay which was already growing in complexity beyond the chase and the race to the rescue), then we must find it curious indeed that the FIAF group's findings for 1905 show a dramatic *drop* in the percentage of films with intertitles – only 15 out of the 327 films viewed – and that the same trend was visible in the 1906 sample, where 17 out of 103 films were intertitled. I expect to show, however, that this drop is consistent with the assumption of a growing nickelodeon market.

The causes of Williamson's apparent abandoning of intertitling after *A Reservist Before and After the War* and the sudden drop in intertitles in the FIAF films after an equally sudden rise in them were I think similar, even if not identical. Evidence for this is an unusually telling remark by Alfred H. Saunders, editor of the American trade paper *The Moving Picture World,* in that periodical's issue of February 22, 1908. Saunders, an Englishman, had edited the British trade paper *Optical Magic Lantern Journal* from 1902 until he went to America in 1907 to help found *Moving Picture World.* The occasion of the remark was a debate in the paper's pages over a recent drop in attendance at American nickelodeons. Of course the real culprits – mentioned by nobody – were the business recession of 1907 combined with the over-expansion of the nickelodeon part of the trade; but no doubt other factors did contribute to it. Most of the debaters put the blame on film narratives which failed to make themselves intelligible to their audiences. One of them, an Iowa exhibitor who identified himself as W.M. Rhoads, suggested the problem could be solved if film manufacturers increased the number of intertitles they were putting into their films. 'If, instead of [having] a few words of explanation of [their] films about every 100 feet, as most of them do, they would have explanations come in at (...) every place an explanation is necessary', the result, he wrote, would be increased attendances at theatres. Saunders' reply to this was as sharp as a reprimand. Putting in more intertitles, said he, 'would unnecessarily add to the cost of the film and [it] is a little too much to ask the exchanges to pay 12 cents per foot for title'. His reading of the situation was that the exchanges did not object to paying for more picture material – as indeed they were doing in a market of longer and longer films – but that they would resent paying for more intertitles. This makes no sense unless it is understood that exchanges were buying films from their makers *by the foot* and renting them to exhibitors *by the reel*, a length which could vary considerably. Before 1904, and in some venues even after 1907, it was considered the option of the *exhibitor* to use title-slides or any other exhibition aid – or combination of aids – he felt he needed to bring in business. But when in 1904 manufacturers suddenly began titling their films, that innovation may well have seemed to the exchanges a collusion of the manufacturers and exhibitors against themselves. Saunders imagines them as feeling that the cost should, in fairness, have been borne by the exhibitor, in whose *interest* it was to show films which made sense to his customers! And some such reaction – expressed to manufacturers by their client exchanges – probably did occur. It would account for the sharp drop, noted by the FIAF group, in the percentage of intertitled films in 1905. But the slight rise which occurred again in 1906 just as probably represents a decision by the exchanges to tolerate the practice provided the titles remained few and brief. This was probably not altruism but a grudging admission that their own prosperity – indeed their very existence – depended on a thriving nickelodeon sector. It is clear nonetheless that they continued to exert enough pressure on manufacturers and film importers to make those groups shy of using titles except where they could not be avoided (indeed, some of D.W. Griffith's Biograph films have no intertitles at all – *A Country Cupid* for one), though in all too many cases it was the narrowest self-interest which determined where they could be avoided and where they could not. And it was exactly this pressure which contributed to the crisis in nickelodeon exhibition of 1907 and 1908.[6] This is the situation which prevailed in the United States at the time of the exchange between Saunders and Rhoads.

Yet the case of Williamson's unrepeated experiment in intertitling suggests that a quite different situation existed in Britain, where, for a long time after 1902, the rental business remained far less developed than in America; where exhibitors were still apt to be proprietors of travelling shows, and where it was still common for them to order films directly from manufacturers. This being so, it seems the British exhibitor continued jealously to guard his right to choose his own exhibition aids (and, incidentally, to refuse to raise his expenses by buying intertitled prints from film-makers) long after the American exhibitor had learned to take for granted the presence of intertitles in the films he rented from the exchanges. Now this would mean that British film-makers were releasing their films in a form ready for showing in every respect save that they lacked the intertitles they needed to clarify action on those occasions when the visuals failed to do it by themselves – a failure the exhibitors themselves were expected to compensate for. And since the United States with its booming nickelodeon sector already constituted the chief market for British film-makers, it would would also mean that when the latter sold their films to America they would normally be expected to insert into their export prints that minimum of titling demanded by exhibitors and tolerated by exchanges.

To test this theory I made a sample of British films released in the United States by the three largest importing companies, Kleine Optical Company, Miles Brothers and Williams Brown & Earle, using as my source their advertisements in the *Moving Picture World* for the 24-month period beginning March 9, 1907, when *MPW* began publishing, to March 7, 1909, by which time the Edison patents trust, as a concession to its most powerful member Charles Pathé, had effectively stopped the flow of films into the United States. Principally from these ads, but also from *MPW*'s plot summaries and release-lists, I was able to identify 66 films with certainty as British imports and to obtain the lengths at which they were advertised. Comparing the information thus obtained with the corresponding information in Gifford's *British Film Catalogue*, I found that of these 66 films, 23 were advertised in longer lengths than their U.K. originals; in 32 cases in lengths unchanged; and in eleven cases in shorter lengths. My data are given in the appendix to this essay.

Shorter lengths may in some cases signify the importer's thrifty insistence on re-measuring the prints, and his correction of the maker's declared length; for not only was he paying their maker for them by the foot, he was also paying duty to U.S. Customs on each declared foot of each imported print. But probably just as often these shortenings had other causes: in an article on the Great Northern Film Company,[7] Ron Mottram describes a letter from Miles Brothers to that company in which Miles asked for a cut of 50 feet of 'the least interesting parts' of a film Great Northern was offering them.

Somewhat less usual, surely, was an instance reported in *Kinematograph & Lantern Weekly* for July 25, 1907. In its trade news column, the paper noted that the 'Williamsons are now offering the *Brigand's Daughter* in a shorter length (...) omitting the unhappy ending'; the film was accordingly advertised at two different lengths in the issue of August 8 (at '670 or 806 feet'). Nevertheless, some of these shortened versions could have contained intertitles. Similarly, longer U.S. lengths, besides representing added intertitles, could also represent new picture material. Lewin Fitzhamon remembered that one of his jobs at Hepwix was to shoot extra footage for re-releases of films made prior to his association with the company. Certainly many of these were for export to America.[8]

James Williamson advertises a title compositor, *Kinematograph & Lantern Weekly*, December 10, 1908

When I broke the 1907 portion of the sample down according to importers, I found that of the seven British films released that year by Kleine Optical, all were longer than their U.K. originals (by at least five feet and by as much as 57 feet). The seven films imported by Miles Brothers tended to divide about equally between those which were longer (three films, by from eight to 90 feet), those which were shorter (two films, by two and 59 feet), and those of equal length (two films). Of the nine films imported by Williams Brown & Earle, however, *seven were of equal length;* one was longer (by 73 feet) and one shorter (by 50 feet). Which certainly suggests that variation in the titling policies of American importers could be considerable.

The configurations of the sample altered when I subjected the 1908 and 1909 films to a similar breakdown, weighting the overall result toward films released at equal lengths; but this is accounted for by the disproportionate number of imports by Williams Brown & Earle in those years, for they and Kleine Optical and Miles Brothers continued to show the same characteristics as they had in the 1907 part of the sample; the lengths of the Kleine imports suggesting that they were conscientious revisions which might include not only the addition of intertitles but additional picture material as well, all presumably calculated to the needs of nickelodeon exhibition, while the Williams Brown & Earle lengths on the contrary suggested an overriding concern for thrift and an all but total indifference to those considerations at work in the Kleine revisions. Without intertitles many of the British films Williams Brown & Earle were selling to the exchanges could easily have puzzled nickelodeon audiences, given the assumption of their British makers that it was the exhibitor's task to give them whatever exhibition aid he had in use to make them intelligible and entertaining, an assumption more and more meaningless in the United States after 1904.

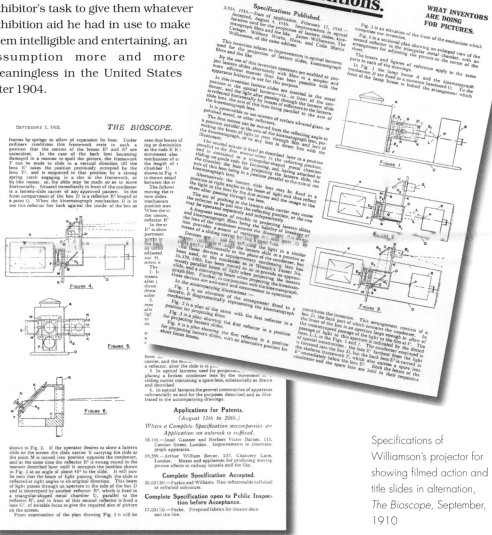

Specifications of Williamson's projector for showing filmed action and title slides in alternation, *The Bioscope*, September, 1910

The evidence presented by James Williamson's career is interesting. Usually involved in several activities at once, Williamson devoted much of his energies to an exhibition service which gave shows in institutions and private houses throughout Sussex. Probably because of this activity he was one of the earliest filmmakers to give serious attention to the problems of exhibiting movies, first as a lecturer in the magic lantern mode, and in 1902 with the successful but unrepeated experiment in intertitling noted above. Several years later, however, the aid of intertitling seems to have made some headway among British exhibitors, and Williamson responded by inventing and, in the *Kinematograph & Lantern Weekly* of December 10, 1908, advertising a device he called a Title Compositor with which exhibitors could themselves make professional-looking intertitles.[9] His continuing concern with the problems of exhibition is shown by a projector he patented in 1910 which could project filmed action and title slides alternately, at the discretion of the projectionist, a cumber some device which may, however, have met the needs of some exhibitors (see appendix).[10]

The evidence points to the conclusion that the policies of American importers regarding intertitling to some extent followed those of U.S. makers and that, because of different assumptions about exhibition practice in both countries, films in the U.S., whether domestic or imported, were likelier than their British counterparts to have intertitles in them when they were released to the trade.

I would expect this view of both markets to hold generally for the years from 1904 through 1910, after which there were probably important changes, especially in the U.K. market, which, to judge from the British trade papers, would soon be importing intertitled U.S. films in quantity.

About Williamson's titling device, one must furthermore assume that it was a response to changes already occurring in British exhibition practice – changes toward a more self-sufficient film show – which could imply a rise in the number of what in America were called nickelodeons. One would expect that intertitled films imported from America, in combination with the editing revolution launched by Lewin Fitzhamon in *Rescued by Rover* – a revolution which was itself, in my opinion, commercially driven[11] and whose lessons were being assimilated by film-makers on both sides of the Atlantic – would after 1910 have transformed British film exhibition into something closer to the American model, in effect eliminating the obvious differences which marked the release prints of the U.K. and the U.S. before 1911.

But inadequate or defective exhibition practice could also explain why it was that the British film trade, which thanks to its links with the magic lantern probably had a head start over every other in the world, was soon left behind by the American trade, and not by it alone. Imperfect as the American system was, it still provided safeguards against miserly or careless or uncomprehending or unimaginative or incompetent exhibitors, and the British system did not. These vulnerabilities prevented the British trade from achieving the same level of prosperity as its American counterpart, which was able to support – and eager to accommodate – the film-makers of Europe as well as its own. The foundation of its success was a thriving exhibition sector, whose prosperity in turn rested on standardised and generally adequate intertitling for which the initiatives of American manufacturers and film importers were responsible.

NOTES

1. *Cinema Journal*, Evanston, Ill., fall 1978; also *Cinema 1900-1906: an Analytical Study*, FIAF, Brussels, 1982.

2. See the forthcoming publication of papers given at the 1994 Domitor Conference (New York City) on Early Cinema.

3. 'The Nickelodeon Era begins', *Framework*, nos. 22/23, Autumn 1983, pp. 4-11, reprinted in ed. Thomas Elsaesser, *Early Cinema: Space, Frame, Narrative*, BFI, 1990, pp. 256-273. See also Charles Musser's *High Class Moving Pictures*, Princeton, 1991, and the numerous paragraphs on exhibition services to vaudeville theatres in *The Emergence of Cinema*, University of California Press, 1990.

4. Locare Research Group, Los Angeles, 1968.

5. Williamson's three-shot chase *Stop Thief!* (October 1901) had no imitators till 1903, but that year was the chase film's *annus mirabilis*. Notable examples of the genre were produced during the year by Frank Mottershaw (*Daring Daylight Burglary*, *The Robbery of the Mail Coach* and *The Convict's Escape from Prison*), William Haggar (*Desperate Poaching Affray* and *A Dash for Liberty, or A Convict's Escape and Capture*), Alf Collins (*The Pickpocket – A Chase through London* and *The Runaway Match*), by Williamson himself (*The Deserter*, now lost but apparently containing a virtuoso sequence in which a chase was combined with a race-against-time) and, in America, by Edwin Porter (*The Great Train Robbery*).

6. As for the use made here of the FIAF sample of 600-odd films, its meaning cannot of course be fully validated until account is taken of the provenance of each print and the evidence for each intertitle has been properly evaluated from its negative, information which was not included in the second volume of *Cinema 1900-1906*, Brussels, 1982, which is my source. It is used here, therefore, not to illustrate titling practice in any particular country but, on the contrary, simply as a broad index of titling practice before 1907. As an index, nonetheless, it does agree with Niver's findings, which refer specifically to American titling practice.

7. 'The Great Northern Film Company: Nordisk Pictures in the American Motion Picture Market', *Film History*, vol. 2 , no. 1, winter 1978, pp. 71-86.

8. See Denis Gifford's 'Fitz: the old Man of the Screen', in ed. Charles Barr, *All our Yesterdays*, BFI, 1986, pp. 314-320.

9. The print of *Two Little Waifs* (November 1905) at the National Film and Television Archive contains an intertitle reading 'The Search for the Gypsies', which has a somewhat typewritten look and whose print in any case is unlike that of any of Williamson's front titles, including the one for this particular film, or, for that matter, the two intertitles in *A Reservist*. The assumption is reasonable that it was inserted into the print by an exhibitor.

10. Not included in the sample of 66 films is a separate sample I made of 20 Williamson films released in the U.S. between March 1907 and October 1908 by Kleine Optical, Miles Brothers, and the Charles E. Dressler Company. Comparison with the U.K. data revealed that the U.S. advertised lengths were: 13 longer, four shorter and three of equal lengths.

11. Fitzhamon's filmic constructs were released themselves without intertitles but their stories, which were often about animals and infants, were pre-plotted with a visual logic so rigorous that they were, if not entirely self-sufficient, then so close to it that an occasional title would make them perfectly so when projected on a screen. While costing no more than other films, *they simplified the task of showing* for the exhibitor, and that alone gave them a strong competitive edge over the product of other British film-makers. That these film-makers began imitating them almost at once is a matter of record and shows, I think, a desire to give their own films the same market advantage.

APPENDIX

A Comparison of U.K. and U.S. Advertised Lengths

This sample consists of 66 British films released in the U.S. between March 1, 1907 and March 1, 1909. Since their exact release dates were irrelevant to what I was trying to determine, and since I wanted only an index of when they were in distribution in the United States, I felt free to assign a date for each film which was simply that of the issue of the *Moving Picture World* in which I found it. After some hesitation I included three Cricks & Martin releases which showed surprisingly wide variation, though I did not include Urban's *Two Little Motorists*, whose July 18, 1908 length, exceeding that of its original U.K. release by an unprecedented 310 feet, could suggest an error in the data.

To get an idea of the magnitude of the differences when they occur, figure that each foot closely approximates one second of playing time. For each film, the U.K. data – advertised length, with month and year of release – is given first, followed by the corresponding data for its U.S. release, once again understanding the date to be an index of when it was in distribution, plus the initials of its importer: KO for Kleine Optical Company, WBE for Williams Brown and Earle, and MB for Miles Brothers. The films are listed by their U.S. titles under the names of their U.K. maker.

	UK LENGTH in feet	UK MONTH	US LENGTH in feet	US DATE	US IMPORTER
UK MAKERS AND TITLES					
ALPHA TRADING COMPANY					
1. *Oh! That Molar*	215	Jan-07	220	May 18, 1907	KO
CLARENDON					
2. *Absent-Minded Professor*	504	Sep-07	504	Jan 18, 1908	KO
3. *Artful Dodger*	346	Nov-06	367	Apr 6, 1907	KO
4. *Follow Your Leader & the Master Follows*	220	Jun-08	224	Aug 1, 1908	KO
5. *Memory of his Mother*	490	Mar-08	500	May 9, 1908	KO
6. *Paying Off Scores*	192	Jan-07	200	May 18, 1907	KO
7. *Pied Piper of Hamelin*	755	Dec-07	790	Jan 18, 1908	KO
8. *Poor Aunt Matilda*	275	Mar-08	240	Apr 25, 1908	KO
CRICKS AND SHARP, later CRICKS AND MARTIN					
9. *Drink and Repentance*	570	Jul-05	570	Apr 20, 1907	WBE
10. *Father's Picnic*	256	Aug-05	256	Apr 20, 1907	WBE
11. *For the Baby's Sake*	375	Feb-08	375	Mar 7, 1908	WBE
12. *Freddy's Little Love Affair*	525	Mar-08	345(sic)	Apr 25, 1908	WBE
13. *Horse Stealers*	346	Nov-05	346	Apr 20, 1907	WBE
14. *How the Artful Dodger Obtained a Meal* (retitled *How the Dodge Obtained a Meal* in US)	320	Jul-08	520(sic)	Jan 9, 1909	WBE
15. *Interrupted Bath*	345	Apr-08	175(sic)	May 9, 1908	WBE
16. *Mission of a Flower*	360	May-08	360	Apr 25, 1908	WBE
17. *Professor Bounder's Pills*	380	Apr-08	380	May 9, 1908	WBE
18. *She Would Sing*	285	Jun-05	235	Apr 20, 1907	WBE
19. *Slippery Jim the Burglar*	220	May-06	220	Apr 20, 1907	WBE
20. *'Twixt Love and Duty*	455	Feb-08	455	Mar 21, 1908	WBE
21. *Catch the Kid*	270	Apr-07	270	Apr 27, 1907	MB

	UK LENGTH in feet	UK MONTH	US LENGTH in feet	US DATE	US IMPORTER
UK MAKERS AND TITLES					
22. *Ice Cream Jack*	516	Oct-07	524	Apr 18, 1908	KO
23. *Napoleon and the English Sailor*	530	Jul-08	530	Aug 29, 1908	KO
24. *Railway Tragedy*	325	Sep-04	320	Apr 18, 1908	KO
25. *Revenge*	375	Sep-04	380	June 29, 1907	MB
GRAPHIC CINEMATOGRAPH CO.					
26. *Gambler's Wife*	535	Apr-08	540	May 9, 1908	WBE
27. *His Sweetheart when a Boy*	550	Oct-07	545	Mar 7, 1908	WBE
28. *Sacrifice for Work*	345	Oct-07	340	Apr 25, 1908	WBE
29. *Tricky Twins*	455	Feb-08	265	Mar 7, 1908	WBE
HAGGAR & SONS					
30. *Red Barn Mystery*	685	Jul-08	685	Oct 24, 1908	WBE
HEPWIX					
31. *Artful Lovers*	300	Oct-07	300	Jan 23, 1908	WBE
32. *Baby's Playmate*	375	Jul-08	375	Jan 2, 1909	WBE
33. *Black Beauty*	475	Aug-06	475	Mar 30, 1907	WBE
34. *The Busy Man*	525	Jan-07	525	Apr 20, 1907	WBE
35. *Catching the Burglar*	525	Mar-08	525	May 16, 1908	WBE
36. *Curate's Courtship*	140	Jan-08	140	Mar 7, 1908	WBE
37. *Den of Thieves*	425	Oct-04	431	Oct 30, 1908	WBE
38. *Doctor's Dodge*	250	Feb-08	256	May 9, 1908	WBE
39. *Drink*	200	Jul-07	200	Feb 1, 1908	WBE
40. *Father's Lesson*	500	Mar-08	500	June 6, 1908	WBE
41. *Hidden Hoard*	600	Apr-08	600	Sept 5, 1908	WBE
42. *Jack in Letter Box*	300	Jul-08	300	Nov 28, 1908	WBE
43. *Soldier's Jealousy*	400	Aug-07	400	Feb 1, 1908	WBE
44. *Tell-Tale Cinematograph*	400	Feb-08	400	Apr 25, 1908	WBE
45. *Thief at the Casino*	600	May-08	600	Oct 3, 1908	WBE
46. *The Tramp's Dream*	450	Jun-06	450	June 1, 1907	WBE
47. *Viking's Bride*	400	Nov-07	400	Jan 18, 1908	WBE
48. *When Women Rule*	600	Jun-08	600	Nov 28, 1908	WBE
49. *The Child Accuser*	250	Mar-07	260	June 8, 1907	KO
50. *The Gamekeeper's Dog*	460	Aug-07	467	Jan 18, 1908	KO
51. *Getting his Change*	305	May-07	320	Jul 20, 1907	KO
52. *Turning the Tables*	290	Dec-06	347	Nov 23, 1907	KO
53. *Chef's Revenge*	238	Feb-07	236	Apr 27, 1907	MB
54. *Fakir and Footpad*	214	Mar-06	287	Apr 20, 1907	WBE
55. *Knight Errant*	480	Mar-07	421	Apr 27, 1907	MB
56. *Robber and the Jew*	320	Dec-08	320	Apr 25, 1908	WBE
SHEFFIELD PHOTO CO.					
57. *Blackmailer*	585	May-07	585	Jan 18, 1908	MB

	UK LENGTH in feet	UK MONTH	US LENGTH in feet	US DATE	US IMPORTER
UK MAKERS AND TITLES					
WALTER TYLER					
58. *Kind Old Lady*	395	Sep-08	395	Nov 29, 1908	WBE
URBAN TRADING CO.					
59. *Baffled Burglars*	360	Jun-07	414	Apr 27, 1907	MB
60. *Following Mother's Footsteps*	465	Dec-08	475	Feb 20, 1909	KO
61. *Guard's Alarm*	430	Dec-08	463	Feb 6, 1909	KO
62. *Sammy's Sucker*	295	Oct-07	357	Jun 6, 1908	KO
WALTURDAW					
63. *Eggs*	300	Feb-07	300	Apr 27, 1907	MB
64. *Murphy's Wake*	335	Aug-06	343	Apr 27, 1907	MB
WARWICK					
65 *Dick Turpin*	500	Apr-06	525	Sep 28, 1907	KO
66 *Lazy Jim's Luck*	485	Feb-08	395	Nov 28, 1908	WBE

14 'NINE DAYS' WONDER': Early Cinema and its Sceptics

Stephen Bottomore

> 'Young man…you should be grateful, since although my invention
> is not for sale, it would undoubtedly ruin you. It can be exploited
> for a certain time as a scientific curiosity but, apart from that, it
> has no commercial future whatsoever.'[1]

So said Antoine Lumière, turning down an offer from an enthusiastic
Georges Méliès to buy a Cinématographe, which Méliès had just seen
for the first time. This anecdote is well known; indeed it has entered
into the legend of cinema history, and though possibly apocryphal it is
not incredible, for there are many other such examples in the early
period of people suggesting that the cinema had no real future. While
such pessimism may not typify early attitudes to the cinema, it seems
to me to represent a significant body of opinion, and offers an
interesting corrective to traditional, 'linear' accounts of the
development of the new medium.

Of course it is scarcely surprising that a new device should be
greeted with scepticism, and many other inventions, from
automobiles to television, have initially had their doubters, but in the
case of the cinema these seem to have been especially numerous, and
include a surprising number of people in the entertainment and
'media' professions whom one might have thought would have been
more sanguine about the new invention. In this essay I will quote from
some of these early Jeremiahs, and attempt some explanation of their
views.

My approach is partly based on a large body of research which has
appeared in recent years on the emergence and social context of
technologies.[2] Few film historians have made much use of this work
and of the theoretical models which it offers. A rare recent exception to
this neglect has been Deac Rossell's important paper on the influence
of the magic lantern and its practitioners on early film, partly based on
the theoretical work of historian of technology, Wiebe Bijker.[3] Writers
such as Rossell and Bijker remind us that inventions are not simply
born in the inspired minds of lone inventors and then launched upon
an expectant world; the development and introduction of a technology
will be affected by the experiences, goals and needs of the people
concerned in its gestation and initial use.[4] Perhaps the early doubts
about the cinema can be seen in this context? This is what I have tried
to do in this essay, examining such attitudes through the experiences
of four 'interest groups': lanternists, music hall managers, producers

of actualities, and 'theatrephiles'. I have also attempted to show why the views of these groups proved over-pessimistic.

THE LANTERN PROFESSION: 'plain porridge' and 'highly-flavoured meats'

By the 1890s the magic lantern had become an important medium of entertainment and instruction, and there was an entire industry of firms producing slide sets, projectors, and associated paraphernalia. In the hands of a cadre of professional lanternists projection had reached a very advanced standard. When film arrived on the scene in 1896, it was clear that there were many parallels with lantern projection and practice, and an immediate business opportunity presented itself to the lantern community. Should they invest in cinema or not? Was this a technology with a future? There was considerable uncertainty on these points.[5]

In 1896 the two partners in the British photographic firm Newman and Guardia disagreed about the new 'animated photographs', Guardia apparently believing that 'in another two years no more would be heard on the subject', while Newman was eager to start working with this new technology. Newman appears to have won the argument, for by the following year the firm had entered the film business, making their own apparatus.[6] Such differences of view about the future of film were probably not unusual in this early period. One lantern and postcard manufacturer based near Paris jumped first one way, then another: in 1897 the firm planned to take up film work, and one of their employees, M. Elbourn, was trained as a cameraman to be sent to Egypt and Palestine in order to make a series of films. Some weeks later Elbourn was all packed and ready to go to Cairo along with his film camera and permits, but was told at the last minute that the job had been cancelled:

> 'I was gravely informed by the heads of the firm that after further consideration they had come to the conclusion that there was no money in cinematography, that the proposed trip to Egypt would never pay for itself, that living pictures were simply a scientific curiosity and a passing fad, and would never be a commercial success.'[7]

Such doubts seem to have persisted in the lantern world for many years: as late as 1904 Fred Balshofer's employers, the Shields Lantern Slide Company, told him movies were 'just a passing fancy'.[8] At about the same time a British trade journal manifested the volatile flux of opinions on the subject, simultaneously suggesting that the interest in cinema might merely be a temporary fashion – like children's crazes for marbles or hoops – while also maintaining that audiences might be seduced away from the older technology: 'If you feed a person on highly-flavoured meats he will not go back to plain porridge if he can help it'.[9]

The struggle between the 'plain porridge' of the lantern and the 'highly-flavoured meats' of the cinema finds its most interesting expression in the attitudes of Cecil Hepworth, who was to become a leading light of the British cinema in the teen years and early 1920s. He was the son of a well known lantern lecturer, T.C. Hepworth, and himself a keen and devoted disciple of the lantern. For a time he wrote a column for the magazine *Amateur Photographer*, entitled 'On the Lantern Screen', and in November 1896 used this column to launch a virulent attack on the cinema craze, partly based on the poor technical quality of film projection:

> 'That the present boom in these animated palsy-scopes cannot last for ever is a fact which the great majority of people seem to be losing sight of altogether, and yet it is only common sense to suppose that it will not be so very long before the great British Public gets tired of the uncomfortably jerky photographs. Living photographs are about as far from being things of beauty as anything possibly could be, and they ought not to be expected to be joys for ever.'[10]

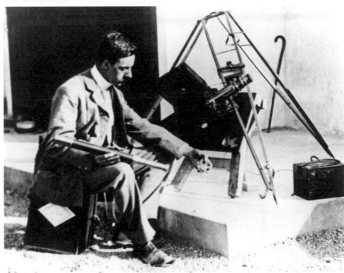

Hepworth was not alone in noticing the poor quality of the early projected film image, and other commentators criticised flicker, low levels of screen illumination and poor prints. A lantern trade journal wrote in 1901: '...the novelty of kinematographic shows is wearing off...the flickering and the occasional flashes due to a scratched film seriously detract from the effect of the exhibition'; and even in 1906 a lanternist was complaining that film's 'incurable habit of winking brings on a headache'.[11]

Cecil Hepworth, 1900

But in March 1897 Hepworth turned his attack away from the quality issue to another front, predicting financial disaster for many of the film companies which had been launched like ships 'upon the troubled waters of public approval':

> '...if, as I fear, the flood tide is over, what a sorry fate is in store for them!...It will be a sad time for many when the waves of public opinion, grown tired at last of their favourite plaything, rise in fury

and destroy in a week what has taken a year to perfect...What are the odds against the finish of next lantern season witnessing the wreck of many cinematographs, and the shores of Time strewn with a tangled mass of sprocket wheels?'[12]

It was an evocative image, indicating Hepworth's passionate feelings on the subject, but by the following week he was having to dilute his pro-lantern views. The *Amateur Photographer* had decided to terminate Hepworth's lantern column (henceforth his weekly musings went under the neutral banner, 'The Idler's Notes'), and Hepworth sadly declared that, faced with the evident 'boom' in living photographs, 'the time for lantern work has come to an end, and the screen must be rolled up and put away'. By May Hepworth had recanted in full, finally convinced that film did indeed have a long term future:

> 'More than once I have aired the opinion in this column that animated photography is getting played out. That I was utterly and hopelessly wrong in so soliloquising is now proved – or nearly proved...animated photography is *not* played out by any means.'[13]

The 'proof' Hepworth cited for his change of heart was that film pioneer R.W. Paul had just formed a company with forecast profits of £15,000 per annum, indicating that perhaps film could be a profitable and respectable business after all. It is also likely that Hepworth's about-turn was partially triggered by a couple of technical innovations that he had come up with, and which might have suggested to him that the poor quality of film projection could be improved. The first invention was a new kind of arc lamp, which would help to increase low screen illumination levels. The second was a means he had devised to alternate animated films with his beloved lantern slides: this combination was an important development in this period, not unique to Hepworth, with which extended lantern/film shows were often compiled.[14] Whatever the reasons for his change of heart about film, Hepworth's *volte-face* was total: he wrote the first ever textbook about the subject in 1897, entitled *Animated Photography*, in which he enthusiastically advised those wanting to take up film-making that: 'There is a tremendously vast field before you, and up to the present it has scarcely been touched at the very edges'.[15]

The initially sceptical attitudes of Hepworth and other members of the lantern community toward film were clearly founded on a desire to protect their own vested interests and professional reputations. Having built up a profession based on high quality image projection, they were naturally uncertain, when film came along in 1896, whether to adopt this unknown technology which was producing rather shoddy results and might give their calling a bad name. And in any case the lantern industry was presently doing rather well; in such circumstances why should they 'retool', at great expense, for a new technology which might not be all that lasting? It was this latter point which also preoccupied another group of cinema's early doubters.

SHOWMEN, ATTRACTIONS, & THE 'NINE DAY WONDER'

Some of the first business decisions about cinema were taken by managers who ran the halls where films were shown, and many of these individuals proved to be notably cautious about the new 'animated pictures'. At the Grand Café in Paris where the Lumière films had their first commercial screening, the manager preferred to take a straight 30 Francs a day in rent rather than the 20% of takings that the Lumières offered him,[16] though in the event the show turned out to be a major success, attracting large crowds.

In Britain the view of many experts was that 'animated pictures' were little more than a passing fad. As early as June 1896 the *Photographic Review* began a report on the Edison Vitascope by saying 'The craze for moving pictures is not yet over', implying that the end was only a matter of time,[17] and many showmen initially took the same view. The impresario, Sir Augustus Harris, planned to feature Robert Paul's Theatrograph projector at Olympia in 1896, but believed that 'It won't draw the public for more than a month. They soon get tired of these novelties.' The manager of the Alhambra Theatre of Varieties, Alfred Moul, was even more pessimistic about the Theatrograph, putting its likely appeal at 'a week or so' (though eventually it stayed at the Alhambra for many months). Moul regarded the Theatrograph as a 'nine-days' wonder', a phrase also used by John Nevil Maskelyne of the Egyptian Hall in referring to the Lumière Cinématographe, a device which he initially averred 'was not worth troubling about'.[18]

The German film pioneer Max Skladanowsky had the outlook of both a showman and a lanternist. His show experience came from touring a mechanical theatre, and his lantern background was equally significant and is evident in the design of his double-film Bioskop projector. This played at the Berlin Wintergarten from 1895 as a variety act, and indeed Skladanowsky seems to have conceived of the cinema simply as a new act or attraction, and when he had 'done' this as a performance the cinema was over for him. He had ceased exhibiting by the Spring of 1897.[19]

Probably what lay behind many showmen's equivocal attitude to early film was this tradition of variety entertainment as a programme of 'attractions'. By the late 19th century, to fuel the act-hungry music-halls and vaudeville shows, new novelty acts and entertainment sensations were continually appearing. Serpentine dances, X-ray demonstrations, performing animals: no sooner was one act exhibited than it was discarded in favour of something new. In this context why regard any new sensation as more significant than the previous one? For the variety manager film projection was a new act, but scarcely a revolutionary one. A music hall paper wrote in April 1897: 'The animatographe is essentially the craze of the moment, and the probability is that in a year hence it may be as moribund, from an entertainment point of view, as boxing kangaroos or talking horses.'[20]

Showman William Brady made a similar point to Adolph Zukor when the latter tried to persuade him to invest in 'the movie racket': '"Why Adolph," I said kindly, "you're out of your head. These pictures are just a fad. They won't last much longer than the Mutuscope [sic] – or the skating rink racket."'[21]

The comparison with skating rinks is instructive. The roller skating craze had swept America and then Europe in the late 19th century. In the first decade of the 20th century rinks attracted a large investment in Britain, but, after peaking in 1909, the rink business suffered a collapse the following year. Variety entrepreneurs at the turn of the century thought that film would peak and then virtually disappear in a similar way, and that they could maximise the benefits and reduce the necessary investment by the usual practice of milking it while the appeal lasted as merely one act on the variety bill. On the other hand, establishing cinema as an independent medium with its own venues would, like the rink business, call for a major investment with associated risks. At the turn of the century the nature of cinema did not warrant such an investment, but things were changing fast.[22]

'THE END OF THE MOTION PICTURE BUSINESS' & THE 'MADE UP SUBJECT'

Most of the films made in the early period of cinema were non-fiction, showing views of everyday life, contemporary events and the like. At first such views were greeted with wonder and appreciation and often headed the variety bills. But how long before the public would be sated with such slices of life? One trade journal in 1898 was sanguine on this point:

> 'It may be urged that people will before long tire of express trains, of children pillow fighting, of divers ascending firework-like from the water to the diving board, [i.e. films shown in reverse] but these things can easily be set aside and others of equal interest shown. There is a vast field open yet to the enterprising film taker.'[23]

Others were not so hopeful. By 1900 the *New Zealand Photographer* was claiming that the kinematograph was about 'played out', and argued that 'the average sightseer soon tires of paying for the exhibition of scenes similar to those which he can see every day for nothing.'[24]

Perhaps the answer was to show the 'sightseer' things which he or she couldn't see every day? Foreign views for example. The Lumières sent cameramen all over the world to 'collect' such scenes on film, but even they considered that the taking of views of the world was a temporary calling. They told one of their first cameramen, Félix Mesguich: 'what we're offering you here isn't a job with a future; it's more like the work of a travelling showman. It may last six months, a year – maybe more, maybe less.'[25] And in 1900, when another Lumière operator, Francis Doublier, returned to Paris after taking scenes all over the world, he considered the game was up:

> 'I thought that was the end of the motion picture business. I had photographed nearly everything there was to be photographed in the world and didn't think there was anything left of importance.'[26]

To this way of thinking, the world was to the film-maker as wild animals were to the hunter. In hunting animals there comes a point at which there are no more to be bagged; everything that is of interest has been shot – the species is extinct. Likewise with cinema, there are only so many events out there which can be filmed; only so many folk rituals, processions, street scenes, royal occasions. In this sense Doublier had a point, and in his terms 1900 might well have been the 'end of the motion picture business'.

If the public had seen enough of actuality on the cinema screen, where if anywhere could motion pictures go from here? By 1899 the *British Journal of Photography* was predicting that the future of the cinema was in commerce rather than in entertainment:

> 'By-and-by it is safe to assume that animated photography will secure great patronage at the hands of large advertisers, and then farewell to it as an attraction at music halls and suchlike places. At any rate as a "draw" it may be safely relied upon to have its day and no more.'[27]

There is some independent evidence to confirm that turn of the century audiences and exhibitors really were experiencing this sense of ennui, for in some locations films started appearing lower down the bill than in earlier times. In the United States this era of retrenchment is called the 'chaser period', when movies often became the final act in a show. Charles Musser has found this pattern in several U.S. regions, and in Rochester between 1901 and 1903 films virtually disappeared from the bills.[28] Films also moved down from the top of the music hall bills in Britain, and probably in other countries too, though there is some evidence that especially in country areas in Britain the appeal continued well into 1902 (in some places films were said to have a 'magnetic power' to draw an audience).[29]

How did the cinema rise again from this dip in its fortunes? It now seems fairly well established that salvation for the film industry came in the form of acted films. In the United States these appeared in large

Making "Movies"

A FILM PRODUCER
SAYS THEY ARE
ALREADY ON THE
DOWNWARD ROAD

Oliver Morosco.

Oliver Morosco, the theatrical and motion-picture manager and producer, is an all-around athlete. This unusual photograph shows him doing an air-spring.

Photograph by
Stagg, Los Angeles

I HAVE come upon a situation that seems to me to be quite novel—a motion-picture manufacturer who believes—and has the courage to say what he believes—that the motion pictures are doomed as a rival of the spoken drama. But he is, it is true, also a theatrical producer.

"My own photoplay-producing company has been successful from the beginning," Oliver Morosco, the Los Angeles theatrical magnate, told me, "but I feel that it and every other film-producing company will soon go into a decline. The motion pictures will go down fighting, but they will go down nevertheless."

He went on to say to me that conditions had proved to him that the spoken theater always would hold the ascendancy; that he intends to fight the films from now on even if he wrecks his own film-company in so doing.

This was Mr. Morosco's declaration of war:

"I intend to give battle to the motion-picture business with every ounce of strength at my command. To the successes I now have in the field of spoken drama I propose to add more successes. This will be one of my weapons.

"Already the sun of the motion pictures is setting. I do not believe it will set entirely; I believe that motion pictures will last forever, but that they will exist in their proper groove, which will in no way conflict with the great demand of the people for the spoken drama.

" 'But,' people say, 'how about your own photoplay plant?' That is another situation. My film-company has been a big success, and so long as there is money to be made in the picture game, I will stay in it. But if, as I believe the future will show, the moving-picture industry is on the wane, then my photoplay-company will go down with its guns firing and its flags waving.

"There is no question that the moving-picture demand and popularity is waning," he continued; "and by the same sign the spoken drama is returning to its former commanding position in leaps and bounds.

"There is no proof of this needed. You have only to look at the hundreds— in fact, thousands—of moving-picture houses throughout the land that have

and Fighting Them

By Miles Overholt

Mr. Morosco making a broad-jump.

Photograph by Stagg, Los Angeles

Walking on his hands.

Photograph by Stagg, Los Angeles

closed within the past six months; you have only to read your daily paper every morning to see the announcements of the crumbling of great moving-picture companies that a year or even six months ago were paying their stockholders great dividends; you have only to read of the dozens of picture-concerns that are dashing desperately into a merger scheme to cut the tremendous expenses that are not justified by the returns from their sales.

"It takes no expert to see that the public is rapidly tiring of the sameness of theme, inferior production and punchless sort of film that compose eighty per cent of the present moving-picture output. There are about twenty per cent of motion-picture releases that are worthy. This one-fifth part is just about the proportion of the moving-picture business that will survive. The rest will go.

"The moving-picture game is not going to die out and be forgotten. Its novelty simply has worn off. Its popularity was based on novelty, and gone. Moreover photoplays are limited to the expression of emotions by facial or physical acts,—barring the voice,—and that means its downfall. The people are tiring of just that. There will continue to be good moving pictures, for the public will always want them, but there will be but a small percentage of the output, and they present will be based upon a real appeal to the people and not upon a basis of novelty.

"There will be a place and a demand for photoplays containing good stories, good acting, fine production and all that goes to make a good picture; and it will be the companies and producers capable of giving these pictures that will survive."

numbers from about 1903, and a couple of years later hundreds and then thousands of nickelodeon theatres started opening to screen this wave of chase comedies and other 'made up subjects' (as the new type of acted films were sometimes called). Thanks largely to the rise of fiction, the cinema enjoyed a second wind, becoming more than a mere attraction on the vaudeville bill: it became a medium in its own right.

'SHIVERY SHADOWS' VERSUS 'FLESH AND BLOOD PERFORMANCES'

With these changes in subject matter and profitability, and improvements in technical quality, most of the reasons we have examined which had motivated predictions of the cinema's early demise disappeared. After its first decade, the main criticism of the cinema was not that it was doomed, but rather that it was all too successful, and that its trivial and amoral influence was permeating society. Assorted moralists and clerics penned articles about 'the debasing picture theatre' and the like.

Probably the only people who continued to maintain, against all the evidence, that the cinema would not last were a group which would have had a direct benefit in its passing: the theatrical community. The argument often used was that Art in the form of the theatre would ultimately win out against the cinematic bauble, and those who had a rosier view of the future of film were probably a minority in theatrical circles. At a dinner party some time in 1900, when the proprietor of the dramatic journal *The Encore*, Edgar Lee, predicted that the cinema had a great future and would prove a major competitor to the theatre, the assembled company 'pooh-poohed him, and dubbed him a Jeremiah.'[30]

But as time passed it became harder to refute the movies' success. Within the first decade of this century film production companies were building studios and investing heavily in acted films. By 1910 the cinema was thriving, with dozens of one-reelers being churned out, which were being seen on thousands of screens around the world. A building boom in permanent cinema sites was under way. Yet in this same year a writer for the respectable *Munsey's Magazine* stated: '...this big absorber of low price patrons appears to have done its worst...It is inconceivable that any amusement seeker would prefer these shivery shadows to flesh and blood performances...Already the "picture" houses are introducing more and more vaudeville "turns" into their programs.'[31] In fact, according to historian Robert Allen, exhibitors had been adding vaudeville acts to their film programmes since 1907, partly because there were not enough films to satisfy demand, not because of audience dissatisfaction with movies.[32]

Illustration, previous pages: Oliver Morosco Making Movies and Fighting Them, in *The Green Book*, Chicago, 1916

By this point increasing numbers in the theatre world were turning traitor. At just about the time *Munsey's Magazine* was holding forth on the doomed motion picture, Mary Pickford was abandoning her stage career in favour of the movies. Theatrical producer William C. deMille, brother of Cecil, recalled his concern at Mary:

'...throwing her whole career in the ash-can and burying herself in a cheap form of amusement which hasn't a single point that I can see to recommend it...I pleaded with her not to waste her professional life...So I suppose we'll have to say good-bye to little Mary Pickford. She'll never be heard of again and I feel terribly sorry for her.' [33]

But DeMille's contempt for the movies was itself temporary, and he was soon to become an important film director. Others also experienced this change of heart. The Russian theatre director, Vsevolod Meyerhold wrote in 1912: '...in the field of art there is no room for the kinema even when it might take only a subordinate part'. But by 1913 Meyerhold had altered his view of cinema, possibly through meeting Apollinaire and d'Annunzio, both keen cinema fans, and in 1915 he directed his first film, *A Picture of Dorian Gray*. His compatriot Vladimir Mayakovsky also later entered the film industry, but in 1913 he was asking: 'Can the cinema be an independent art form? Obviously not...Art produces refined images, whilst the cinema, like the printer's press for a book, reproduces them and distributes them to the remotest and most distant parts of the world.' [34]

This idea that the most suitable function for the cinema might be as a kind of animated printing press for the other arts had already been mooted by British theatre critic Max Beerbohm. In 1902 he contemptuously described films as 'quivering cold grey photographs' and suggested that if the cinema had any role it might be in combination with the phonograph to record for posterity the performances of great actors like Samuel Phelps and Dan Leno.[35] A more reasoned argument for the view that cinema could not be an independent art form, but did have a role as a medium of archival record, had first been presented as early as May 1896 in the *New Review.*[36]

In 1916 the cinema boom reached new heights, with some 20 million tickets a week being sold in Britain, and several times that in the United States. Yet the theatre folk had not given up the campaign against the movies. *The Green Book*, a Chicago dramatic periodical, published an extraordinary interview with Oliver Morosco, a motion picture and theatrical producer, who suggested movies were 'on the downward road':

'My own photoplay-producing company has been successful from the beginning... but I feel that it and every other film-producing company will soon go into a decline. The motion pictures will go down fighting, but they will go down nevertheless...There is no question that the moving-picture demand and popularity is waning... and by the same sign the spoken drama is returning to its former commanding position in leaps and bounds...There will continue to be good moving pictures, for the public will always want them, but there will be but a small percentage of the present output...' [37]

CONCLUSION

Morosco's outburst was effectively the swansong of the doom mongers.[38] They had had a good run for their money, for some twenty years arguing that the cinema was a kind of 'flash in the pan' of the entertainment world. Their doubts about the long-term future of the cinema had been based on a variety of grounds, but all of the sceptics spoke from the particular vantage points of their own interests and professional backgrounds. The lanternists maintained that the cinema was a sensation of the moment, comparing it unfavourably to the quality and solid tradition of the lantern; many in the variety professions suggested that the movies were but another sensational act, which could only last for a brief time on their bills; early actuality producers wondered whether, once all the world's sights had been recorded on film, there would be anything left for the cameras to do; finally, representatives of the legitimate stage maintained that spectators would never prefer mere celluloid entertainment to the presence of live performers.

Clearly all of these doubting Thomases were proved wrong, and in passing it is worth contrasting their pessimism with the views of many other individuals, from a variety of backgrounds, who had a much rosier opinion of the future of the cinema right from the earliest days. Theorists such as Boleslaw Matuszewski, literati like George Sims, ordinary members of the audience, and of course many of the pioneers of the new industry itself. The excitement that some of these 'visionaries' felt in the infant cinema was an important factor in its rapid rise.

And given the nature of the cinema, was it really so incredible that it should succeed? If one had been trying to predict the future of the new invention, there were surely a number of quite novel qualities which made its triumph likely, qualities which were even realised, if dimly, by some at the time. These would include the inherent fascination for spectators in looking at a moving representation of reality. Also the ability to cut instantly, indeed almost magically, from one time and space to another. But most of all there was the economic advantage of the cinema medium: each film could be copied onto many prints, and each print seen by several audiences of scores or hundreds of people each day. This multiplication factor meant that the cost of a highly expensive original negative – of a foreign voyage, for example, or the performance of an exclusive star – could be subsidised by millions of people, each paying a small fee.[39]

But we should not push this argument of inevitability too far. If the doubters of the early cinema era teach us anything it is that film history, like all history, should not be seen as a smooth, linear progression from one point in the development of an idea or device through to another: in this case, from the birth of film to its ultimate triumph. Rather, the process was full of argument, controversy and doubts, in which vested interests vied one with another, and the precise result was by no means a foregone conclusion: it only seems that way when we look backward in time, and choose the events to highlight with this benefit of hindsight. It would be too easy in retrospect to represent the opinions of cinema's early sceptics as short-sighted prejudice, or to deride them as follies. But we should remember that no new technology arrives in a vacuum, and that the opinions and actions of those in professions which impact on a new invention play an important part in shaping its development (whether or not they considered that it had a long term future).

For some years historians of technology have striven to study 'the roads not taken' as well as the roads which were – inventions which failed as well as those which succeeded – and Deac Rossell rightly suggests that we should introduce this 'symmetrical' approach into film history. In this context, perhaps the doubters of the early cinema period may be seen as the mirror image of the visionary pioneers who predicted and worked for the cinema's recognition and success, and who are so loudly trumpeted in conventional film history. While the sceptics may not deserve the same attention, neither, surely, should they be forgotten.

NOTES

1. Quoted in various sources; this one in Maurice Bardèche, Robert Brasillach, *History of the Film*, Allen and Unwin, 1945, p. 10. The Lumières originally showed the Cinématographe along with a demonstration of their colour photography, and were apparently surprised that the former was received with greater interest.

2. See for example, John M. Staudenmaier, *Technology's Storytellers – reweaving the human fabric*, M.I.T. Press, 1985.

3. See Deac Rossell, 'Double think: the cinema and magic lantern culture', paper delivered at the conference *Celebrating 1895* at the National Museum of Photography, Film and Television, Bradford, June 1995. Bijker's arguments are nicely summarised in his 'The social construction of Bakelite: towards a theory of invention', in eds Wiebe E. Bijker, Thomas P.Hughes, Trevor J.Pinch, *The social construction of technological systems: new directions in the sociology and history of technology*, M.I.T. Press, 1987.

4. Bijker calls the pre-existing attitudes, knowledge, cultural values, and goals of these groups' 'technological frames' (to simplify his definition somewhat). See also Claude Fischer, *America*

Calling: a Social History of the Telephone to 1940, University of California Press, 1992, pp.10-17, who has suggested that we should drop the concept of the *impact* of a technology on a society, but instead examine its different consequences for different groups.

5. Both David Francis and David Robinson have discussed the influences of lantern stories on British and French film-makers in *The New Magic Lantern Journal (NMLJ)*, passim. See also Laurent Mannoni, 'Elbow to elbow: the lantern/cinema struggle', *NMLJ*, January 1993.

6. *Photographic Journal*, December 1942, p. 409.

7. 'Letters to the editor', *British Journal of Photography (BJP)*, August 1, 1941, p.352. See also 'An old man's film memories', *Cambridge Daily News*, September 6, 1938, p.3 (courtesy N. Hiley).

8. Fred J. Balshofer, Arthur C. Miller, *One Reel a Week*, University of California Press, 1967, p. 3.

9. *Photographic News*, October 2, 1903, p. 626.

10. *Amateur Photographer (AP)*, November 6, 1896, p. 371. In his autobiography Hepworth records his first sight of projected films in 1896: 'I do not remember being greatly impressed with the pictures...' *Came the Dawn: Memories of a Film Pioneer*, Phoenix House, London, 1951, p. 27. He wrongly states that this was in July 1893.

11. *Optical Magic Lantern Journal (OMLJ)*, December 1901, p.105; Roger Child Bayley, *The Complete Photographer*, Methuen, 1906; see also *AP*, December 15, 1899, p. 476. On low screen illumination see *BJP*, November 6, 1896, p. 82.

12. *AP*, March 19, 1897, p. 226.

13. *AP*, May 7, 1897, p. 374; 'rolled up': AP, March 26, 1897, p. 247. The column changed name on April 2.

14. One writer for example suggested that lantern shows could be 'spiced up or flavoured with living pictures': OMLJ, October 1901, p. 68. Hepworth devoted a whole chapter to this combination in his textbook, *Animated Photography, the ABC of the Cinematograph*, 2nd ed., Hazell, Watson and Viney, 1900.

15. *Animated Photography*, p. 98; also see Deac Rossell, op. cit., on lantern/film combinations, and *Came the Dawn*, pp. 30-33. Hepworth's other inventions included an automatic film developing machine.

16. Georges Sadoul, *Lumière et Méliès*, Lherminier, Paris, 1985, p. 35.

17. *Photographic Review*, June 1896, p. 205.

18. Frederick A. Talbot, *Moving Pictures: How They Are Made and Worked*, Heinemann, 1912, pp. 40-42. See also Leslie Wood, *The Miracle of the Movies*, Burke Publishing Co., London, 1947), p. 101. David Devant, *My Magic Life*, Hutchinson, 1931, pp. 70-72.

19. Thanks to Deac Rossell for this information.

20. *The Music Hall*, April 30, 1897, p. 1.

21. William A. Brady, *Showman*, E.P. Dutton and Co., New York, 1937, pp. 160-1, 262-70. As Jim Corbett's manager, Brady had attended his 1894 fight with Peter Courtney before the Kinetograph. Adolph Zukor was to become the head of Paramount.

22. On rinks, see Nicholas Hiley, unpublished manuscript on early British cinema.

23. 'Has the cinematograph come to stay?', *OMLJ Annual*, October 1898-9, p. 100.

24. Quoted in *BJP* Supplement, November 2, 1900, p. 84.

25. *Lumière et Méliès*, op. cit. p. 52.

26. Speech to the National Board of Review, reported in *New York Times*, February 2, 1940, p. 12.

27. *BJP*, June 16, 1899, p. 369.

28. Charles Musser (and reply by Robert Allen), 'The "Chaser Theory"', *Studies in Visual Communication*, Fall 1984, pp. 23-52. George Pratt in *Image*, December 1959.

29. See *The Showman*, July 19, 1901, p. 457; July 12, 1901, p. 445; August 2, 1901, p. 497; January 10, 1902, p. 283; January 24, 1902, p. 314.

30. George Gray, *Vagaries of a Vagabond*, London, 1931, p. 206.

31. 'The Stage: what 1910-1911 may set forth', *Munsey's Magazine*, August 1910, p. 706.

32. Robert Allen, *Vaudeville and Film*, Arno Press, 1980.

33. *Stage,* August 1936.

34. Quoted in Jay Leyda, *Kino: a History of the Russian and Soviet Film,* Allen and Unwin, 1983, pp. 58-9, 80.

35. See Max Beerbohm, *More Theatres,* London, 1969, p. 498, and *Around Theatres,* London, 1953, pp. 45, 352: references are from 1899 and 1904. Another English drama critic was even less sanguine about the cinema by 1913, suggesting that 'the interest even of the threepenny public' would soon be exhausted and that 'Ten years hence it would not be necessary to talk at all about the kinematograph'. John Palmer, *The Future of the Theatre,* London, 1913, p. 17.

36. O.Winter, 'The cinematograph,' *New Review,* May 1896: reprinted in *Sight and Sound,* Autumn 1982. See also Ian Christie, 'Has the cinema a career?' *Times Literary Supplement,* November 17, 1995, pp. 22-23.

37. 'Making "Movies" and Fighting them', *The Green Book,* vol. 16, August 1916, pp. 330-331.

38. Though I have found one last prediction of the demise of cinema in *Scientific American* for March 1930, in which a 'public official' claimed that damage to eyesight from the movies would provoke public demands for their abolition within ten years.

39. In this sense film shared the economic advantages of other forms of industrial mass production (and the disadvantages for those previously employed). See Harry Braverman, *Labor and Monopoly Capital: the Degradation of Work in the Twentieth Century,* Monthly Review Press, New York, 1974. For information on the number of prints struck for each film, see *Licht Bild Bühne* March 1, 1913, p. 16.

15 THE ATTRACTIONS OF CINEMA, or, How I Learned to Start Worrying About Loving Early Film

Roberta E. Pearson

Last August, seeking a cure for a healthy case of jet lag, I sat in the coffee bar of a former Soviet leisure complex in the seaside resort of Jurmula, outside of Riga in the Latvian Republic. A reporter from a local paper, working on a story about the summer school on silent screen acting organized by Yuri Tsivian and the Riga Film School, struck up a conversation with the obvious foreigner. Despite her youth she had some experience of scholarly conferences and observed that early cinema scholars seemed to enjoy each others' company rather more than adherents of other disciplines. Why might this be the case, she asked, and why do we love these old films so much? Not feeling terribly lucid, I offered a quick and perhaps rather glib response having to do with our passion for history and a bygone age and then forgot about the encounter until Christopher Williams asked me to contribute to this volume. In the midst of a trans-Atlantic relocation, facing numerous time-pressures and the imminent removal into long-term storage of all my research materials, I gave further consideration to the young reporter's query, the question of the attractions of early cinema seeming perfectly suited for the 'thought-piece' rather than the 'research piece' that I felt capable of producing under the circumstances.

Upon further reflection, it struck me that early film scholars meet more frequently than any other band in the cinema studies tribe: the Giornate del Cinema Muto at Pordenone every year; the Domitor conference every other year; the Nederlands Film Museums workshops that have for the past two years focused on aspects of the silent cinema; as well as one-off occasions in commemoration of the medium's hundredth birthday – the Lumière Conference in Lyons and the *Celebrating 1895* Conference in Bradford. 1996, Britain's official cinema centenary coming after the United States' and the rest of Europe's, sees yet another round of gatherings – *Moving Performance: The British Experience of Early Cinema* in Bristol and the Lumière Festival at the University of Westminster which has occasioned the publication of this volume. Joined by a passion for a dead art, the few but devout celebrants in the moveable feast of early cinema migrate between two continents, seeing the same faces on both sides of the Atlantic. And my young interlocutor was right – the inevitable clashes of personality and theoretical orientation aside, we get along remarkably well in a profession known for its petty infighting.

Perhaps this equability relates both to the size and age of early cinema studies, the youth and smallness of the field causing us to band together for mutual protection and support. The revival of interest in early film is now usually dated from the famed Brighton conference of 1978, the early cinema equivalent of Woodstock or Glastonbury: if you didn't attend you're tempted to pretend that you did. In the seaside resort town where the luminaries of the British cinema, George Albert Smith and James Williamson, made their incredibly inventive films at the turn of the century, a group of youthful enthusiasts under the guidance of knowledgeable archivists such as Eileen Bowser of New York's Museum of Modern Art, surveyed all known surviving prints from 1906 and before. Engaging in the close textual analysis characteristic of the period's film studies, the Brighton conferrers began an on-going cataloguing of the formal conventions of the early cinema.

Energized by the gathering's reevaluation of these previously neglected films, the young scholars scattered to their homelands to continue the work they had begun in Brighton. André Gaudréault, then at the Université Laval, Charles Musser and Tom Gunning then at New York University, working under the inspired guidance of Jay Leyda, and others all over North America and Europe began an archaeological investigation of their respective countries' early cinema history. Soon a second generation of scholars, myself among them, succumbed to the fascination of these brief but compelling films, as well as to the cultures that had produced them. Now, a hundred years and more after the first public showing of projected moving images, established scholars and their graduate students produce a small but steady stream of early cinema publications that deal with everything from issues of race and gender to the minutiae of early film exhibition in their various home bases.

The growing interest in early cinema history in the late 1970s was not entirely fortuitous. At a moment when auteurism and structuralism had begun to recede from their high water marks and the onrushing tide of psychoanalysis threatened to engulf all before it, a Kuhnian analysis would have predicted the imminent emergence of a competing paradigm rising like Botticelli's Venus from the waves (if I may be permitted to swim in my watery metaphor for a moment longer). Two key books of the mid 1970s, Robert Sklar's *Movie-Made America* and Garth Jowett's *Film, the Democratic Art,* signalled a taking up of an historical perspective that had fallen into desuetude after the pioneering efforts of a previous generation including Lewis Jacobs in the United States and Rachel Low in Britain. Cinema studies' turn to the past took place within the context of the burgeoning popularity of a social history that had grown increasingly strong within the academy since the publication of E.P. Thompson's *The Making of the English Working Class* in 1963. This kind of history expanded its vision beyond the economic, the political and the activities of great men that had constituted the subject matters of traditional histories to embrace the culture and the activities of ordinary people. The growth of cultural studies in the late 70s, spearheaded by the activities of the Birmingham Centre in the United Kingdom, gave further impetus to the effort to place film texts within their historical contexts. Explaining the emergence of either social history or cultural studies is beyond both the scope of this essay and of my competences, but I do wish to give more serious consideration to the young reporter's inquiry about the attractions of early cinema than I did that day in the Latvian bar.

Resued by Rover,
Cecil Hepworth, 1905

At the risk of unkindness, I must admit that the field does attract hobbyists, the trainspotters who might otherwise spend their time in role-playing games or philately, who delight in collecting facts about obscure production companies and can recite by heart the production dates and variant titles of countless films. Despite these anorak tendencies, however, there is something rather grand and exciting about studying the infancy of the world's first and arguably most influential mass medium, a period when film practitioners made up a new mode of communication as they went along and audiences experienced the thrill of viewing projected moving images for the first time. Seeing these films and delving into the historical records of the cultures that produced them provides a portal to a bygone age, a time machine of sorts. As one sees more and more films from the pre-Hollywood period (roughly 1894-1915, though periodisations of this kind do constitute a source of much debate) and reads contemporary printed material ranging from production company records to novels, the elaboration of one's intertextual frame provides an ever deeper understanding of a lost culture. When, for instance, I first began work on my dissertation dealing with the transformation of performance style in the Griffith Biographs (subsequently published as *Eloquent Gestures*), I saw a film in which a male character stands on the lawn beneath the porch of a large Victorian house, gesturing rather wildly at the female character who stands above him. Not until several weeks later, after further immersion in turn-of-the-century culture, did I realize that he was suggesting an elopement, a standard narrative trope of the period that any member of the original audience would have readily comprehended.

At least I think that they would have had no difficulty in understanding the scene, but of course we know very little about early cinema audiences. In fact, there is very much about the early cinema about which we know very little, given that the majority of prints, of studio records and of exhibition related materials have been lost. This is particularly the case as regard the original conditions of performance for these films. What speed were they projected at? What were their original colours? What lectures and sound effects accompanied them? What did the nickelodeons look like and who went to them? Some of the thrill of early cinema studies derives from the detective work entailed in trying to answer these questions, as we strive to come ever close to reconstructing, at least imaginatively, the experience of cinema going in the pre-Hollywood era.

My own book on Griffith once more provides an example, perhaps even an extreme example, of this tendency. In the introduction I sought to induce an imaginative sympathy for the period and to convey the vast changes in both films and exhibition venues that took place during the five years D.W. Griffith worked at Biograph. I invited my readers to do a little armchair time-travelling and accompany an imaginary New York City lawyer on visits to the cinema in 1909 and again in 1912. This device permitted me to detail the period's cinema-going experience through the eyes of a contemporary, albeit fictional, figure. While my second book, *Reframing Culture: the Case of the Vitagraph Quality Films* (co-authored with William Uricchio) refrained from such literary conceits, it nonetheless sought to understand contemporary audience reactions. You can imagine my delight when a reviewer in the unlikely location of the *American Cinematographer* commented that the book 'provides a contemporary audience-eye viewpoint' and 'offers the next-best thing to being there'.

These comments are not intended merely to publicise my books, but rather critically to interrogate my own motives in order to locate the attraction of early cinema studies within the cultural zeitgeist. Two contradictory impulses motivate the field. First, there is the longing for connection in an uncertain, fragmented and, if you will, postmodernist age, leading to the obsession with history that has paradoxically become paramount in this most dehistoricised of periods. The passion for reconstruction exhibited by early scholars is shared by what is broadly termed the 'living history movement' which produces everything from museums to reproductions of ancient instruments. On both sides of the Atlantic, enthusiasts re-enact Civil War battles (both the conflict between North and South in the United States and that between Roundheads and Cavaliers in Britain), tourists visit numerous 'heritage' museums like those in Williamsburg, Virginia or the Viking Museum in York, and musicians endlessly debate the exact means of tuning a Renaissance viol before their performances at St. John's, Smith Square or St. John the Divine. The field of early cinema studies in fact shares with the field of early music the passionate search for the 'real' and 'authentic' in the face of incomplete texts and scanty information about actual performance conditions. We worry about original projection speed whilst our musical counterparts worry about original tempi.

The occurrence of these parallel activities within what Michel Foucault might refer to as different discursive régimes signals an episteme in which painstakingly reconstructed historical simulacra, 'correct in every detail' as John Wayne says at the end of *Fort Apache,* disguise past conflict and serve the agendas of present regimes. Certainly the British heritage movement, officially instigated and subsequently supported by successive Tory governments, has been accused of a sanitised representation of history creating a false unity of the glorious, and largely English, past that excludes the experiences of the Welsh, the Scots, the working classes, women and writes out the appalling legacy of imperialism and exploitation. The anorak impulses of early cinema enthusiasts may stem from this broader epistemic tendency, as may indeed some of my own work, but much early cinema research is motivated not by affirmation but by contestation, not by the passion for reconstruction, but by the questioning of previously dominant paradigms.

This paradigm questioning constitutes the flip side, as it were, of the delight in historical detail. The young scholars convening in Brighton mounted a first assault upon the evolutionary master narrative written by previous generations of film scholars. These scholars viewed the films of Méliès, Porter, Williamson *et al* as the cinematic equivalents of the Neanderthals, interesting not in their own right but rather as the primitive precursors of the fully developed and superior classical Hollywood cinema. Countering this demeaning view, early film scholars argued that the so-called 'primitive' cinema should be considered a fully realised mode of filmic communication, constructed around alternative, not inferior, conceptions of story-telling and spatio-temporal continuity.

These scholars eagerly embraced these early films not only in recognition of their delightful novelty but, in some cases at least, because they had a parallel interest in a contemporary avant-garde cinema which also challenged Hollywood's dominance. Positioning the Hollywood cinema between the early cinema and the avant-garde led to its being seen not as the measure of all films but simply as yet another cinematic mode.

While an initial concern with the formal elements of the texts permitted drawing connections between the early cinema and the avant-garde, researchers quickly realised that these films could fully be understood only in relation to the turn-of-the-century popular culture from which they sprang. Now researchers turned their attention to the theatre, the press, and other visual media such as the magic lantern and the stereopticon. These initial extra-textual forays into allied media led, perhaps inevitably, to a general broadening of the field's remit, such that by the late 1990s much of early cinema studies may be seen as a sub-field of the larger social history movement. Many early cinema scholars now engage in historical projects that pay attention to the experiences of those marginalised by dominant hegemonies, attempting to reclaim a complex and even messy past hitherto written out of the official record. Miriam Hansen, in her exploration of women's experience of the nickelodeon, William Uricchio and I in our investigation of the probable conditions of reception for the Vitagraph quality films, as well as other early film scholars, have shifted the focus from the cinema as an aesthetic and formal phenomenon to the cinema as a social and cultural phenomenon that fits within contemporary structures of power and domination. Even more recently, researchers, among them 'traditional' historians as well as film scholars, have begun to explore the connections between the new film medium and the emergence of modernity, seeing the cinema as an integral component of the vast and wide-ranging transformation of human experience that occurred in the late nineteenth and early twentieth centuries, when, among a myriad of other factors, consumption began to take priority over production and the image to take priority over direct experience.

Sortie d'usine, 1895

But are we now film scholars doing social history or social historians doing film studies, taking the films merely as entry points for broader investigations and sometimes dispensing with them entirely? When history dethroned the preceding reigning paradigms of auteurism, structuralism, and psychoanalysis, it simultaneously dethroned the texts that the previous three had taken as their primary object: auteurism extrapolated an author from his/her texts; structuralism extrapolated combinatory rules from groups of texts; and psychoanalysis extrapolated readers from texts. Given its necessary intense concern with history and historiography, the sub-field of early cinema studies played a crucial role in this decentering of the text since the absence of complete or 'original' films, and sometimes the absence of any films at all, precluded the fetishisation of the object characteristic of much previous film studies. Early film scholars, having established the general conventions of an alternative mode of cinema, rapidly moved on to exploring intertextual and intermedia connections. The absence of studio production records and the other kinds of hard data beloved of the more 'hard-headed' traditional historians constituted an even greater challenge than the absence of texts, forcing us to face the historiographical implications of broadening the range of evidence to encompass previously neglected sources.

Even more importantly, our interest in a period marked by social strife and cultural upheaval forced us to face the ideological implications of 'doing' history not as distant and objective observers but as politically aware individuals whose current concerns meshed with and often motivated their historical investigations.

I and many of my colleagues welcome the reconfiguration of cinema studies in which early film history has played such an important role, yet in his keynote address at the third Domitor conference, Jacques Aumont expressed concern about the abandonment of the text, urging us not to reduce films to the status of historical documents by concentrating on the social and the cultural but rather to see them as aesthetic objects, returning our attention to their formal aspects. Whilst I and others in the audience took umbrage at what we viewed as a retrograde call for dehistoricisation and aestheticisation, Aumont's opinion perhaps signals, if not a crisis of faith, then perhaps the perception of a crisis not limited to early film studies as film scholars face the absence of a master narrative that defines not only the discipline but ourselves as intellectuals.

Some now believe that a film studies not defined by the object of study subjected to rigorous expertise in textual analysis and aesthetic criticism raises serious questions for the future of the discipline. From a purely pragmatic perspective, what now sets film studies apart from other disciplines and justifies its separate space within higher education? Even taking on board television, how are we to defend the maintenance of screen studies departments, journals, and conferences together with the accompanying academic infrastructures of post-graduate studies, the job market, and, in the United States and increasingly in Britain, issues of job security and promotion? And from the perhaps more important theoretical perspective, does the abandoning of the text and the leap into history attest to an overall lack of coherence? Certainly the opportunistic theoretical borrowing that now characterises much of the 'cutting-edge' work within the field signals a degree of radical interdisciplinarity that might seem to undercut any claim to separate disciplinary status.

I wish to conclude this essay not with Cassandra-like prophecies of doom, but rather by suggesting the celebration, not the condemnation, of the imposition of a radical contingency that we should embrace as liberating rather than reject as threatening. Far from leaving us rudderless and drifting helplessly in a sea of competing and discredited paradigms, the ascendance of history has provided us with a new navigational chart, enabling us to reassess the old paradigms in light of the overarching and metacritical historical paradigm. Thus, for example, French scholars such as Roger Odin have developed the new field of *sémio-pragmatique*, which contextualises the traditional textual concerns of semiotics within the historical context. Developments such as this, together with the other new directions film scholars are now exploring, can indeed give us faith, not in any single intellectual paradigm, but much more importantly, in the continued intellectual vitality of a screen studies which takes the world as its purview.

16 RE-CREATING THE FIRST FILM SHOWS

Stephen Herbert

There is no-one now alive who remembers the first film shows; no-one to tell us how it was. One method that can help us to understand something of what it must have been like to see moving pictures in 1894/6, is to attempt to re-create the experience, so far as we can. It was my belief in the value of re-creating early cinema presentations which led to this being a major strand in the *Countdown to Cinema* series of events at the Museum of the Moving Image, London, from 1992 to 1996. With the wealth of relevant knowledge of Brian Coe (who presented most of the lectures in the series) to call upon, and the support of Leslie Hardcastle, MOMI's curator when the series started, I planned a fairly ambitious range of presentations.

Ellis Pike as Emile Reynaud, operating the replica Théâtre Optique for MOMI's centenary celebration

Examples of much of the original equipment used for filming and projecting at that period survive. A surprisingly large number of the films have, somewhat miraculously, come down to us. We have a good idea of the way in which the films were presented; the screen size, types of music and narration, the use of the films between music hall 'turns' on a variety bill. Contemporary accounts give us clues as to the nature of the original presentations, and their reception by the audiences; we know enough to be able to produce a reasonable facsimile of the experience. From there, our imagination must take over. For what we can never re-create is the 'innocence' of those 19th Century cinemagoers. We cannot delete a lifetime of moving images from our minds, and look on these animated photographs with a perception free of the knowledge of film language, Hollywood, live television, computer imagery. But in recreating the original presentations, we go as far as we can towards understanding the experience of the first audiences.

REYNAUD'S THÉÂTRE OPTIQUE

The work of Emile Reynaud, inventor of the praxinoscope optical toy, has been of importance to MOMI since the museum opened, as a replica 'Théâtre Optique' projection arrangement is one of the popular working exhibits. This device was designed by Reynaud to project the first animated cartoons (and later, photographic sequences) onto a theatre screen. With the approaching centenary of the opening of Reynaud's *Pantomimes Lumineuses,* at the Musée Grévin in Paris in October 1892, the first official *Countdown* event was planned; a reconstruction of part of that first show, at the conclusion of a lecture about the artist/inventor and his important pre-cinema inventions.

The machine was set up behind the MOMI Cinema's unique rolldown screen gantry, and the rear-projection screen lowered. Due to the depth limitation 'back-stage', a small moving image was projected from the picture band (superimposed over a background projected by a magic lantern, as with the original arrangement). Both to enlarge the picture area and add a sense of *fin-de-siècle* Paris, a magic lantern slide of an ornamental proscenium and curtain was front-projected from the projection booth, the centre blacked out to accept the rear-projected images. The audience was unaware of any of this preparation, and listened to the slide lecture for an hour, at which point Brian Coe announced *Pauvre Pierrot.* A singer and pianist, both suitably costumed, began to perform Gaston Paulin's specially composed music – and the projected proscenium appeared on the screen, quickly followed by the background and characters of the story: Harlequin, Columbine and the eponymous Pierrot.

For a few magical minutes we really did seem to be back in the *Cabinet Fantastique* at the Musée Grévin of 1892; the performance was quite delightful. One of the audience said to me afterwards, 'I thought you had a 16mm projector back there' – but at the conclusion of the little play, the screen rose slowly to reveal 'Monsieur Reynaud' himself (actor Ellis Pike) rewinding his precious picture band. He then stepped forward and introduced himself, and answered a few questions before inviting the enthusiastic audience to examine the equipment for themselves. Several visitors took the opportunity to try their hand at projecting with the rather difficult mechanism.

How close were we to experiencing the real thing? Well, the result flickered rather more than it may have originally. The machine is designed from a popular engraving, as the original was destroyed by its inventor before the First World War, and may not be quite as efficient as Reynaud's. The images are not original, but are very close – photographic copies of recently painted facsimiles of the two surviving strips. Our actor certainly had the necessary presentation skills; it isn't simply a question of turning a handle, as the animated sequences are 'created' on screen for each performance, cycles of action being repeated by a deft manipulation of the mechanism.

So how useful was the exercise? Perhaps we didn't learn much from a technical research point of view – this learning had taken place when the reproduction machine and picture band were first produced for the opening of the museum – but undoubtedly our audience gained something of the experience of the *Pantomimes Lumineuses.*

Following on from this modest success, in January 1993 the *Countdown* continued with a special Magic Lantern Presentation, using a tri-unial (triple-lensed) lantern with mechanical slides, and actors' participation, to give our audience a sense of 'screen practice' before cinema.

MUYBRIDGE'S ZOOPRAXISCOPE

In May 1994, ninety years after the deaths of motion picture analysis pioneers Eadweard Muybridge and Jules Marey, a special presentation of *The Chronophotographers* celebrated their work. The museum's working replica of Muybridge's Zoopraxiscope projector (a 'magic lantern run mad – with method in the madness'), was set up to conclude the lecture. In its usual position in the museum, this machine shows a galloping horse (replica disc) when activated. For our special show, it was decided to extend the repertoire by at least one more moving image sequence.

Shortly before the event we visited Kingston Museum and Heritage Centre, where Muybridge's original machine is displayed, and photographed a number of the painted discs. From these photographs colour laser transparencies were produced, and the images cut out and mounted around the edge of a perspex disc. Using a bi-unial (double-lensed) magic lantern, 'two-phase' animation of a horse image was demonstrated to our audience – a technique used by Muybridge in his original lectures – before Brian noted wistfully that we had everything ready for our motion picture demonstration except the old chronophotographer himself; at which point, almost on cue, 'Mr. Muybridge' made his entrance from behind the screen; a startlingly

good lookalike appearance by the multi-talented Ellis once again, to the general bemusement of the audience. Robbed of his store of prepared Muybridge anecdotes – they had all been related by the lecturer prior to 'Muybridge's' appearance, which is one of the hazards of unrehearsed ad-lib performance – our actor nonetheless conducted the demonstration of his machine, with trotting elephant to compliment the galloping horse, to great effect, his general air of ill-temper seeming quite authentic.

And how valuable was this performance? In terms of the audience's experience, it was entertainment rather than historical education. However, in the course of our preparation for the show we had gained an intimate knowledge of the original Zoopraxiscope machine which would lead to further research, and should eventually result in a publication about the machine and Muybridge's animated projections – a comparatively neglected area of his work – including much new information and material.

THE EDISON KINETOSCOPE

Britain's first Kinetoscope parlour opened in Oxford Street in October 1894. To celebrate the centenary of film in this country, Brian Coe's lecture on the Kinetoscope, with new information from researcher Frank Gray on its introduction into Britain, was concluded with the raising of the cinema screen to reveal a row of Kinetoscope machines, evoking the ambience of those first peepshow arcades. An actor dressed as a period 'barker' invited the audience 'inside' to see 'Edison's Latest Marvel'. Four replica Kinetoscopes showed copies of original Kinetoscope films on the insertion of a coin. (There are probably not more than a dozen or so original machines extant, and all far too precious to bring back to a working state). Two of the replicas had been made for the Museum's opening by Ray Phillips, author of a book on the subject, whose interest in the machine spans fifty years. The other two machines were produced in London by cinematograph engineer William Bell.

Four phases of Muybridge's 'elephant' disc (the images drawn elongated, as they were compressed on projection), laser copied for MOMI's replica presentation

Watching Kinetoscope films projected onto a screen demonstrates their technical quality, and the results were greatly enjoyed by the audience during our October 1994 lecture. Seeing the films in the Kinetoscope is a very different experience. One approaches the machine and peers through the eyepiece, while pushing a coin into its slot. A whir, and there is a blur of movement within. After a few seconds of confusion we are able to recognise what we are seeing – a skirt dance, or bar-room scene. The figures are unmistakably human but miniature – 'smaller than Lilliputians', as one contemporary reviewer put it. For the original viewer, there must have been a sense of surprise and wonder at these photographically perfect representations moving with absolute semblance of life. Something of this can still be appreciated by the empathetic modern viewer, but the picture is small and distant, and the subjects are inextricably locked in the past, ghosts of a world now disappeared.

To see the films in a replica peepshow Kinetoscope is an authentic experience, and reveals how miraculous the result must have appeared to many of the original viewers, but also demonstrates why they would have quickly abandoned the machine once given the alternative of motion pictures on a big screen. There are only a small number of working Kinetoscope replicas, and MOMI is one of the very few places where the public have the opportunity to see the world's very first motion picture films in the way in which they were originally presented.

THE LUMIÈRE CINÉMATOGRAPHE

My own first experience of seeing an early film on an original machine was in 1971. As a young projectionist at the NFT, I briefly assisted Dr. Paul Genard of the Lumière Institute in Lyons, who brought a complete original machine to London to celebrate the seventy-fifth anniversary of the first Lumière shows in Britain. I was surprised at the picture quality and steadiness of *Sortie d'usine* (Workers Leaving the Lumière Factory) shown on the Cinématographe, but also aware that the image flickered rather more than the rest of the Lumière programme, shown on the NFT's modern projectors, due to the less efficient projection shutter of the early machine; a limitation mentioned by the first reviewers.

In Bologna in 1994 I was fortunate enough to see the complete December 1895 Grand Café programme, presented on an original machine in what must have been a very close recreation of the original shows.

It was decided to use the Lumière Cinématographe on display in MOMI to project *L'Arrivée des Congressistes* at the conclusion of our

July *Countdown to Cinema* show, within a day or two of the centenary of its first showing at the Photographic Congress in Lyons in 1895. I had heard that projection tests at the National Museum of Photography, Film and Television at Bradford with one of their Cinématographes had failed to produce a result with modern 'Edison' perforation filmstock, so was rather concerned that our machine would also prove impossible to use. A trial quickly proved this concern to be groundless. I knew that the machine used for Bradford's trials was an early model, and MOMI's a late number (though both superficially the same design), and concluded that perhaps the first batch of machines had been able to project Lumière-perforation films only, whereas the mechanism was altered slightly with later models to allow the projection of films perforated to the Edison standard. (A subsequent discussion with Michelle Aubert of the Centre National du Cinéma Film Archive in Paris confirms this.)

The MOMI machine, from the Sarosh Collection, has some cracks in the casing and chips in the glass aperture plate, so for conservation reasons a limited amount of light was used to keep heat to a minimum, and consequently a small picture was projected. Nevertheless the presentation was enjoyed by our audience who, having heard of the machine's versatility – being camera, printer and projector – were impressed by its simplicity and efficiency. They were also able to examine it after the show.

THE KAMMATOGRAPH DISC MACHINE

Not everyone, in the very first years of the movies, fully embraced celluloid film as a medium. Inventor Leo Kamm launched a machine for taking and projecting motion pictures of up to 45 seconds duration

The Kammatograph camera/projector of 1900; a spiral of images on a glass disc

– approximately the same running time as the first films – using a spiral of small images on a glass disc. The Kammatograph camera/projector (patented in 1898 and for sale from 1900) is quite rare, but we thought it would be of interest to demonstrate this alternative to flexible filmstock, to determine its strengths and weaknesses.

An approach to Pollock's Toy Museum, where an example was on display, was favourably received and we were given permission for a short-term loan of their machine, and discs, for display – and one public demonstration. There were several thin glass discs, all photographed in the very early years of the century; some negatives, some positives. If we were to see these images in motion, we had to make the original machine work once again, perhaps for the first time in ninety years. After fabricating a replacement crank handle and disc retainer, we rummaged in our spares boxes for a suitable lens (which was also missing from the machine). The 'new' lens was too big to fit behind the original shutter, so an extended substitute shutter also had to be made. Finally, all moving parts were lubricated and, over a period of several days, the mechanism gradually eased into motion. We were soon able to appreciate its novel and clever design, with a worm gear providing intermittent movement to the discholder, and the gradual automatic progression of the entire discholder/disc across the lens during projection, to ensure centering of the spiral of images.

The machine was loaded with a disc on our test bench, with a slide projector used as a light source; we crossed our fingers and turned the handle and – somewhat to our surprise, it must be said – a domestic back-garden scene, with young child in frilly frock petting a shaggy-haired dog, came to life on our small test screen.

Once again there was concern about possible damage; this time our fears were for the discs. It was certain to be something of a shock for Victorian glass to be once again subjected to the stresses of intermittent projection at 12 frames per second or more. For all of our tests we used one of the discs which was already in two pieces (and repaired with sticky tape several decades ago). To eliminate any possibility of heat damage we projected a small picture for the public demonstation too, which was video-relayed up onto the big cinema screen.

It was, and is, an enthralling experience. As the projection lamp is lit a misty image can be seen, of an organ grinder on a street corner. Cranking the machine brings the organ-grinder to life, his action seeming to mimic that of our projectionist. A young woman passes with a child. She looks into the camera. A horse and cart pass by. The picture is jumping and weaving around on the screen. It's not perfect – but it works (as Willie Friese Greene says in *The Magic Box).*

KINEMACOLOR

Something which often surprises those new to research in early film is that 'natural' colour films date back to before the First World War. The Kinemacolor system used black and white filmstock, with whirling red-and-green colour filters on camera and projector providing the colour information. It was successful enough for films up to two hours long to be shown at London's Scala Theatre around 1912.

The surviving Kinemacolor shorts in the National Film and Television Archive are of variable quality, with only one or two giving a good idea of the potential of the system. They are mainly early test films, which their producer G.A. Smith thought 'not good enough to be worth printing up', as he told Brian Coe half a century later.

As part of our *Beginnings of Film* course in September 1995, a *circa* 1910 Kinemacolor camera was used to shoot two short tests, of staff and students fooling around by the Thames embankment in vari-coloured clothing. The intention was to learn something of the difficulties of shooting and projecting Kinemacolor, and to see whether we could reproduce a wider range of colours than the original examples that we had access to. We cheated slightly by using a more sensitive filmstock for our shoot than would have been available in 1910; a necessity as it was a cloudy day. Original exterior filming sessions must have been limited to very sunny weather.

There was some excitement when the 'rushes' were returned, and after working out which frame represented the red information (a red dress in the scene showed as 'clear'), the first red frame was carefully threaded in the projector to correspond with the red portion of the spinning filter disc – and the motor started, with the speed gradually being increased to around 32 frames per second. It worked. We were surprised by the subtleties of skin tone and hair colour, and by the fact that the absence of blue was generally only apparent when one consciously looked for it. We were also aware of the colour fringing inherent to the system with fast-moving subjects. Despite our appalling filming technique – not helped by having to frame our subjects 'blind' due to technical problems with using the original viewfinder – the results were encouraging, indicating that perhaps Kinekrom, the proposed improvement of the system that was about to be launched in 1923 but wasn't, would have prolonged the life of additive colour systems in the cinema.

THE WRENCH CINEMATOGRAPH

Before the *Countdown* events started, I had attempted to create interest in building a replica of an 1896 Robert Paul projector, so that when the time came we would be able to celebrate the centenary of cinema in Britain with a show of early Robert Paul/Birt Acres films on a suitable machine. This proposal didn't receive the necessary funds, and won't now happen. Luckily I did find, in the MOMI collection, a Wrench projection outfit of 1896, which we used to project – in a rather 'mixed' tribute – the Lumières' *Sortie d'Usine* on the exact centenary date of that original presentation in Paris, March 22, 1895 – the world's first film projection to an invited audience. The machine was also used by students on MOMI's *Beginnings of Film* course, where they were able to learn how to project a film on an 1890s projector, and during which we discovered that by means of a very ingenious and novel arrangement, the mechanism of the projector moved forwards – whichever way the crank handle was turned!

THE EDISON SPOOLBANK PROJECTOR

In the wilds of Arizona in the 1890s, C.M. 'Valley' White was one of the travelling filmshow operators who took moving pictures to the towns and settlements of the American West. His brief career ended tragically when he was run over by a railroad train in 1898, but his spirit lived again at MOMI in September 1995 when 'Professor' George Hall, ragtime pianist and film historian, gave a show using a replica 'spoolbank' projector, the type of machine used extensively in the U.S.A during the first year or two of cinema. Home in Arizona, George uses an original early Edison mechanism and lamphouse with his replica 'spoolbank'. The latter is a wooden frame that attaches to the back of the machine and consists of a bank of film rollers, through which the film is threaded over and under, in the manner of the Kinetoscope peepshow arrangement. In this way, some fifty feet of film can be accommodated in a loop, enabling the same half-minute Kinetoscope productions to be shown repeatedly until, in the words of one of the pioneers, the audience is 'fed up on it'.

Apparatus and audience of Reynaud's Théâtre Optique, Christmas 1892

For the London show the MOMI technical team constructed a replica Spoolbank attachment, the Projected Picture Trust provided an American mechanism (a Powers machine), and to complete the arrangement we brought into service an 1890s lamphouse from the museum collection, which concealed a modern Xenon lamp, giving approximately the same light output as the original light source. The construction was finished on the afternoon of the show, and I had the 'interesting' experience of re-threading it twice during the performance – without the benefit of a trial run! Baby suffering a soapy tub-bath, and a fire engine galloping towards the camera could be studied at leisure by the audience during several runs through the projector. *Feeding the Doves* – one of the first Edison films to be shot outside the Black Maria studio – was threaded with a twist in the film, so that the image was reversed each time the splice went through, giving opportunities for gags about earthquakes shifting the buildings. This idea was probably quite authentic, being prompted by a report that White showed one round of a boxing match twice, reversing the film to give it the appearance of a different round.

The only known original spoolbank this side of the Atlantic is in the Cinémathèque Française, and our show was probably the only time that such a reconstruction has been used in Europe. If nothing else, this experience taught us that the early American travelling showmen worked hard during their performances.

This was one of the last of the museum's re-creations of the earliest film screenings. The modest success of our 're-constructed' shows has been a result of combining a number of elements. By using the surviving technology, or – where this is not practicable without compromising a scarce or fragile artefact, a replica – the original effect 'on the screen' has been reproduced as closely as possible, and has added an element of novelty and 'theatre' which interests specialist and general audiences alike. As well as the hard technology there were always the people: the inventors, the showmen and women who brought the moving image to the audiences of the world. With their special training in interpretation and skills in public interaction, the actors – all ex-members of the MOMI Actors' Company – have added the 'soft' element of history.

This method of presentation could be extended, and has particular value in the field of early cinema. Just looking at the films isn't enough; the way in which these one-minute productions were built up into a show by the addition of interspersed magic lantern slides, music, live narration, and sound effects, provides endless possibilities for research, exploration, and re-creation.

PART
THREE

TOWARDS
THE FUTURE

17 CUT AND SHUFFLE

Barry Salt

Films are made up of shots, and to make the films you shuffle the shots around and cut them together.

FIRST SHUFFLE

But in the beginning, films consisted of only one shot, which showed only one scene, and ran continuously from the beginning of a standard roll of film negative to its end (65-80 feet). These films could be shown in any order by the showmen who bought them, and this was usually done without much regard for the content of the individual films. The spoken commentary which usually accompanied the projection of films in the early years could support any assemblage.

FIRST CUT

The first known cut from one shot to another was in the Edison Company's *The Execution of Mary, Queen of Scots*, which was made by Alfred Clark in 1895 for exhibition in the company's Kinetoscope peepshow machines. In this film, the actor playing Mary, Queen of Scots is brought up to the execution block, and his head laid down on it. At this point, the camera was stopped, the actor removed, a dummy in the same clothes substituted, the camera was restarted, and the headsman brought his axe down, cutting off the head. Afterwards the negatives of the two sections of the scene were joined (or 'cut') together to give a complete negative from which prints could be made.

This cut was meant to be invisible, so as to create the illusion that the character had actually had her head cut off, but actually the cut was evident on close inspection, since the bystanders watching within the scene moved their positions while the camera was stopped and the substitution made. When Georges Méliès took up this 'stop-camera' technique in 1896 after Edison Kinetoscopes and their films had reached Europe, he did a much better job in making such trick cuts invisible in his *Escamotage d'une dame chez Robert-Houdin*, and many other subsequent films.

SECOND SHUFFLE

However, exhibitors did sometimes show the first one-shot films in an order that made sense. Francis Doublier, one of Lumière's travelling cameramen/exhibitors, claimed that in 1898 he showed a series of actuality shots of soldiers, a battleship, the Palais de Justice, and a tall grey-haired man, as a film of the Dreyfus case. If this event actually happened, rather than just being a good story, it happened no earlier than the first film actually made up of more than one shot, and sold as such.

SECOND CUT

The first real step in film construction was the use of a cut from one shot to another different one, and in this case the cut was meant to be seen. This first happened in R.W. Paul's *Come Along, Do!*, shot around April 1898. This film was undoubtedly made up of two scenes, each consisting of a single shot, and was filmed on constructed sets. So far only the first shot, which shows an old couple lunching outside an art gallery, and then following other people in through its doorway, survives. However, there also exist stills showing both of the two scenes, and it is clear that the second scene was shot on a set representing the interior of the gallery, where the old man closely examines a nude statue, until removed by his wife.

Later in 1898 Méliès made a film entitled *La Lune à un mètre* which was closely based on one of the miniature fantastic shows that he had previously staged in his theatre. *La Lune à un mètre* was made up of three scenes, representing first 'The Observatory', in which an aged astronomer looks at the moon through a telescope and then falls asleep; next 'The Moon at One Metre,' in which the moon descends from the sky and swallows him up; and lastly 'Phoebe', in which he meets the goddess of the moon. The second scene and the beginning of the third were intended to be understood as the dream of the astronomer, who wakes up in the middle of the final scene when the goddess he is chasing vanishes by a stop-camera effect.

This was the first of a long line of films made over the next couple of decades which used the device of a dream story turning back to reality at the crucial moment, but the most important thing about *La Lune à un mètre* was that this whole concept was not immediately apparent from the film itself. This was because there were only small changes made in the décor between one scene and the next, so that there was no way for the viewer to instantly notice the transition between what took place when the astronomer was awake and what took place when he was asleep. Since films in those years were nearly always shown with an accompanying commentary by the showman who projected them (just as in the earlier lantern-slide shows), this was not such a great handicap, but Méliès must have felt that the way he had treated the matter was not ideal, for in his next fantasy film, *Cendrillon* (1899), he joined all the scenes by dissolves, just as was the practice in most slide shows. In this and all subsequent long films made by Méliès during the next seven years, dissolves were used indiscriminately between every shot, even when the action was continuous from one shot to the next – that is, when there was no time lapse between shots. The dissolve was used in the same indiscriminate way in the slide shows which pre-existed the cinema, and hence in both cases the dissolve definitely did *not* signify a time lapse.

THIRD CUT WITH SHUFFLE

The next film after *Come Along, Do!* developing action continuity from shot to shot, was G.A. Smith's *The Kiss in the Tunnel*, made before November 1899. The Smith film shows a set representing the interior of a railway carriage compartment, with blackness visible through the window, and a man kissing a woman. The Warwick Trading Company catalogue instructs that it should be joined into a film of a 'phantom ride' between the points at which the train enters and leaves a tunnel,

Attack on a Chinese Mission: according to the Williamson catalogue, the first scene shows the outer gate of the China Mission Station, with Chinese Boxer rebels breaking through it. In the Imperial War Museum print, this scene occurs second, and the last frame of it shows the jagged splice across the middle of the frame – a tear really – where the alteration was made

an event which many 'phantom rides' included, and this is indeed the case with the surviving copy of this film. (G.A. Smith had made a 'phantom ride' film, which was the result of fixing a film camera on the front of a train, the year before, as had other film-makers, but it is difficult to tell which 'phantom ride' is which amongst the few that still remain out of the many that were made in the first decade of cinema.) In any case, the catalogue instruction as to the point at which the cut should be made shows that the concept of action continuity was understood by Smith. A few months later, the Bamforth company made an imitation of Smith's film with the same title, which developed the idea even further. Bamforth & Co. were a well-established firm making and selling lantern slides and postcards in Holmfirth, York-shire, before the owner, James Bamforth, took them into film-making. Their version of G.A. Smith's *The Kiss in the Tunnel* was made at the very end of 1899. This put their restaging of the scene inside the railway carriage between two specially shot scenes of a train going into a tunnel, and then coming out the other end. Since these shots in the Bamforth film were objective shots, with the camera beside the track, rather than 'phantom ride' shots, they made the point of the continuity of the action quite clear, rather than forcing the viewer to work it out by logical deduction.

STACKING THE DECK

The further development of movement from one shot to the next was carried out by James Williamson in films like *Attack on a China Mission*, which was released at the beginning of 1901. For a long time it seemed that this famous film, which originally consisted of four scenes according to the Williamson sales catalogue of 1902, only survived as a single shot, but a more complete version turned up several years ago at the Imperial War Museum. This version contained the four scenes described in the sales catalogue, but two of them were spliced together in an order different from that in the catalogue. Close examination of the National Film Archive viewing copy print made from the master preservation material showed a cut or splice from one shot to another which was quite different from, and much cruder than the ones joining the other shots. This made it clear that at some time after the shots of the film were first joined together, someone had recut the film. It was also clear that the single shot form of the film was, as various people had conjectured, an uncut print of the unedited camera negative for what was eventually edited by Williamson into shots two and four of the film. That is, he was doing what G.A. Smith recommended the buyer of his *Kiss in the Tunnel* to do: to cut a shot into two parts and join another shot in between so as to construct a multi-shot film. This was real film editing in its fullest possible sense, and done long before

Edwin Porter had any idea about it. I regret to say that Americans are *still* publishing books saying Porter invented film editing.

As my examination of the unedited single shot from the film showed it was longer, and contained more action at its beginning and end than the material in the Imperial War Museum version (which had been shortened through the wear and tear of repeated projection, as usually happens with prints of very old films), I used it to make a reconstructed version of the film. This contains the shots in the original order, and by using the unedited material combined with the rest of the Imperial War Museum version, creates a more nearly complete version. But this reconstructed version is still not complete, because the original film had five shots in it, not the four remaining. The fifth shot, about 80 feet long (i.e. a full reel of camera negative) continued the fourth scene, and originally was joined onto the fourth shot by an 'invisible' splice, since it was shot with exactly the same camera position and direction as the fourth shot, and at a brief break in the action, when the scene had briefly cleared of actors by their exit off-screen. I very much hope this shot will eventually turn up as well.

The second scene was originally the garden in front of the house, with the mission and family attacked by the Boxers. Again, the last frame of the shot from the Imperial War Museum copy shows another rather crude splice made to put this scene first, rather than second as it should have been

FOURTH CUT

G.A. Smith also invented the practice of dividing a continuous scene shot in the one place up into a number of shots, in a series of films beginning with *Grandma's Reading Glass* of 1900. In this film, a small boy is shown looking at various objects with a magnifying glass in the first shot, and then Big Close Ups of the objects seen from his Point of View (POV) are cut in in succession. As the Warwick Trading Company catalogue put it at the time: 'The conception is to produce on the screen the various objects as they appeared to Willy while looking through the glass in their enormously enlarged form'. In the Big Close Ups of the objects the view through the actual magnifying glass is not used, but its field of view is simulated by photographing the object of interest inside a black circular mask fixed in front of the camera lens. Smith repeated this device in *As Seen Through a Telescope* (September 1900), which shows a man with a telescope spying on another man who is taking advantage of the act of helping a woman onto a bicycle to fondle her ankle. Into the Long Shot incorporating all this action is inserted the ostensible view through the telescope, which is represented by another Big Close Up showing the lady's foot inside a black circular mask. Unlike the previous film, there is only one cut-in POV Close Up rather than several, but in the development of *As Seen Through a Telescope* made in 1901 by the French Pathé company, *Ce que je vois de mon sixième*, the man uses his telescope to spy through a number of different windows in succession, so combining the structures of both earlier Smith films.

Also in 1901, G.A. Smith initiated the other major form of scene dissection with *The Little Doctor*. In this film, which now only exists in the essentially identical restaged version he made in 1903, *The Sick Kitten*, there is a cut straight in down the lens axis from a Medium Long Shot of a child administering a spoon of medicine to a kitten, to a Big Close Up Insert of the kitten with the spoon in its mouth, and then back to the Medium Long Shot again. As this is an objective shot of the kitten there is no masking as in the other films, and the matching of the position of the kitten across the two cuts is not perfect, as is hardly surprising given the nature of kittens, but it could be worse.

ANOTHER LITTLE SHUFFLE

The last sign of the variable film for a long time was *The Great Train Robbery* that Edwin Porter made for the Edison company towards the end of 1903. As the sales catalogue announced, the close shot of the bandit Barnes firing straight into the camera could be placed at either the beginning or the end of the film. This shot was not part of the story, and *I* say it was handled thus because Porter did not know what to do with the kind of Close Ups he had seen in the films of other film-makers in the previous two years.

FINAL CUT

By 1901 all the basic techniques for joining individual shots to construct a film had been introduced by the leading English film-makers, and it remained only to add the final refinements of the way cuts related to the shots on either sides of them. For instance, the only kind of Point of View shots which were used in the early years was those in which the watcher in the film looked through something that had an aperture in it, and his view was then shown with a black mask round its edges of the same shape as the hole through which he was looking. The more usual kind of Point of View shot nowadays is that in which a watcher looks at something with his unobstructed vision, and his view is then shown with ordinary full film frame. The use of this sort of POV shot apparently represented some kind of conceptual problem to early film-makers, and did not really begin to develop till about 1910.

The third scene shows the reverse angle through the gate, with the British bluejackets coming to the rescue, kneeling and firing, and then rushing past the camera to engage with the Boxers

TRACK LAYING

Around 1910, another major development for film construction was the introduction of 'spoken titles' between shots, which gave the text of some of the crucial things that the characters in the film would say in the succeeding shots. When these spoken titles came to be cut into the middle of a shot at exactly the point at which they were spoken, which happened around 1913, the result was equivalent to a modern film with sound track.

MARRIED PRINT

Theories about how the film screenplay should be structured began to be articulated at least as early as 1908, when film production and exhibition had standardised into programmes of single reel films. All of these theories were variants and adaptations of the basic ideas that had developed in the nineteenth century about writing stage plays. These ideas about play construction were in their turn a development of the original Aristotelian conception of what drama should be, and were well known to, and thoroughly internalised by, most writers of plays.

The essential mechanism was the conflict between one character striving to accomplish some purpose in which he is thwarted by another character. This initial situation is developed purely by a logical process of cause and effect. Further than this, there were other essential ideas which can be found in most of the American manuals on play construction and film script writing from the end of the nineteenth century through the early twentieth century.

Variation of mood was most important, both from scene to scene, and also within scenes. To quote Alfred Hennequin's *The Art of Play-writing* (Houghton Mifflin & Co., 1890), which was the first complete exposition of these ideas: 'Pathos must be followed by humour, wit by eloquence, talky passages by quick-succeeding scenes of incident, soliloquies by the rapid give-and-take of dialogue. The entire act should be a rapidly shifting kaleidoscope, presenting new features at every turn'. This alternation of mood was associated with the device of suspense – 'In some form or another, it must exist throughout the entire progress of the story. At various points of the play, generally at the close of each act, it may be partially relieved, but it must always be done in such a way as to give rise to new suspense, or to leave one or two particulars still unsettled, etc.' – and a progression of climaxes – 'A dramatic story should be full of climaxes from beginning to end. Every act should have several lesser ones scattered through it, and should invariably end with one of greater importance. Toward the end of the play should occur the great climax in the technical sense of the word, i.e. the point at which the interest of the play reaches its highest stage.' The final major constituent of the standard stage and film plot was the 'heart interest' as it was called before World War I. (Later this came to be called 'the love interest'.) This required that the hero, as well as solving his problem, or defeating the villain, should also get the girl. (The reversal of sexual roles was also possible, though quite rare.) By the 1930s the vast majority of American films had this double plot action.

In the American one reel film the requirement that the character or mood of succeeding incidents be varied was usually not met, though it *is* actually possible for really skilled film-makers to do this with a certain amount of effort. Some of D.W. Griffith's Biograph films do contain one or two lighter incidents, verging on comedy, among the more dramatic scenes that make up the bulk of his films, and he and other people also made some comedies that involved suspenseful scenes amid the more usual fooling.

Then, once films became several reels long, and had their dialogue rendered in inter titles, it became fairly easy for them to accommodate all the desirable dramatic features just mentioned. The full assumption of theatrical methods of dramatic construction by American motion pictures took place at the same time that the final

The fourth scene reverts to the same camera set-up as the first, and is actually filmed continuously with it as one shot. It shows the bluejackets rushing past the camera (shooting in the opposite direction), and engaging with the rebels hand to hand

features of continuity cinema were being generally polished and diffused, during the First World War. The perfection of standard film dramatic construction particularly involved people like Mary Pickford, who had starred in Belasco plays in New York, and who worked to incorporate features from such plays into her films when she became an independent producer. 1917 was really a crucial year for some of the new leaders of the American film industry, because, besides Pickford finally getting these things right from *Rebecca of Sunnybrook Farm* onwards, Chaplin began to introduce pathetic scenes into his comedies, and Douglas Fairbanks moved beyond his stodgy early works like *His Picture in the Papers* to better shaped constructions.

The proven success of this formula for ordinary commercial film-making has meant that it has been the standard ever since, even if some film-makers, particularly outside the U.S, have not always completely adhered to it.

SHUFFLING ALONG

Alternative versions of films have been produced for commercial reasons from before the First World War, but nearly always this was just a matter of changing the ending from happy to unhappy (or vice versa), or of shortening the film. Both of these practices were most common in the silent period, with the American market demanding a happy ending, and the pre-Communist Russian market an unhappy one. Film-making for export could produce both endings for the one film. In general, that small number of European films imported into America tended to be cut, and not just for censorship reasons, but because American audiences considered them slow and boring. This sort of cutting was usually done by omitting whole scenes, but occasionally there were cases like the British distribution print of Fritz Lang's *Kriemhilds Rache* (1924), which was shortened by cutting the beginning and end off every shot. It has been claimed that some Western films were completely re-edited for the Soviet market in the 1920s, but since no-one has ever produced a print of these films as evidence, this may just be more show-business exaggeration.

Inevitably, the practices in other advanced art during the 1960s had an effect on avant-garde film-making, and films made up of sections which could be shown in any order appeared. The best-known example is Andy Warhol's *Chelsea Girls* (1967), but this is not really a narrative film, and I think my own *Six Reels of Film to be Shown in any Order* (1971) was the first truly variable film with a story, or rather 120 stories. Five of the reels each contained a couple of scenes involving a selection of four principal characters in which a few dramatic interactions took place between them, and one or two facts about their past were disclosed. (One of the reels was neutral with respect to any possible narrative.) The interactions, which involved such dramatic favourites as sex, marital infidelity, nervous breakdown, and suicide, were selected so that they might give rise to some of the events in some of the other reels. I checked the plausibility of the different stories arising from the different possible orders of the scenes by writing them on five cards and shuffling these into a substantial proportion of the total possible number of permutations. Since this produced satisfactory results, I trusted that the rest of the permutations would also produce convincing sequences of events.

My miscalculation was to think that other people enjoyed this sort of thing as much as I did. So the film was not much of a success, partly because, as one critic suggested, people like himself preferred to do their own inventing of interpretations of the films they saw. In other words, your average critic with intellectual pretensions preferred to do his or her own shuffling of the content, and didn't want the maker doing it for them. Another way of approaching my creation was to suggest that the film in fact had only one story, and all the 120 alternative versions were just the same story told through different arrangements of flashbacks (and maybe flashforwards). It hadn't occurred to me that anyone would take this attitude either. Part of the lesson of this incident is that most members of the cinema audience prefer films the way they are, with the scenes in a fixed order.

However, there have been a few recent indications that the wisdom of ages about the best approach to script construction may not be completely correct. The idea of alternating scenes with greater dramatic tension, such as action scenes, with scenes with a more relaxed tone, such as romantic or comedy scenes, seems to have been dropped in some action films that have been extremely successful at the box office. They might be thought of as 'robotic action movies'. The one of these which most caught my attention was *Total Recall* (1990), though an earlier Schwarzenegger film, *Commando* (1985), is pretty much the same. Incidentally, both of these films have only the most perfunctory hint of a love interest. On the other hand, other recent films which break the ancient commandments of script construction in other ways, for instance *Henry and June* (1990), which has effectively no plot at all, have been commercial failures.

THE NEW DEAL

So what does all this presage for the multi-media creations of the future, be they on CD-ROM, or some other medium?

Factual multi media works are already truly variable in the way they can be used, but I think those which involve a narrative element are generally not. Many current computer games have a plot, or narrative, or story aspect, but so far as I am aware they usually have only one end to the game, and only one way of reaching it, with no truly alternative paths through them. Those games which are basically a matter of puzzle-solving, such as *Lemmings* or *The Incredible Machine* sometimes have more than one way of solving their earlier, simpler stages (or 'levels', as they are called), but as the puzzles grow more complex, there is usually only one way to solve them. So-called adventure games also include puzzle elements at various points, and these puzzle elements require a unique solution to an even greater extent. Games which might appear to be strategy games, with a large number of possible solutions, such as *Populous*, usually turn out to respond to a fairly simple-minded brute force solution. (In this last case, raise as much flat land around your populations as fast as possible.) Only games which are really simulations rather than games, such as the Maxis 'Sim-' series, are truly infinitely variable in their progress. And they are not going towards any particular goal, and have no story at all in the conventional sense. Their mass appeal is also far less.

The games with the greatest mass appeal are of course 'shoot 'em ups', 'beat 'em ups' and the related driving games ('crash 'em ups'). Here brute force and speed are of the essence, and these are of course very similar to the new trend in action films noted above, with more or less continuous action, explosions, and noise, without relief.

One recent variety of the 'shoot 'em up' is the kind of game that presents a three-dimensional representation of a world that the player sees, apparently from the his/her point of view, as he/she moves around inside it. The point of the game is to blast as many as possible of the moving figures which appear before one, as well as solving the occasional puzzle to enable one to get from one area of the labyrinth that makes up the game's world to another of its three dimensional areas. In general, such games, of which *Doom* is currently the best known example, are only seen from what is referred to as 'the first person perspective', though in film terms this means that they are one long POV shot, like Robert Montgomery's *The Lady in the Lake* (1947). As that film proved, continuous Point of View presentation of a dramatic narrative slows it down considerably, and negates one of the major virtues of film cutting. POV shoot 'em ups like *Doom* have continuous blasting at any moving thing that appears as a way of retaining the participant's interest.

There has recently been an attempt to make it possible to switch between an objective view of the action and the player's POV in one of these games, *Bioforge*, but this still falls a long way short of the true 'interactive movie' that some computer game creators dream about. This hypothetical form, which would involve not only different objective angles on the scene as well as Point of View presentations, and also variable reactions to the actions of the player's persona from the other figures appearing in them, is theoretically possible, but requires a vast increase in the computing power available to any ordinary person playing them. Sometime, but not yet.

The most recently developed computer games, which involve scenes digitised from filmed live-action sequences, have the same kind of narrative mechanisms underneath them as the games I have discussed earlier. The economic imperative says that money spent on creating expensive alternative scenes of this kind is wasted if the scenes might not ever be seen by someone working their way through the game by alternative paths.

From all this I make the prediction that the older form of audio-visual creation, with its fixed structure varied in the ways established long ago, will continue to be the favourite for audiences large and small, whatever medium it is delivered on, but that the 'shoot 'em up', in its direct, disguised, or developed forms, may take a larger share of the recreational market. But I could be wrong, so deal your own hand from the cards on the table.

18 LITTLE BIG SCREEN

Mark Shivas

Kevin Brownlow once said to me: 'Television? Don't worry about it, Mark. It's just a passing phase'.

I was brought up on the movies. Once upon a time I thought that heaven would be working as the film critic of the Sunday *Observer*. I wrote about film for a magazine called *Movie* in the 1960s and tried to get a job in films. Instead, I got a job in television and thought I was lucky to get it. I'd been trying to find something of that sort for three years.

I continued to watch a lot of movies and write about them and not to watch enough television. I was a bit snobbish about it even though I worked for Granada. I wasn't fond of the look of it - black and white at the beginning, with studio lighting which was often ugly and studio sound which was flat.

The first drama I produced for the BBC was *The Six Wives of Henry VIII*, one of the first big series in colour, but made mainly in the studio. We taped six 90-minute shows in three days each. *Henry VIII* was a huge hit in 1970, won awards, and sold in sixty countries.

I continued, while producing drama for the BBC in the early 70s, to write showbiz interviews for the *New York Times*, until a moment came when I visited the location for Dick Lester's film *The Three Musketeers*. I'd met Dick before, and he waved at me across the set, then later came over and said, 'I understand you're here for the *New York Times*. What are you still doing *that* for? I thought you were here as a producer to steal some of my crew.' I was mortified. Later the same afternoon I met one of his cast to whom I took an immediate dislike. I'd have enjoyed taking him apart in print for his arrogance, stupidity and fascist views, but I realised that I might need to employ him some day and concluded it was time to give up film journalism. I was reluctant to do so – it had, after all, over a very few years, brought meetings with Chaplin, Fellini, Hitchcock, Polanski, Visconti, Wilder and Welles, not to mention the Burtons, Anna Magnani, Mia Farrow, Burt Lancaster and Boris Karloff.

Was all this film side, as opposed to television, to be closed to me? I'd seen quite a lot of film sets, big movies being made, great directors at work. Just how different, after all, was it from the programmes and films we were making?

In the 1970s, we began making more 'plays on film', as they were sometimes, to my great distress, called. I produced two or three directed by a brilliant and funny man named Alan Clarke. I produced

Alan Parker's only 'feature length' television film, *The Evacuees* (1974). I produced two or three films directed by Clive Donner, who taught me an amazing amount about story-telling on celluloid. At the same time, at the BBC, Ken Loach, Stephen Frears, Michael Apted, Mike Newell, Roland Joffé, Richard Eyre and Waris Hussein were in frequent employment as directors. Innes Lloyd, Ken Trodd, Irene Shubik, Louis Marks, Graeme McDonald and Tony Garnett produced them. I thought, and many of us did, that the work made at the BBC in the 70s, film and tape but primarily film, was worthy of decent critical attention, not just jokes by Clive James.

But it didn't get it. *The Monthly Film Bulletin*, the British Film Institute's then organ of record, reviewed any piece of feature-length celluloid which opened theatrically, but nothing that had its première on television. And the boast that the British cinema was alive and well and living in Shepherd's Bush remained exactly that, a boast. The attitude of critical journals and the press in general annoyed a lot of us making television films. As Alan Bennett said of *An Englishman Abroad*, made in 1983 for the BBC:

'None of my previous TV films have received anything like the attention devoted to this one. Some of this was undoubtedly due to its being shown first at the London Film Festival and reviewed by a better class of critic. And then the upper classes and espionage are always dear to English hearts, more so certainly than the touching stories of sudden incontinence north of the Trent in which I generally specialise. *An Englishman Abroad* is bolder and more polished than my earlier films thanks entirely to John Schlesinger, but I did feel that if some of my earlier stuff, particularly the films directed by Stephen Frears for London Weekend, had been put in a similar film festival showcase they would have fared almost as well. As it is they now languish in the archives [sic] of LWT with no prospect of ever being seen again.'

By 1984, when Alan wrote this piece in *Sight and Sound*, Channel 4 had been running *Film on Four* for two years. I had produced one of them, *Moonlighting*, starring Jeremy Irons and directed by Jerzy Skolimovski. We made the film in four six-day weeks. The script had been written in two weeks. From a discussion in January 1982 to a screening at the Cannes Film Festival, with sub-titles completed by mid-May, was some kind of record.

At the time, I was not used to contact with the actual sources of finance. At the BBC, the money to make a film had either been there or not. It came from no one individual. With *Moonlighting* I knew Michael White who had, with amazing speed and daring, come up with half the budget. I had to look him in the eye, be responsible to him, get him to sign cheques. I had to sign cheques myself for every item of expenditure. We were in a hurry to complete the film for Cannes. That,

Skolimovski's ruthlessness and the financing were the major difference as a production experience from, say, *The Evacuees* eight years earlier. The surrounding publicity and Cannes hype *were* something else again, and made use of the film's speed of production and daringly low budget. But otherwise the film wasn't greatly different from the television work I'd done thus far.

In 1980, I'd been privileged, as perhaps the best result of making a film with the director Anthony Harvey, to meet Katherine Hepburn at her home in New York. I'd asked her about *Bringing Up Baby*, and she allowed as to how it had gone over budget and schedule in a rather outlandish way. 'Yes, it eventually shot for six weeks,' she marvelled, in contrast to the others she'd done at the time in four or five.

This was a formative converation for me in that house on (was it?) 44th Street one afternoon. Here was I sitting at the feet of this legend and she was telling me how these classics she'd made had been produced at the same speed we'd made our television films.

A Private Function, 1984

I felt I need never again apologise for the short schedules or low budgets of the films I produced, whether they were for the cinema or television. They were films, simple as that. What mattered was whether they were any good, whether they worked.

In the 80s I produced two more features films after *Moonlighting* – *A Private Function* (1984) and *The Witches* (1989) – as well as two television series and a pilot called *The Storyteller* (1986). The only one where we seemed to be unpressured by money was *The Storyteller*, a 30-minute piece financed by American television.

A Private Function was budgeted at $2 million and *The Witches* at $13 million. Neither seemed to be enough, any more than were the television film budgets I'd worked on. *The Witches* was American-financed, and needed animatronics. Both films needed real animals, pigs and mice/cats respectively.

The business of producing, small or medium budget, seemed much the same. As someone once said, 'It's like trying to keep a truck on a downhill road when the brakes have failed.'

When I took the job of Head of Drama of BBC Television in 1988, one of my aims was to get the BBC into the business of feature film financing, and to an extent I succeeded. We now co-produce and invest in more than ten of these a year.

Tony Garnett congratulated me. 'We've all been trying for ages, haven't we? Finally, it happened, after twenty years.'

Even then, the atmosphere in the Corporation was not conducive to feature film making, a mixture of coolness, jealousy and incomprehension. The most difficult problem to overcome was to persuade the Controllers, strapped for cash, to postpone television transmissions of films they had already paid for long enough to give those films time for proper theatrical and video exposure and therefore make them attractive to distributors in this country. Channel 4 had conquered this problem, though it took them a few years (I remember the confusion and feelings of betrayal exhibitors expressed when they were told that *Moonlighting* was to be shown on Channel 4 very shortly after its London première).

Truly Madly Deeply (1991) was the first BBC film to be bought by an American company (Goldwyn) for theatrical release. It had been made for television, under television union agreements, on 16mm,

Truly Madly Deeply, 1991

with a different title, *Cello*. All the contracts had to be renegotiated for its new incarnation, at a cost of several hundred thousand pounds. It opened first in America to decent reviews and business (though it would have been better if *Ghost* hadn't emerged just before it). Then it did well here, too, running in London up to a week before its television screening. I wish that the cinema owner had tried running it right across that screening and out the other side, to see if the TV screening might have positively helped its cinema business. It is received wisdom that one damages the other, but *The Snapper* disproved this to some extent. *Truly Madly Deeply* achieved huge ratings on television thanks to its cinema pre-publicity (and, of course, that is one of the arguments for cinema release prior to television showing).

More of our made-for-television films were bought for cinema release. *Antonia and Jane* had two strikes against it as a cinema film - it had already been shown on BBC-2 and only ran 65 minutes. This didn't stop Miramax buying American rights in the film and making a success of it there. The same company bought *Enchanted April* (1991) while it was in production and negotiated a brief theatrical window here. The London reviews were poor ('Cut-price Merchant/Ivory', said one) and it did no business, but in the U.S. it took $15 million and got three Oscar nominations.

The last example I'll use is *The Snapper* (1993). Stephen Frears, coming off the back of a $40 million film studio picture with Dustin Hoffman called *Hero*, agreed to direct *The Snapper* so long as it was written into his contract that the film could not be shown in cinemas. He felt it was too small a piece to work there. Reluctantly, we agreed, though distributors couldn't believe us when we told them the cinema rights were unavailable. *The Snapper* played successfully to a large audience on BBC-2 in April. Stephen had agreed that the film could open the Directors' Fortnight at Cannes in May. The screening played

so well that he was persuaded to change his mind and allow it to be sold theatrically. Amazingly, and courageously, Liz Wrenn of Electric Pictures decided she'd like to release it theatrically in the U.K., thus bucking tradition. It did decently, but we had problems persuading the newspapers to write about it (they'd covered it already in April, they said). One reviewer ignored it completely, another said it looked like a television film.

Thus bringing us back to the old question, 'What makes a film a film for the cinema?' It seems to vary from country to country - hence the different appeals of *Enchanted April*, or, more recently, *Persuasion*, which played here first on television, won't sell in non-U.S. English-speaking territories, and reached number 20 in the U.S. box-office

Small Faces, BBC Films, 1996

charts. Should *Vanya on 42nd Street* have been for television first, or *Ladybird, Ladybird*? You'd get different answers in the U.K. and France. What's the difference between *Kramer versus Kramer* and a television film except for Hoffman, Streep and Benton? Between *Quiz Show* and good television, except care in the direction and a better budget, bringing the audience a large picture and richer detail?

Problems occur at Oscar time. *Enchanted April* could qualify because its first screening anywhere was in the cinema. *The Snapper* couldn't, and nor could *The Summer House* run for a nomination for Jeanne Moreau in America because its first screening was on BBC Television as *The Clothes in the Wardrobe* (1993). You see how these supposed differences can affect a film's commercial chances.

In some countries, the barriers between cinema films and television films are high. In France it's hard to show a TV film in the cinema. There, cinema seems to be Culture and TV to be commerce. In America a few films made for Home Box Office and cable have had cinema release, but not many. In Britain we're more flexible - there's neither the huge cultural or commercial differences between the two, and the snobbery between them is much less than it was 20 years ago.

The obvious, and true, answer is that there are good films and bad films, dependent on many factors, and they almost all now start or finish on television. And more people now watch films at home than go out to see them in the cinema.

19 THE SOCIAL ART CINEMA: a Moment in the History of British Film and Television Culture

Christopher Williams

British cinema has four reputations and a problem. The first reputation is for a kind of built-in mediocrity, a supposed lack of interest in visual style or formal elaboration which can also be perceived as emotional inhibition. Satyajit Ray's argument was that the medium compels its user 'to face facts, to probe, to reveal, to get close to people and things; while the British nature inclines to the opposite; to stay aloof, to cloak harsh truths with innuendoes'.[1] Ray thought British film-makers lacked the creative imagination to produce visible filmic equivalents of the conflicts, clashes or tensions which may or may not (he was not sure) have existed in British culture. The argument has been advanced in broadly similar terms by many other writers, though with structural or intellectual terms replacing Ray's 'natural' one.

The second reputation is for realism. Many British films from different periods have engaged substantially with some of the conventions of artistic realism. The film criticism of the 1940s and 50s was generally in favour of these engagements, taking them as evidence of seriousness, and seeing some measure of success in their products; the theoreticism of the 1970s and 80s damned them, though without doing much to sort out the extent to which they varied or acknowledging the subtleties of how they worked. British realists could be faulted for trying at all, because realism was a waste of time, or for not trying hard enough, because the versions of realism they dealt in had too many blind spots, were too concerned with finding ways round what the critics took to be the principal issues: sexuality, politics, class-conflict.[2] This strand tended to conflate modes and concepts which had substantial operational differences, reducing them into univocal theoretical entities like 'the documentary-realist tradition'.[3]

Thirdly, we come to the concept of quality, which has different faces in criticism and professional practice. V.F. Perkins, writing just at the time of the (very circumscribed) new wave social realism of the early 1960s, summarised the British quality film as combining an important subject (meaning, at that time, serious human relationships and social problems), a popular story (undefined, but it could mean one which had either topical, available subject-matter or an exciting shape), a degree of balance ('a fair representation of all points of view'), a thought-compelling resolution, the use of figures of filmic style which were not necessarily motivated by anything substantial in the material, and some personal idiosyncracies. Perkins derided this combination, setting it alongside modes which drew on more assured senses of language, style and creativity.[4] This negative definition of quality set the tone for much discussion of British cinema (until Charles Barr's mid-1970s work on Ealing[5] began to open up the possibility of a broader view), and was further sustained by John Ellis's late 1970s recycling of it to blend critical humanism with some forms of 1940s realism into another unconvincing entity whose name was Quality.[6] These static visions of British film culture can be contrasted with Alan Lovell's scrupulous, differentiated account of how in the middle of the same period its strands resembled and yet did not resemble each other.[7]

The professional face of quality is more sympathetic. It proposes that there have normally been reservoirs of craftsmanship and talent among British film artists and technicians, and that these qualities have found their expression in a range of work of different kinds (though principally mainstream film and television), but without their exponents ever being called into a commanding position or achieving the critical or artistic recognition they merit. These are the famous 'best technicians in the world' who toil away as expensive hired hands on films which originate in other cultures or do their well-meaning bit on serious national productions which don't quite make it, perhaps, as Ray thought, for lack of creative imagination, perhaps because of British cinema's subordination and lack of confidence. From this point of view the professional quality of British film-making is seen as the victim of economic structures or aesthetic and cultural systems inadequate to sustain a national cinema.

The fourth, and to my mind the most significant, reputation of British cinema lies in its social character. This also has two main aspects. To pick up Ray's metaphor and consider the idea it introduced more closely, the apparent aloofness of some aspects of British culture masks an almost frenzied curiosity about social life and its systems, differences and observances. The British are obsessed with social functions and performances of all kinds. They are not thoroughly open about this (much less open for instance than Americans or Australians), nor may they have devised art forms which express or explore the social nature of existence to its fullest or most formal extents. Despite these limiting factors, pronounced commitment to sociality and social usage are evident in many of the representative individuals who have left their marks on British film culture - Grierson concerned with social purpose, Balcon involved with national identity and social responsibility, and Puttnam's version of responsibility, which has involved combining practices based in advertising, attempts to maintain a British perpective and the development of internationally-based material. Parallel pursuit of elevated conceptions of the social can also be found in some of our best known institutions – in the British Film Institute in many of its incarnations, whether representing traditional views about the dangers (cultural and social corruption) and rewards (good communication) of the medium or, on the other hand, the formalist, experimental anti-realism which still claims to put social function first.[8] These positions, both individual and institutional, are not indifferent to the aesthetic or entertainment values of film, but they prioritise the instrumental values which can be associated with it. The social is not reduced to the instrumental, but it takes on an instrumental face.

The second aspect of this commitment to the social expresses itself quite differently, in the form of a relative lack of interest in the individual or in subjectivity. This is most evident in the mature British feature film (from about the 1930s onwards), which demonstrates a tendency to attempt to build narrative structures around groups of characters rather than protagonists, and where it does have clear protagonists, still normally to attempt to socialise them, to present their emotions, motives and ideas in a version of a social context, which the film usually takes some pains to establish even if it may not elaborate all its details very succinctly. This tendency is very clear across films which have been grouped critically in quite different categories and have quite clear stylistic differences: for instance, Launder and Gilliatt's *Millions Like Us*, Powell and Pressburger's *Black Narcissus*, Relph and Dearden's *Victim*, even Reisz's *Saturday Night and Sunday Morning*. This has the effect of implying that what the individual feels or thinks, though relevant and part of the material, is not the primary focus of the work, nor can the narrative structure be articulated essentially around his/her goals or desires, but rather that his/her trajectory will be one element in a broader network of issues. Even when the individual is the primary vehicle, he/she is placed in a context towards which the machinery of the work is also drawn. This constant leaning of the British feature film can annoy devotees of active style and impact, emotional pertinence and centredness, and seem to confirm Ray's judgement by not probing, revealing or getting close to people. My contention is that instead, it actually explores something else, which is either a sense of the social or a set of images (which may be precise, but don't *have* to be) of the social, and that this, by and large, is what British cinema has been and is good at doing. There are artistic benefits as well as drawbacks in this leaning towards social context. Documentary, propaganda and argumentative films are also immediately drawn to a parallel notion of context, indeed often have one provided by the terms of their material, but this does not mean that the main British tradition is documentary-realist. The main British tradition is social. But to mark the facts that film-makers do not feel compelled to say things that are sociologically accurate, historically stimulating or politically correct, and that they work in a variety of mixed forms to represent and use these perceptions, it may be useful to re-define this social as being social-diffuse in structure and expression. I'll return to its main characteristics a little further on.

The problem of British film-making is also long-standing, but it has become more acute recently. British film-making is caught between Hollywood and Europe, unconfident of its own identity, unable to commit or develop strongly in either direction. On one side an economically and artistically powerful industry, using a broad range of elaborated genres and generic principles, popular with audiences around the world, frequently exercising controlling functions in our own production, exhibition and distribution, expressed in a different dialect of the same language, but with markedly different modes and diction. On the other a number of national cinemas which no longer have strong industrial bases but do in some cases represent perceptible senses of national identity. The strongest link between them is the concept of 'art cinema', which, although born much earlier, acquired critical mass in the 1950s and has since attracted the 'continental' adjective as a sort of generic principle: one can talk of European art cinema or 'European art-type' cinema. The art film deals with issues of individual identity, often with a sexual dimension, and aspires to an overt psychological complexity. Because it sees the individual as more important than the social, the social (which must normally figure in the films, if mainly by way of contrast) tends to be presented in terms of anomie or alienation, from a point of view which has much in common with that of the consciousness of the unhappy or doubting individual. It is more interested in character than in the plot aspects of story, which in keeping with the interest in anomie can be allowed to drift and follow each other in a loosely defined episodic fashion. It tends to interiorise dramatic conflicts; in some sense to give us the feeling that they are happening inside the protagonist's own mind. It aims at a distinct, intentional feeling of ambiguity, and its ending is typically unresolved; these lacks of resolution are valued for their 'life-likeness' and provocativeness. At the same time, and as an external mark of the subjectivity with which it is thematically concerned, the art film is expected to bear the marks of a distinctive visual style, which may be associated with the individual authorship of the director.[9]

Cinema in Europe speaks different physical languages. The idea of European cinema has acquired political relevance if not yet any real political energy through the development of the European Community and the collapse of the Warsaw Pact, and in practice European film-making now frequently depends on relationships with national and regional television* companies; despite these problems, European cinema has a general shared basis in terms of cultural affinity. To this cultural affinity the British subscribe reluctantly: they are Europeans despite themselves. In filmic terms they have stood confused between a popular culture whose rhythms and vigour they could not espouse (in part because of the comparative diffuseness and decentredness which are the mark of the British social tradition) and a European culture whose forms have been near but elusive.

One can summarise this situation by saying that the British, traditionally, had no art cinema, and later no specific equivalent of the European art cinema, no medium in which the leading issues of subjectivity (individual identity, sexuality, personal relations) or of socio-cultural developments and consciousness (history, community and national relationships) could be directly addressed in image-related forms. The nearest substitute was the documentary; but it could not convince in these capacities because (with a few exceptions which tended to demonstrate the main rule) it had downplayed the individual during its first flowering, lost prestige during its local decline between the 1940s and 1970s, and only developed an explicit interface with fiction from the 1970s onwards (by which time the very principles of documentary, though still crucial in the media, had incurred much theoretical displeasure). On one level this lack did not matter, because by the mid-1940s the British cinema had other things going for it. As Charles Barr has put it, 'By the end of the second world war, a positive reading of "mainstream" British cinema for the first time became convincingly available, both in Britain and abroad'.[10]

To my mind this positive interpretation should be attached to the social-diffuse characteristics of British cinema rather than to the realistic or quality domains where Barr, following Ellis, though with nuances, puts it.[11] The social-diffuse is a blend of the following factors: the debating of issues of present social and media concern, often explicitly, sometimes rather maladroitly; elements of observational, cultural and stylistic realism (Ellis was not wrong in seeing realism as an important element, just in misinterpreting its multiplicity and in linking his simplified version with the concept of quality); melodramatic features, which again may be handled maladroitly - lack of punch or conviction; interest in group rather than individual entities and identities, hence the apparent evasion of subjectivity, as I've already suggested. This British mainstream – one which properly incorporates Gainsborough and Launder and Gilliatt, Ealing and Powell and Pressburger and might even, recent work has suggested, be extended to include Rank[12] – certainly existed in the 1940s, was in fact still flourishing in the early 1950s, but after this fell into disrepair. By the 1970s a polarisation had taken place: the mainstream had shrivelled up and almost disappeared and so had any trace of broad-based reputation. A portion of the field was occupied by two rival concepts of 'independence', one based essentially on negation (it thought the mainstream did not exist, except as a set of backward-looking ideas and a few surviving decrepit practices), the other on the hope that mainstream ideas could be reanimated in terms of individual expression. Thus the content of independence was a few ideas about individual expression and artistic form, sometimes linked to overtly radical stances (as in the previously cited case of the formalist, experimental anti-realism which claimed to put social function first); but both strands functioned off narrow socio-cultural bases. Between the wasted body which had lost any plausibility as a form of popular culture (an area in which it had in any case never been confident), and the thin, voluntarist whines of independence, British film-making was gasping for air.

A measure of help – which was also part of a real cultural change – was at hand. It came about through the establishment, after 1979, of Channel 4 Television, with an active commitment to cinema and film-making, and the specific forms this commitment took. Jeremy Isaacs, who was to be the Channel's first Chief Executive, had already signified an interest in film by making the series *Hollywood* for Thames Television and chairing the BFI Production Board. In his letter of application he formulated the following as his ninth and last aspiration for the new channel: 'If funds allow, to make and help make films of feature length for television here, for the cinema abroad.'[13] The involvement of television companies in the production of films for cinema screening had already been successfully pioneered in Germany and Italy. Of Channel 4's £80 million start-up budget, £6 million was committed to film production and a further £2 million to other film-related activity, such as the buying of rights and measures of funding for independent and regional film workshops and other groups.

The principal vehicle for film production was the programme slot *Film on Four*, for which David Rose, Commissioning Editor for Fiction, commissioned quite a wide range of film projects. The initial aim was to 'make or help make' twenty films a year and to spend an average of £300,000 on each. In practice fewer films have been made (about fifteen per year), and usually with greater expenditure. The huge majority of these films have been co-financed, in partnership with such bodies as British Screen, other television companies both British and international, independent film companies (in some cases with a more or less continuous production activity, in others set up to make a specific project), or the British Film Institute. We are thus talking essentially about co-productions, in which Channel 4 is evidently a major, often the principal facilitator, but the substance of its aesthetic or cultural contribution may still be debatable. Its percentage contribution to budgets is spread out fairly evenly between the small (6% of *Hope and Glory*), the perceptible (19% of *On the Black Hill*), the substantial (50% of *The Draughtsman's Contract*), the major (75% of *Wish You Were Here*) and the total (100% of *My Beautiful Laundrette*).

The development of *Film on Four* heralded two important structural changes in British film and television culture. Firstly, it marked a

My Beautiful Laundrette,
1985

pronounced step towards the intensification of the relationship between the two media. Hitherto television companies had depended on film to fill large slices of its entertainment and some of its cultural slots – buying the TV rights to large quantities of film company product. Film companies had become used to regarding the accumulation of these sales as a significant proportion of their potential income. But now television companies were actually making films, and the intention was for them to be shown in both media. Isaacs' original proviso that they should only be shown in cinemas abroad was reversed when it was realised that a successful screening in British cinemas could lead to increased public interest and audience for national TV screenings. And films which were not commercial enough to secure cinema release could be shown on TV without delay, so long as they cost less than £1.25 million. Secondly, the success of *Film on Four* accelerated the trend to do away with the institution, popular and respected over the previous two decades, of the single television play, typically performed in a TV studio, with film or video inserts made on location when appropriate. Films made for television, perhaps showable in the cinema, and grouped under a loose series title, came to replace single untransferable television plays (also grouped under such titles). Television drama remoulded itself into the formats of series, serials and soap-operas. Television lost and gained by this development: losing (or putting on hold) one of its characteristic forms, but gaining a dynamic, participatory relationship with the world of cinema. Cinema regained a portion of the ground lost as a result of social and economic change, but acquired important new production and diffusion possibilities. Neither medium lost its identity through the change, but its effect was to make them less extricable from each other.

How should we assess the films which have been produced out of this change? They need to be set alongside the other substantial British films of the same decade: the work of Puttnam, Parker, and Bill Forsyth and the bulk of the films directed by Stephen Frears, Peter Greenaway and Derek Jarman, which were produced elsewhere. A reasonable proportion of the *Film on Four* work is at the same level, and two of them, Greenaway's *The Draughtsman's Contract* (1982) and *My Beautiful Laundrette* (directed by Frears, 1985) seem to me to rank with *Chariots of Fire* (produced by Puttnam, 1981) as the three defining British films of the decade. In his account of his stewardship at Channel 4, Isaacs struck two deprecating notes while laying claim to a measure of achievement:

> 'Some talk, though we [Rose and himself] do not, of a 'renaissance' of British film. In my view, reports of that birth are somewhat exaggerated. Film-making in Britain remains a chancy business. There is no conceptual framework [in *Film on Four*] to which I can point that defines a body of work. Yet something of substance has been done.'[14]

To my mind Isaacs was too modest. There was a conceptual framework of sorts, and it developed out of the relations between the social and the artistic – static, antithetical forms of which had contributed to the stifling of British cinema by the end of the 1970s. Although criticism has been feeble in developing generic classifications or principles appropriate to British film-making, I think it possible to devise some rough and ready categories (part thematic, part stylistic) to classify the output of *Film on Four*.[15] In the first 10 years (1982-91) of the series, 138 feature-length films were transmitted. Of these, seventeen (12%) were primarily concerned with addressing political issues. *The Ploughman's Lunch* (directed by Richard Eyre, 1983) and Karl Francis' *Giro City* (1982) are good examples of this. A further sixteen (12%) can best be described as Human Interest dramas – films which seem to have taken over many of the attributes of the serious, socio-culturally concerned single television play. *Good and Bad at Games* (directed by Jack Gold, 1983) and *The Good Father* (directed by Mike Newell, 1986) can represent this tendency. Eleven films (8%) were conspicuous literary adaptations. There were nine films representing observational forms of realism (including Mike Leigh's *Meantime*, 1983), nine thrillers and nine films addressing primarily historical topics (6.5% in each category). Eight films (6%), including *Experience Preferred But Not Essential* (directed by Peter Duffell, 1982) were part of *First Love*, a sub-series which originated with Goldcrest. Seven (5%) were comedies, thirteen (10%) are unclassifiable (Leigh's *High Hopes*, 1988, the most notable of these), a further five (3.5%) seriously weird, and two avant-gardish (quite a lot of avant-garde material was shown on Channel 4, but not in the *Film on Four* slot). But the largest single category is that of the art film, as defined above: individual identity, sexuality, pyschological complexity, anomie, episodicness, interiority, ambiguity, style. It accounts for 33 films (24% of the total), of which the most prominent examples are Neil Jordan's *Angel* (1982), Jarman's *Caravaggio* (1986), Terence Davies' *Distant Voices, Still Lives* (1988), *The Draughtsman's Contract*, Chris Petit's *Flight to Berlin* (1983), Jerzy Skolimovski's *Moonlighting* (1982), *My Beautiful*

Letter to Brezhnev, 1985

Laundrette, *Reflections* (directed by Kevin Billington, 1983), *Letter to Brezhnev* (directed by Frank Clarke, 1985) and David Leland's *Wish You Were Here*. These last two are debatable.

Some necessary comment on these categories. They are not mutually exclusive, and some films could probably be categorised under several of them. The *First Love* material could be reclassified as Human Interest, realism or comedy. The 'primarily political' category clearly corresponds to the perception that Channel 4 was expected to provide radical and/or socially committed material. The number of films which I regard as unclassifiable may bear witness to the further expectation that the new Channel was to be fresh, different and attempt to pull within the frame 'what had previously been either excluded or treated in a bland or simplistic way.'[16] The real but modest proportions of literary adaptation and historical evocations simply continue long-standing sub-traditions in British film-making. The relative paucity of thrillers is not surprising (the genre was never strong here and has been in decline for a long time); the lack of comedy may seem so, but can perhaps be explained by (a) the seriousness with which film-making took itself in the context of a new, innovative channel, (b) the institutional tendency within television to think of comedy in terms of light entertainment, and (c) the presence of some humour in the Human Interest, realist and even unclassifiable categories.

It may be possible to amalgamate the Human Interest and realist categories into one larger grouping (18.5%), roughly equivalent to the 'social-diffuse' category that I have argued is the traditional core of British film-making. It might also be possible to stretch a point by further adding the primarily political grouping to create a larger 'social diffuse-and-oriented' category which would then, at 30.5%, become notionally the largest category. But the most important point is that the art film grouping (a new feature in the early 1980s) is the single most substantial element, and that more traditional combinations of the Human Interest, the realist and the political (in which perhaps only the form of the political is rather new) carry about the same weight. Films like *Angel, Caravaggio, Distant Voices, Still Lives, Flight to Berlin, Moonlighting, My Beautiful Laundrette, Reflections* address the principal concerns of the European art film – loneliness, who am I?, social and moral confusions, the importance of the stylish exterior, in ways which are both direct and hitherto unknown in British film-making, but they also begin to shift these concerns toward the group, the context and the social-diffuse, to some extent through using diction drawn from television. This seems most evident in *Laundrette*, in which central questions of sexual identity are mixed with discussion of race, economics and generation difference and where the action constantly swings back and forth between the social and the individual in a manner which may not always work (in terms of relations between the parts) and in which the ideas may be rigged to some extent, but which compels admiration for its vigour and attempt at comprehensiveness.

Wish You Were Here is rooted in a classic Human Interest theme: a teenage girl's sexuality and its problems in a social and familial world.

Wish You Were Here, 1987

Leland's treatment grapples with combining all these elements, trying to say things (artistically) about sexuality and society in general before subsiding into art images of a less satisfying kind: *Soave sia il vento* on the sound-track to get us over an unconvincing plot point, cute images of defiance rather than addressing a tragic situation. There is something postmodern about this choice of language rather than substance, as there is also in *Letter to Brezhnev*, which is a successful combination of social realism (treated in a rather broad, shallow fashion), popular romance and political fantasy. Unlike *Laundrette* or *Wish*, *Letter* opens up the possibility of a relationship between British film and popular culture. But all three attempt a blending of the British social-diffuse with some of the concerns of the European art film. This social art cinema was a new formation. It also provided the conceptual framework which defined the substance of Channel 4's contribution to British film-making.

NOTES

1. Satyajit Ray, *Our Films Their Films*, Orient Longman, Bombay, 1976, p. 144.

2. See John Hill, *Sex, Class and Realism*, BFI, 1986.

3. See, for example, Andrew Higson, 'Britain's Outstanding Contribution to the Film: the documentary-realist tradition', in ed Charles Barr, *All Our Yesterdays*, BFI, 1986, pp. 72-97.

4. V.F. Perkins, 'The British Cinema', in *Movie*, no. 1, 1962.

5. Charles Barr, 'Projecting Britain and the British Character', *Screen*, vol. 15, nos. 1 and 2, 1974; Ealing Studios, Cameron & Tayleur/David and Charles, 1977, 2nd revised ed., Studio Vista, 1993.

6. John Ellis, 'Art, Culture and Quality: Terms for a Cinema in the Forties and Seventies', *Screen*, vol. 19, no. 3, 1978.

7. Alan Lovell, 'The British Cinema', *Screen*, vol. 13, no. 2, 1972.

8. See for example eds Rod Stoneman and Hilary Thompson, *The New Social Function of Cinema* (the Catalogue of British Film Institute Productions 1979/80), BFI, 1981.

9. This summary of the characteristics of European art cinema draws on the accounts in David Bordwell, 'The Art Cinema as a Mode of Film Practice', *Film Criticism*, vol. 4, no. 1, 1979 and in Steven Neale, 'Art Cinema as Institution', *Screen*, vol. 22, no. 1, 1981.

10. Charles Barr, 'Introduction: Amnesia and Schizophrenia', in ed Barr, *All Our Yesterdays*, p. 11.

11. ibid., pp. 13-26.

12. See Geoffrey Macnab, J. *Arthur Rank and the British Film Industry*, Routledge, 1993.

13. Jeremy Isaacs, *Storm over 4: a Personal Account*, Weidenfeld and Nicolson, 1989, p. 25.

14. ibid., p. 158.

15. The factual information for my account of *Film on Four* draws on John Pym, *Film on Four: a Survey 1982/1991*, BFI, 1992. The generic categories have evolved from discussing British film culture, art cinema, realism and genre with students of the M.A. course in Film and Television Studies at the University of Westminster.

16. Sylvia Harvey, 'Channel 4 Television: from Annan to Grade', in ed. Stuart Hood, *Behind the Screens*, Lawrence and Wishart, 1994, p. 117.

20 DON'T CRY FOR ME WHEN I'M GONE:
Motion Pictures in the 1990s

Paul Schrader

Lectures about 'the state of motion pictures' are the occasion for self-promoting pieties about 'art', often given by businessmen for whom art is a slogan, not a way of life. If movies were better, people would be better, and what a wonderful world it would be. You know the routine.

It's time to take the longer view. Movies are a hundred years old. Movies took off in this century and the century is coming to an end. Just because film has been the popular art form of this century doesn't mean it will be of the next century. Discussions about the problems of contemporary film tend to slip down the slope of the unstated assumption that film's 'problems' began yesterday and can be solved tomorrow. The opposite is true. The problems that film faces today were present from the very beginning of the art form.

History repeats and loops around itself and at times it appears there's nothing new under the sun. Everything new is old. There are, however, two tendencies which stand apart: two linear, chronological lines running from the beginning of recorded history to the present. One is technology, the other democracy. They are progressive, not cyclical, and are the yardsticks by which art, religion and social conduct can be measured.

Technological progress – man's knowledge of the physical world and his control over it – is not only continuous but exponential: the more we learn the faster we learn it. One discovery begets ten. At one time an educated person could master both the arts and the sciences; today a scientist, to be on the forefront of knowledge, must choose a specific science, a field within that science and a subfield within that field. Our tools are equally exponential and progressively more sophisticated: mechanical, combustive, electronic. Man's mastery over his environment has grown to the point where he is able to destroy it, both in evil and benign ways.

Democracy, or, more accurately, the empowerment of the common man, is another powerful thread. The events we associate with democracy, the Magna Carta, French Revolution, emancipation of slaves, universal suffrage – Democracy's Greatest Hits – are political symbols of a broader social evolution. History can be defined as an accretion of individual rights, civilisation by civilisation, century by century. Democracy has had its setbacks, as has technology, but the overall trend is irrefutable. The individual has successively gained knowledge of events around him, a greater voice in government, more say in his religious life, increased participation in the arts. Rules by definition resist empowerment; over time they invariably fail. To stand against the individual is to stand against history.

Individual empowerment and technological progess are not exactly isolated tendencies. They are handmaidens. They assist and feed each other. Individual curiosity spurs technological progress, technology empowers the individual.

This is where cinema comes in. At the end of the nineteenth century, during the so-called 'Second Industrial Revolution', the tools of technology turned from heavy industry to consumer needs. The invention of the linotype machine and cheap newsprint created a pervasive popular press, the combustion engine provided economical travel, the telegraph made it possible to communicate across great distances, the electric light freed millions from dawn to dusk schedules, leisure time democratised sport, cinema brought news events to every neighbourhood. Commoners flocked to cities to enjoy new freedoms. The cities gave birth to a new urban proletariat, doubling, tripling in size. 'Invention runs free,' H.G. Wells declared, 'and our state is under its dominion.'

The upstart film medium dovetailed democracy and art. Scorned by Culture, movies became the voice of the people. The Art Establishment, pigeonholers all, circumscribed moving images. They were clever but strange – good for recording historical events, preserving theatre, aiding scientific research. Cinema was not art. Repudiated, cinema entrepreneurs, creators of the motion picture turned to the public. They owed nothing to the cultural establishment.

Arrivée d'un train en gare de la Ciotat, 1895

'Art' was validated by working people paying to enter the nickelodeons. Art for and by the marketplace. Stories glorifying the the common man. U.S. film entrepreneurs, in the ultimate insult, fled the East Coast with its stultifying patent laws and cultural prejudices and started anew, lock, stock and lens, in Southern California.

The inventors and early critics of cinematography, as motion pictures were then called, were more aware of its democratic potential than of its future as an art form. The debate raged. On one side were cinematic utopians and democrats. Michel Corday, a Parisian journalist, described a 'Cineorama' exhibit at the 1900 Exposition as part of a 'great current of democratisation which offers the masses the precious joys until now reserved for the few'. Thomas Edison, co-inventor of the kinescope, declared: 'I intend to do away with books in the school. (...) When we get the moving pictures in the school, the child will be so interested that he will hurry to get there before the bell rings, because it's the natural way to teach, through the eye.' An 1894 columnist in *Harper's Weekly* wrote, 'Already it has been made quite clear that that in this scientic millennium the public will not have to betake itself to exhibition halls to see and hear a novelette, but will sit at home and take the novelette over the wires, seeing and hearing with the aid of electricity.' By 1916 motion pictures had their first theorist, Hugo Munsterberg, who saw the new art form was a means to democratise the theatre. 'The greatest mission which the photoplay may have in our community is that of aesthetic cultivation.'

On the other side were the defenders of Cultural Values. German sociologist Georg Simmel went right to the point: 'Individuals, in all their divergences, contribute only the lowest parts of their personalities to form a common denominator.' In 1895, Gustave Le Bon was even more dystopian: 'Today the claims of the masses amount to nothing less than a determination to destroy utterly society as it now exists.' Louis Haugmard, a Catholic essayist, countered Munsterberg's optimism. 'Alas! In the future,' he wrote in 1913, 'notorious personalities will instinctively "pose" for cinematographic popularity, and historical events will tend to be concocted for its sake. (...) The charmed masses will learn not to think any more, to resist all desire to reason and to construct: they will know only how to open their large and empty eyes, only to look, look, look (...) Will cinematography comprise, perhaps, the elegant solution to the social question, if the modern cry is formulated: "Bread and cinemas"?'

Sounds familiar? The modernist and postmodernist debate rages on. One hundred years on, similar laments fill the popular press. Critics are outraged that movies have 'gotten worse', corrupted by popular taste. They don't make movies like they used to. Every year is worse than the one before. Film-makers, ironically, and film executives, even more ironically, as they count their gains, have joined the list of complainants.

Anyone who looks behind last week's grosses realises that film is not in a unique crisis of quality. Movies are as good as they ever have been, probably better. Today's debate is an old one and it is the debate which defines mass-produced art: cultural standards versus popular taste. The extent to which popular art can promote social intelligence is the unanswered question of modern history - one which probably cannot be answered, and perhaps need not be.

Film is in a crisis of another sort, however; a crisis dictated by the trends which created its technology and democracy. This is the real crisis, the crisis of whether or not movies will continue to exist. What direction are those mighty horses, technology and democracy, pulling in?

Technologically, film – at least as theatrically exhibited – is very antiquated. We still show moving pictures the way the Lumières did, pumping electric light through semi-transparent cells, projecting shadows on a white screen. These techniques belong in a museum. A change is overdue.

The future of film is coming into focus. Digital technology not only redefines movies, but also the very idea of the image. We were born in an analogue era, we shall die in a digital one. Film is an analogue, that is, a physical copy of something else, it is 'analogous' to what it photographs. A digital image is not a copy, it is an electronic and mathematical translation. Laserdiscs transform images and sounds into binary choices, millions of on-off decisions.

Digital technology is not only transforming exhibition, it's transforming our notion of the image. The dream of the *Harper's Weekly* columnist, of 'novelettes' brought into the home 'with the aid of electricity', has come true. 'In the meantime,' that writer continued, ' we must be content at the halfway house. Certainly the halfway house has proved to be a very interesting place.' Public cinemas have been a halfway house for almost a century. Analogue exhibition has been a good tool. It's done its job. It's time for a new tool. (Digital transmission of images may itself be a halfway house. In the future audiovisual images may be transmitted bio-chemically.)

If you think technology is threatening, take a look at democracy. For a century, artists have been fomenting the desire for artistic freedom among the commoners – Ortega's 'revolt of the masses' – while retaining papal prerogatives for themselves, creating art by *fiat*. In *Hearts of Darkness*, a documentary about the making of *Apocalypse Now*, Francis Coppola comments that being a film director is the closest thing there is, in this democratic age, to being a dictator. And so he is. Twentieth century artists live in the best of both worlds, advocating power to the people, never imagining they will have to give up any themselves. Democracy is a wonderful thing, just don't try it on my film set.

These prerogatives will also be called into question. Digital technology challenges the traditional relationship between the artist and the viewer/listener. A digital image is, in essence, as potentially different from an analogue image as a portrait is from a photograph: portraits interpret, photographs replicate. Analogue images are essentially what they are, immutable; digital images are manipulatable, not only by the artists but also by the viewer. Digital images and sounds can be altered: sounds and images can be added to a recording, digital images can be broken up, colourised, morphised.

In recent years a new form of literature, Hypertext, has evolved. These are novels written exclusively on computer software. A Hypertext novel can have an infinite number of windows: each sentence, each word, each letter can lead to a separate narrative pattern. The reader chooses his own path, interacting as he chooses with other paths. The novelist programmes the paths but cannot programme the interactions – they are the reader's creations. Novelist Robert Coover wrote recently about a 'novel' he and his students were programming. Each successive reader chose a narrative path and added to it, expanding the text. The creative life span of this Hypertext novel, Coover speculated, could be 100 years. The reader was empowered.

Something similar may be in store for cinema. In the digital future, a viewer will not only be able to re-cast an existing movie, replacing Gable with Bogart or Cagney in *Gone with the Wind*, for example, but will also be able to participate in the creation of new films, mixtures of pre-existing and imagined images. The appeal of 'virtual reality' is that it is interactive. The autocratic artist will finally face the consequences of democracy, he will be a creative partner. A film-maker won't direct a movie, he'll instigate it.

Am I saying what you think I am saying? Yes. In the future, movies will not only not look like they do now, the film-maker won't even have autonomy.

An immediate retort is: but audiences *want* the artist to have autonomy. Viewers want structure, they want to be told what to see, what to hear, what to feel. This is the argument which has been made by political autocrats, ecclesiastical czars and cultural mandarins over the centuries: the masses want us to decide for them. The Roman church assumed parishioners *wanted* it to control the Scriptures. They were wrong; individuals wanted to participate – to share and decide – and the Reformation democratised Christianity. The autocrats weren't right in the past, it's not likely they'll be right in the future. Viewers will decide. The child playing narrative video games, the colleague at his computer paint box – they will decide. Most films will be made, as they are now, by authorial *fiat*; but there will also be new films, films made in concert with viewers.

There will always be stories. Humankind has needed to tell and retell itself certain tales from the beginning of civilisation. As long as there are parents and children, men and women, landlords and tenants, the ancient myths will be repeated and updated. Whatever the medium. The media will change, the relationship between the storyteller and the listener will be realigned, but there will always be stories.

There is no cause for despair. It *is* disconcerting. The future is, by definition, disconcerting. That's the fun of it. Without challenge, without change, art atrophies. The only thing more frightening than going forward is standing still.

I'd like to close by quoting Nietzsche, who, as you can imagine, took a dim view of the democratisation of the arts. In 1888, he wrote a statement reflecting his despair at recent developments, a statement which can be repeated, not in despair, but with hope. 'Nothing avails,' he wrote, 'one *must* go forward - step by step further into decadence (that is my definition of modern "progress").'

This essay is based on the Cinema Militans lecture delivered in Holland in 1992. A version of it first appeared in *DGA News*, Los Angeles, vol. 18, no. 1, February-March 1993.

21 READ ONLY MEMORY:
the Re-Creation Of Sensorial Experience in 3D and CD-ROM

David Mingay

Cinematography began exactly 100 years ago, and video is about 60 years old. For over 20 years I have worked as film-maker, film editor and producer in cinema and television. These are two distinct industries which have vied to transcend each other in a struggle between two technologies, film and analogue video. Neither has succeeded, and they live uneasily side by side.

Three years ago I ventured into production in the new medium of the CD-ROM. So what made me turn to the computerised delivery of images, the result of the third great revolution in the field of moving pictures - the Digital Revolution?

One reason is the ability to work with the capacities of computer graphics and three-dimensional images to produce visuals which were previously impossible. The advances made by computer graphics are particularly noticeable in advertisements, and in cinema films like *Jurassic Park*. But nothing prepared me for the combination of fully-rendered 3D animation on the high definition computer screen. The computer screen is comparable in its resolution to High Definition Television. The digital revolution allows the high quality reproduction of electronic art, which is not possible with analogue video, an unstable medium which degenerates in the act of copying the signal. The low quality of the VHS tape and its pictures will be superseded by digital technology.

Filmed images have the appearance of depth, but before the tools and modelling programmes of computer animation existed the animated drawing was relatively flat, two-dimensional and unlike film realism. What 3D animation provides, with the addition of the computer to the animation process, is a scientific tool to allow the artist to work in a 3D mode where it is possible to model the drawings, to render them with textures and then to light them with literally the choice of thousands of colours, shades and effects of light. Computer graphics works within a visual interface which re-creates the sensorial experience of 3D virtual reality. The concept of 'sensorial experience' refers to the way the part of the human brain which controls the senses receives and deciphers the experience of interacting with a visual medium. In the case of the new medium of CD-ROM, where the key function is interactivity, the art of navigating and playing a programme of text, pictures and computerised links and actions is a new sensorial method which implies new modes of entertainment and production. Interactivity has been called the sixth sense.

I am working with a team which makes CD-ROM titles for three platforms – PC, Macintosh and CD-i. The current production, *Virtual Nightclub*, is a technically advanced computer disc exploiting the 640 megabytes of data in a CD-ROM disc when linked to a colour computer screen. The disc takes us to a world which embodies new ideas and working concepts:

– Virtual Reality, which is the technology used to provide an interactive interface between human beings and computer imagery.

– Cyberspace, an independent realm created by the interconnection of the world's information systems.

– Telepresence, the communication between the operator and a robot, where the robot becomes the operator's body and the operator is transported to wherever the robot is working.

–Transparent Systems, which are systems for conveying messages from one human being to another without in any way shaping their meaning. The user's access to a network system allows open communication to the individual.

–Virtual Navigation is the ability to travel freely in an artificial environment. The travel may be powered and guided by use of the mouse or a controller. The environment is an immersive 3D world.

Through the medium of CD-ROM and the interface of 3D worlds the user enters a new universe which is a pure entertainment capable of cyber-experience. *Virtual Nightclub* features highly coloured 3D environments which the user can navigate – in what we call the new CD Experience. This means that the experience of interactivity applied to entertainment on the screen of a computer is different in kind from passive viewing.

The production began as a multimedia project which would exploit all the facets of multimedia – photography, video, sound, music, information, filmed live action and graphics of all kinds. With the addition of 3D graphics and then of virtual navigation - by moving as in a subjective camera through space on a network of nodes between which the user travels, and with the ability to turn 360 degrees in an environment – it also took on the possibilities of the interactive movie and the video game.

There is a clear parallel between these new capabilities and the sense of novelty which attended the first appearance of the Cinématographe. It was the simulation of reality which shocked and delighted the Lumières' first audiences. *L'Arrivée d'un Train en Gare de La Ciotat* may have caused alarm to some spectators who are thought to have feared the train's approach as it gained in size on the screen. It must have seemed technically awesome that such an image could make an illusion like this. The means were persistence of vision, a camera able to take at least 18 frames a second, a projector able to project photographic strips, and the invention of the sprocket hole and the pull-down mechanism. As with much technology, people did not know how the effects were achieved, but they accepted that the means were normal and not supernatural.

We no longer feel menaced by moving images in a physical sense – although Hollywood film-makers make efforts to reproduce such an effect. Every action movie and Disneyland ride is an attempt to recapture the visceral thrill of simulating sensory experience and exposure to danger and menace. Why? Because the effect is cathartic. To experience a performance of confrontation with and escape from danger is a meaningful fantasy. So is the vicarious learning experience of reading a novel.

Current computer effects should be seen as an extension of cinema, and particularly of animation. The apparently mysterious computer world may be nothing more than a combined camera and projector capable of playing digital video and sound, with the tools of computation enabling it to generate computer graphics

Virtual Nightclub is a tissue of movies arranged in layers playing with all the illusions of cinema to create an interactive projector which is operated by the user. Virtual Reality[1] and Video Games do not represent an advance on the Aristotelian rules of dramatic art. If the effect to be achieved is catharsis, they apply to these media as to others.

Can we talk of a qualitative difference in these scientific advances from what is already known? In 1914, the Italian director Pastrone in the film *Cabiria* put a camera on a trolley and moved it past a giant statue of a Sphinx. This was the first camera move to give the impression of subjective movement. 3D animation repeats this effect endlessly. The lurch past the foreground object emphasises the movement and gives the subjective feeling of being there and of moving in a space. When this is added to an interactive interface – i.e. when you press a mouse or a controller to make it happen, to repeat the movement and effect, to turn around in the 3D space in 360 degrees – then you have virtual navigation.

The key function of the CD-ROM is interactivity. But the rules and possibilities of interactivity and their application to virtual reality are still only in their infancy. As one who has sat around trying to think about interactivity, I think it is the case that the passivity of viewing films and listening to music is fundamental to the presentation of these arts. Interactivity produces new concepts not easily applied to existing forms of entertainment. Up till now the twin peaks of interactive application have been the genres of Games and Reference. But behind a catchphrase like 'the Information Superhighway' lie possibilities for new modes of communication. Crafts like that of 'interactive storytelling' are waiting to be born.[2]

A CD-ROM can store and access any data including video. It can be programmed by software to deliver information, sound and pictures in any way the programmer decides. It can perform the function of a database which can be activated by a user on a computer – or in the case of a game or experience it can be programmed with rewards, alternatives, rules, interpretive possibilities so that it becomes a world or an artificial intelligence. These possibilities are what interactivity is attempting to deliver. I can illustrate this by discussing some features of the CD-ROM programme *Virtual Nightclub* and the interactive movie *Burn:Cycle* to which it is related.

Virtual Nightclub is now in final preparation for launch in the market on CD-ROM Mac and PC platforms in 1996. The team behind it is led by interactive designer David Collier and visual designer Olaf Wendt, who are both under thirty years old. While prototyping the concept of *Virtual Nightclub* they were joined by writer/director Eitan Arussi and made *Burn:Cycle* for Philips. *Burn:Cycle* is an interactive science fiction movie with strong game play. It has a linear plot which is divided into levels which the player achieves by successful shooting and puzzle solving. He then progresses in the plot and has to stay alive by shooting opponents. He also works through dialogue scenes to the conclusion of the story. The script has a three-act structure as in a Hollywood feature film. The hero visits bars and houses in his role as a message

Virtual Nightclub:
the Art Gallery

carrier, and has to lay the fuse to blow up a door, visit a Buddhist guru and finally transmogrify into cyberspace.

This movie/game has been successful and is now converted from the CD-i platform, for which it was originally made, to Mac and PC CD-ROM. It shares with *Virtual Nightclub* the surreal and highly rendered graphics of Olaf Wendt. In *Burn:Cycle* the player has the ability virtually to navigate in the architecture of a space-ship, a futuristic city with streets and skyscrapers, and to enter and fly a space carrier plane. By using the controller the player is telepresent in manipulating his way through the environment, performing tasks and collecting items in the inventory in the manner of an adventure video game.

In addition, a time-clock of two hours is set to the user's actions, so that it becomes a beat-the-clock exercise, which greatly motivates the player in the direction of a visceral involvement in a life-like experience of time, space and action. In this sense *Burn:Cycle* conforms to the Aristotelian rules, and they compel immersion in an artificial world and the work to be done there.

The work to be done involves assuming the character of Sol Cutter, a 'Data-Thief' from the pages of a William Gibson cyberpunk novel like *Neuromancer*, in a first-person point-of-view visual shooting style, where the 'to-camera' pieces give way to the player holding the hero's gun in a pretty seamless fashion, and shooting enemies in the style of

Virtual Nightclub:
Cyber-Image

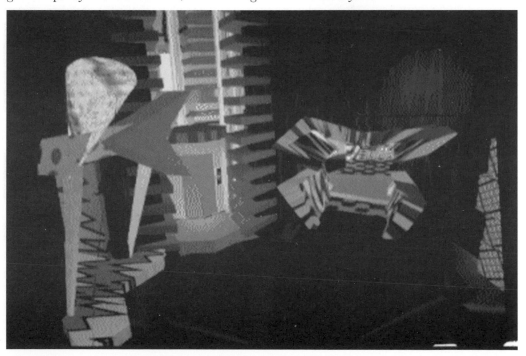

every shoot-out. If shot, the player has to start the movie again. The subjective travelling shot, used for navigating, cuts into dialogue scenes where the hero is seen with the other characters of the story. The time-clock on the user's action is fictionalised as a brain-implant in the hero Cutter's head, set to explode in two hours if he does not deliver his data and win the decommissioning of the explosive charge inside his head. Life-and-death identification for the viewer is implemented by use of the time clock in every computer. The realistic 3D environment sustains the sense of dramatic immersion.

But how immersive is *Burn:Cycle*? We can only see, feel, and experience this by playing. It is not easy for adults unused to video-gaming suddenly to have to take this seriously. The experience is purely visual: it is the visual sense which understands and manipulates the passage through the artificial world. This passage is achieved through manual dexterity. This gives a prosthetic effect. The machine is an extension of the body – as is the keyboard for the typist, and to some extent the car for the motorist. Adults are handicapped until they can achieve skill in co-ordinating fingers, hands and feet in these extended tasks. It is possible to suggest that young people are being trained in re-coordination for the prosthetic future of the human body by the hours they put in training on Gameboy, Sega, and Nintendo – pressing those buttons, beating those scores, in routines which are tricky but simple at the same time.

These software inventions (headed by the flight simulator game) were created as virtual training systems for the military in the US and for the NASA space programme. The Space programme helped to develop the electronics industry on the U.S. East Coast which is now the centre of the computer industry, the Internet and telecommunications networks. It is these developments which have created Cyberspace.

The CD-ROM title *Virtual Nightclub* is an artificial Cyberspace with nineteen rooms. It is arranged in three levels: a street level which re-creates a navigable Soho, a Club level with rooms full of events and personalities in five time zones, and Headspace, which is accessed in a separate network where the user meets Cyber-gurus and music experts.

Virtual Nightclub has attracted several commercial sponsors including Levis, Stella Artois and Dr Martens. The challenge was to invent and create interactive advertisements within the environment of the Club. Protected by NASA, an adverting agency in London was able to create an interactive cyber-advert entirely from resources existing within the immaterial world of the Internet, and to download these goods (potentially valuable ones) at the desk of the operator at his computer. An advertisement for the Levis installation within the

Virtual Nightclub was able to use material (video and audio images of the moon landing) drawn from the NASA site on the Internet.

'The NASA static images and sound samples that BBH [the advertising agency involved, Bartle, Bogle and Hegarty] sourced in order for *Virtual Nightclub* to produce an interactive Levis advertisement within the Virtual Nightclub were downloaded from the NASA Compuserve forum on the 18 December 1994. The NASA Compuserve is owned and administered by NASA. Compuserve Forum contained a notice at the start of logging procedure to the effect that all material contained within it was worldwide copyright free.'[3]

It is the intention to make a two-way connection with the world's information systems, via the "Virtual Nightclub" site on the Internet where Club members will meet each other, and where the transparent systems will allow members to appear in the rooms of the Virtual Nightclub on the Internet. The Internet is the main example of a network in space, a means of two-way communication arising out of a peripheral attachment to the computer of a modem which allows data to be exchanged down telephone wires.

The content of the Club has come from collaborations with music artists, record labels, fashion designers and aspects of youth culture which are wrapped into video-game motivations and fast interactivity. The telepresence of the *Virtual Nightclub* CD-ROM makes a Disc Jockey or Video Jockey of the user. This is because there is an audio component to virtual reality. On the simplest level no video game is very interesting without its monotonous but compelling soundtrack. So in terms of sensorial experience the artificial world is an architectural space capable of generating sounds, triggered through code and software commands. In a 3D model the user can then move freely, generating combinations of the possibilities which have been created mathematically. Similarly, in the real world, sound comes out of various kinds of movement and vibration. Thus sound is perhaps the strongest single factor in creating the illusion of an artificial world.

Virtual Nightclub: Music Room

Cyberspace is not a deaf and dumb world, and significantly it connects with sampling and synthesisers which have taken over the production of both popular and classical music. The key to this is the loop – an electronically-cut sound which is available to the user as a note sequence or a sound effect. When these are seamlessly played together there begins to be a music or soundscape to virtual reality and we are probably only beginning to know what this is, and where it will lead. Hopefully, the *Virtual Nightclub* will be a step in this direction.

AN A-Z OF CD-ROM

a: analogue > digital technology is set to supercede analogue technology. Analogue is a real-time, steady-flow copying system, unstable and impermanent, used in TV, hi-fi, radio, video and the telephone. Digital technology reduces information to a binary number system.

b: bytes/bits > a bit is the smallest unit of digital information representing a single binary digit which can be either a 1 or a O. A byte is 8 bits 1 kylobyte is 1,024 bytes. A megabyte equals 1 million bytes.

c: CD-ROM > the CD was invented by Philips and Sony in the early 1980s as an audio format, and then in 1985 the invention of the ROM added pictures and text. It reads only data which is written or 'burnt' onto the disc by laser. The latest CD-ROM is equipped with double-speed, which refers to the speed at which it reads the data when accessed on a computer.

d: digital data> stored as binary numbers it offers vast storage for infinite time with instantaneous access. The capacity of the standard disc is 650 megabytes. In the future this capacity is set to grow by a factor of ten.

e: electronic art> electronic culture blurs the distinctions between different cultural areas and typically marries science, technology, education and entertainment. CD-ROM can display the electronically produced graphics which are beginning to create their own artform, called Cyber-art.

f: fractals> fractal theory exploits the colour generation and geometry of electronic data to create coloured patterns, which can be stored on the CD-ROM.

g: graphics> computer-generated graphics create the artificial worlds of cyberspace, are the basis of stored electronic information and can be brought to artificial life by movement and sound.

h: hypertext> hypertext is the non-linear, branching 'choices' system used to facilitate access to stored data, typically on a CD-ROM and activated by the mouse of the computer. The sytem offers choices which guide the user to be able to access and browse intuitively through the material on the disc. The user begins to work and live inside the electronic world. The world becomes responsive to the user.

i: interactivity> hardware and software systems which allow the user to respond to the program through the interface which is the point of contact between the user and the machine.

j: JPEG> Joint Pictures Experts Group (an international committee) has laid down the compression standards using data compression algorhyithms, designed to reduce the data to standard formats which match the capacity of the disc – JPEG being for still images. (MPEG is the equivalent standard for moving pictures.) Compression is the key to what can be stored on a ROM. Video and film require enormous volume of storage, and hence compression.

k: kylobytes> kylobytes are the usual measure of data storage and flash up like miles in the real world to describe the dimensions of the data on a CD-ROM.

l: lasers> laser technology is what has made this technology possible, ever since the CD Audio started to replace the stylus with a laser reader. On the CD-ROM the data is written by lasers burning onto the disc before it is read by the microprocessors of the computer.

m: multimedia> Multimedia is a product which combines text, graphics, audio, images, and moving pictures in digitised form. Multimedia makes the user active by the ability to select from a range of information or entertainment which is the result of the non- linear approach. Computer logic allows a non-linear or multi-linearity which is user-friendly, open, and different from enforced modes of the written print medium .

n: networks> CD networks and powerful applications link users in different locations and on separate computers to servers full of CD-stored information with which they can also interreact, or exchange data.

o: optical storage> optical storage is the medium from which the data is read, a digital laser bank of information and other content. It is capable of infinitely greater capacity than the magnetic systems of floppy discs and hard drives.

p: photo CD> this high quality photographic storage medium was developed by Kodak – one Photo CD is able to store up to 100 digitally-encoded images from 35mm film at high definition levels. Currently it is more successful as a professional image bank than as a consumer item.

q: quicktime movies> quicktime is a computer software tool which allows the transfer and playing of video on the computer screen and in multimedia presentations.

r: rendering> rendering is the process by which computer graphics are processed to add colour and texture to computer images, or to 3D wire-frame models, building up the images of computer graphics. Complex rendering can take days to achieve, and requires extra powerful computers.

s: silicon chip> the silicon chip is the basis of a computer processor, and more powerful and faster chips are the key to advances in computer capability.

t: telematics> telematics is the term for the study of the whole field of telecommunications, which is the web of fibre optics and telephone lines down which digital information can be sent to sites and outlets anywhere on the planet. This leads to the Superhighway, the internet and the ability to communicate entirely through machines.

u: user-friendliness> the development of the personal computer, begun by Apple, is an exercise in user-friendliness. This attempted to destroy the idea of computers as restricted to scientists and trained operators. CD-ROMs open up a huge new opportunity to extend this developing story.

v: virtual reality> virtual reality to some is a coarsely rendered neon-coloured artificial world. The allure of this cyberspace is that it is responsive – but also sparsely populated, and it is easy to get lost in the void. This relates to the experience of computer games which are converging on to the CD-ROM, now that the cartridge medium is being superseded because of the lower cost of CD technology.

w: worm> a worm is the professional term for a test disc on CD-ROM, and the process of creating a test disc is called 'burning a worm'. Data from the hard disc of a computer is transferred in the form of files to a CD-ROM in a similar fashion to the transfer of data to a simple floppy disc.

x: generation x> x is the computer-literate generation identified by the American writer Douglas Coupland – people aged between 18 and 30 who have adapted their lives to computer culture.

y: yamauchi> the president of the Nintendo Corporation who is against the growth of the CD-ROM and will fight the 'cartridge war' to maintain the monopoly of his games empire.

z: no listing under this digit.

NOTES

1. The virtual reality systems which involve head-sets or goggles, and where head movements navigate through real-time generated environments created in computer graphics, have disadvantages. There are health issues concerning immersion in headsets for long periods. When wearing a headset the user has to hold the head unnaturally still. This can also be uncomfortable and the main method will probably remain the interaction of brain and fingers using a mouse, controller, keyboard or joystick.

2. 'There is a lot of talk in Hollywood about revolution these days. The revolution discussed has to do with the "Information Superhighway", or the "Infobahn". These abstractions inevitably lead the adventurous in film and television to think about the new opportunities to communicate, to tell a story, as the craft of "interactive storytelling" is waiting to be born. Ultimately the revolution (like all revolutions) will come from outside the system. Which is why new directions are as likely to come from Europe as they are from New York or Hong Kong. This revolution will result in the creation of another level of experience which exists side by side with its sisters, film, television, theatre and literature.' Caitlin Bachman, Hollywood script editor.

3. David Bryant, Levis' account executive at BBH, in a fax to the author confirming the copyright situation in regard to the NASA material. The Internet is in space, where there is no private copyright.

This essay is based on a presentation given in Buenos Aires in August 1995 as a part of a three-day seminar on Perception in the Era of Virtual Reality supported by the European Union and and the British Council.
© David Mingay 1995.

22 BACK TO THE FUTURE:
the Cinema's Lessons of History

John Chittock

As with television, it is unwise to attribute the invention of the cinema to any one person – not even collectively to the two famous French brothers now being celebrated on the centenary of the cinema. Its invention evolved, through an array of contributions from various people and countries. But its very possibility goes back earlier to the invention of photography (also dangerous to attribute and date), which – when it arrived as a practical reality – gave rise to the famous remark by Paul Delaroche that 'from today, painting is dead'.

The comment, which inspired *Daguerreotypomanie*, the famous 1839 cartoon by Théodore Maurisset which showed artists, printers and engravers hanging themselves in the streets of Paris, epitomises the march of image technology over which the cinema has always suffered some sense of paranoia. Every new development in image technology has been accompanied by excitement and controversy, expectation and apprehension. The stories of the arrival of sound in the era of the silent film typify this confusion of attitudes – one commentator believed passionately that sound would destroy true cinema and argued at the time that cinema should have started with the talkies and then evolved into the art of silence.

But there is a leitmotif in the development of the cinema which offers some indication of future trends. Evolution in the cinema has followed a relentless path towards greater realism, despite the aesthetic view that the art of the motion picture is creative interpretation rather than similitude. After sound came colour, then wider and larger screens, engulfing stereo sound, and countless (albeit gimmicky) attempts to provide 3D – all in the quest for greater realism.

In the 1990s, as the centenary of the cinema is celebrated, technology has become a crucial element in keeping the loyalty of audiences – necessary to combat the desertion of viewers to television and video. Fifty years ago, cinema attendances in the UK topped 1,585m, declining to a low of 58m in 1984. Numbers rose again to over 120m in 1994. This small reversal has been possible through overdue improvements in the quality of the cinema experience – partly thanks to new technologies.

TECHNICAL AND ENVIRONMENTAL CHANGES

For the public, the most conspicuous changes in cinema-going in the last 25 years have been environmental – first with the introduction of multi-screen auditoria, then the huge success of multiplexes (with attendant car parking and catering facilities). Not only have these developments provided a wider choice of programming, but they have emerged as a concentrated drive to improve the design, comfort and facilities in modern cinemas.

Less obvious to the average citizen have been the technical improvements. Behind the scenes in the projection box, flat-bed 'platters' able to run a full length feature film without breaks – replacing the clumsy 'changeover' from one reel to another on a second projector – have made the presentation of films seamless (and overcome the irritating jump in picture quality or focusing when projectors are switched). Better projectors with higher powered illuminants have contributed, as has the introduction of digital sound systems able to provide hi-fi quality and surround sound.

Better projectors have meant not only sharper, brighter and steadier pictures on the screen, but (helped by less physical handling for changeovers) a lower incidence of scratching and dirt on projected prints. And the screens on to which the pictures are projected have even undergone their own revolution - no longer simple, white painted surfaces but specially coated fabrics yielding maximum reflection (known as 'gain') so that little of the projected light is lost.

Multiplexes

Screen technology alone has become a complex specialisation with many quite unexpected parameters of which the audience is usually oblivious. Most basic since the days of sound has been the need to have small perforations in the screen to prevent sound from the loudspeakers behind suffering from attenuation. In large auditoria, the sheer weight of even bigger screens has demanded careful mechanical mounting and stretching. And in times when audiences are less passive than they used to be, even the surface of the screen has had to be made from materials capable of being cleaned easily – various kinds of missile do get thrown at their surfaces.

But possibly the biggest improvements in the quality of the cinema experience, apart from digital sound, have come in the production chain – from film stocks to the methods and equipment used in production.

Film stocks have improved immeasurably over the last 25 years, in quality of colour, fineness of grain and resolution, and not least in sensitivity – enabling cameramen to now shoot in candlelight without the aid of artificial lighting. Cameras have become more compact and of higher quality, as have the various contraptions available for supporting them – ranging from dollies and cranes for tracking and craning shots to the ubiquitous Steadicam, a harness-mounted, counterbalanced camera support worn by the cameraman which allows handheld shots to be made with perfect steadiness; similar improvements have been made in camera mountings in helicopters, so that aerial shooting often appears to have been made from rigid supports reaching down to the ground below.

One important change in film stocks has been in the formats – that is the actual picture frame size and its aspect ratio as used in the camera. The early 35mm film had a width to height ratio of 4:3. Over the past 40 years, various new permutations of this were introduced – to yield a wider picture and sometimes a larger frame area to improve the quality of the projected picture. One of the most well-known of these was VistaVision, which actually ran the film through the camera horizontally to allow the normal frame width to become the height and the overall frame size to increase and produce a wider aspect ratio. Cine-

maScope provided panoramic screen pictures by squeezing a much wider angle view in the camera on to normal width film (by using anamorphic lenses) and unsqueezing it again in projection; but CinemaScope was trying to get something for nothing, which rarely works in life or in physics. The quality of picture could not match that of better systems (and the projectionist had less tolerance in maintaining sharp focusing).

Numerous other film formats have attempted to bring greater spectacle to the screen by wider and super-quality pictures. All relied upon making greater use of the available film area in the camera (and projector), or even – as in the case of Cinerama – by using three films run side-by-side in synchronism to effectively more than triple the apparent frame size (each of the three Cinerama prints used a frame higher than its width, also increasing the frame area and quality). Some which survive today use 70mm rather than 35mm in projection, with 65mm film for camera shooting (the 5mm difference being reserved on prints for the stereo sound track).

Another improvement in projected quality was sought by a plan to increase the framing rate from the standard 24 frames per second to 30 frames per second. Very bright areas in the projected scene, especially at the periphery of vision, may suffer from slight flickering at 24 fps, which an increment in the frame rate reduces; the simulation of motion is also improved at 30 fps, and optical faults such as strobing (causing spoked wheels sometimes to appear to rotate in the wrong direction) may be reduced. But re-engineering cinema projectors to handle 30 fps was an expense the industry was unwilling to accept and the idea was dropped for normal cinema use, although in recent times revived for special auditoria.

3D AND SENSORY CINEMA

In its quest to enhance realism in the auditorium, the cinema industry has made numerous, futile attempts to introduce stereoscopic or 3D movies. All commercially practicable systems have relied upon the use of left and right eye images shot in special cameras. In the cinema, in order for viewers to see only the right eye images with their right eyes and left eye ones with the left eye, various systems have been employed. The most infamous, known as anaglyphs, used a red filter over one projected image and a green over the other – equipping the audience with similarly filtered spectacles so that the appropriate image was only seen by the correct eye.

Improvements in the system came with the use of polarising filters instead of colour filters, allowing colour movies to be shown without their reproduction being affected. As well as the same encumbrance of issuing audiences with spectacles, this 3D method also requires metallised screens to be used in the cinema – ordinary fabric screens depolarise the light. Thus the polarised systems have failed to catch on.

Other methods have been tried, none with success. In Russia, one idea has been to use a lenticular screen – effectively built-up from vertical strips that each act like a lens so that the slightly different viewpoint of left and right eyes will see different picture strips focused by each vertical element. Very limited results have also been obtained in trying to import holography – the perfect 3D technology – into the cinema, but there are huge technical difficulties in doing this and a practicable system is still many years away.

The smellies, and even vibrating auditoria (eg during earthquake sequences) have also attempted to enhance the realism of some films in the cinema, but these ideas have remained firmly in the realms of gimmickry.

BIGGER SCREENS FOR BIGGER IMPACT

In the last ten to 15 years, one emerging trend in cinema has been to make the visual experience more of a spectacle. The change to a wider aspect ratio – 1.65:1 and sometimes 1.85:1 – has now become a standard. The aesthetic advantages of this wider format have been enough to even influence the television industry, which is now hesitantly making some use of a wider aspect ratio even at the cost of losing usable picture area at the top and bottom of standard television sets.

But the real impact has come with the development of very large screen systems, of which Imax is the most well-known. Various large screen systems have been tried over the last few decades, but only Imax has been a serious survivor. On projection, the large frame area that the horizontally-run 70mm Imax film provides enables outstanding sharpness and screen brightness to be obtained, on screens as large as 100 ft x 75 ft. With closer than usual raked seating

The Dream is Alive,
Imax Corporation, 1985

in front of a slightly curved screen, the Imax audience is almost literally engulfed by the images. Imax has been a commercial success, although its auditoria are few and far apart – only one still in the UK, and some 152 worldwide.

Imax has introduced variations on the theme, such as Omnimax – which enfolds the audience in a hemispherical screen; and 3D Imax – which again uses left and right eye images with spectacles for the audience (albeit electronically shuttered, not polarised). But Imax is essentially a spectacle, and narrative films do not adapt comfortably to the format, where the eyes of the audience are free to wander across a wide vista and are not drawn so easily into the intentions of the director.

Other systems have appeared to rival Imax, such as Showscan and a number of variations from the American Iwerks company. But these have evolved in response to a public taste for turning the cinema experience into one of sensory involvement – the move towards the simulator and theme park theatre rides.

SIMULATION IN THE CINEMA

In the mid 1990s we have reached the point where the development of the cinema is almost at a cross-roads. On the one hand, movies made for the conventional cinema are increasingly relying upon spectacle to grab the attention, even if – as in the case of *Jurassic Park* – they maintain the traditional qualities of good story-telling and dramatic performances. But there is now the emergence of a strain of movies where special effects *are* the movie and threaten to overwhelm the creative nature of the medium, all made possible by the arrival of digital technologies.

By feeding film-captured images into a computer and changing them into digitised electronic pictures, it has become possible to manipulate images with almost infinite flexibility. This has led to the explosive images now seen in some movies which owe their genesis more to video games like *Mortal Kombat* than to realism and beauty as in Stanley Kubrick's *2001 – A Space Odyssey*. The special effects of these modish movies are of course produced on the computer screen, which is a big enough technical achievement in itself; but the crowning achievement has been in the technology which transfers the electronic images back on to film, yielding results which on projection in large auditoria completely belie their computerised origins.

Back at the crossroads, this begins to suggest that the cinema as we know it may split into two diverging paths. The quality blockbusters which use new technologies merely to enhance the story-telling and the creative power of cinema may survive, perhaps proliferate, and certainly become increasingly expensive to produce. But the technologies bringing greater realism to the big screen may follow a separate path, becoming major spectator attractions at theme parks and specially-built auditoria (the name 'location based entertainment' has been coined to describe these kinds of systems).

Showscan, Iwerks and Imax are all involved in projects of this nature, where the emphasis is on giving the audience a sensory experience like the real thing - whether a whitewater ride down the rapids or aerial combat in the pilot's seat of a Spitfire. Trying to keep traditional cinema close to these new developments, United Artists Theatre Circuit in the US are installing Showscan simulators in some commercial multiplex cinemas over the next five years.

With these new systems, the screen size and the brightness and quality of the projected image all assume primary importance. With Showscan, for example, 70mm film with a larger than normal frame size is projected at 60 frames per second to yield picture quality of unrivalled impact. Synchronised with what is happening on the screen, seats in the auditorium move, tilt and shake with the action, increasing the sensation of actually being there. And, of course, surround sound adds to the impact.

The influence of the theme park and fairground ride has never been far away in these recent developments, as in one installation at a Las Vegas hotel. Here, arriving guests may enter a bogus lift ('elevator') which seems to have in the far wall another set of lift doors which are actually a back-projected image from a large format film. The view through the rear 'doors' starts to move as the lift appears to ascend, with the floor vibrating slightly in synchronism. The speed of ascent then increases as the image of the passing floors speeds up, with the floor vibration also increasing. Suddenly, the lift cable 'breaks' and the moving image of the passing floors is reversed as the lift appears to plunge downwards, the floor rocking and shaking violently. A new experience to offer fear under safe conditions for the bored public, and much more realistic than trains arriving at a French railway station in the 19th century.

In a way, history is repeating itself. The early cinema was a fairground experience, where the novelty of creating an impression of the real thing was the attraction. A viewer of Le Prince's early movie made on Leeds bridge in the 1880s was enthralled by this realism, saying 'it was as if you were on the bridge itself. I could even see the smoke coming out of a man's pipe.'

Sony, Sega and other companies with core activities in the video games business are now involved in special auditoria which provide variations on the simulator theme. In the US, Sony has built a 450 seater 3D Imax theatre in New York with considerable box office success and is planning one in San Francisco as part of a 15-plex centre and another in Berlin - a clear indication of the move of electronic companies into public exhibition. Hughes-Rediffusion is another major company busy in the field, drawing upon its experience as a manufacturer of expensive flight simulators for the aircraft industry.

VIDEO PROJECTION IN CINEMAS

The interest of electronic companies in movie theatres began in a significant way with the arrival of video projection systems. In the 1970s a few cinemas were equipped with video projection, but the quality of the images was poor and generally gave the technology a bad name.

Recently, however video projection as a replacement for film has become almost inevitable because of improvements in the technology and the potential advantages it may offer. Video copies of a feature film are infinitely cheaper than 35mm film prints, very small, lightweight (making transportation costs negligible) and – compared with film – almost unsusceptible to physical damage. In the future, delivery to cinemas may be effected by satellite, completely eliminating the need for multiple copies and also allowing simultaneous release across an entire country.

Improvements in the quality of video projection have now reached a point where the results on a cinema-size screen can be indistinguishable from 35mm film. Video projection systems have generally relied upon the use of three cathode ray tubes (red, green and blue) as their light and image source, but new systems have been developed which are no longer limited in their light output by the use of television tubes; in particular, a completely new technology employing microscopic mirrors is now yielding screen brightnesses to rival conventional film projection. By repeating the scanning lines of the video picture ('line doubling'), the familiar line structure of a television picture can be made almost invisible, and other systems are now using high definition television with line structures as high as 1250, replacing (in Europe) the standard 625 lines of television.

Many video cinemas are now operating around the world using improved versions of cathode ray tube equipment, and the spread of these electronic auditoria is inevitable. The videotape copy-protection company Macrovision – which has a proprietary system to prevent piracy – has been a prime mover and catalyst in the development of video cinemas, involved in projects in countries as far apart as Poland and Malaysia. Not only can Macrovision video copies be encoded to prevent illegal copying by errant projectionists, but they can also have invisible codes that will reveal the source of an illegal copy if shot by a camcorder secreted into the auditorium of a cinema (a practice which has been much too common).

THE INTERACTIVE CINEMA - INVOLVING THE AUDIENCE

Not content with heightening realism on the screen and in the auditorium, the cinema industry has tried to remove the control of the story-teller by allowing the audience to influence what is happening on the screen. There is an assumption, perhaps, that ultimate realism in the cinema can only be experienced if the audience actually participates with the action on the screen.

The idea was first tried in the 1930s, and again in the 1960s, when a Czechoslovak film allowed viewers to make their own choice from alternative endings. In recent times, the idea has been revived with the name 'interactive' cinema, encouraged by the arrival of the so-called interactive video disc.

Interactive video has been made possible by the development of the video disc as an alternative way of viewing movies on television screens. By using the format of a disc instead of tape (or film), instant access to any part of the film or programme is possible, controlled by a PC. Associated computer software allows the user to have almost infinite control over the display of images – with video games an obvious application, but many other extraordinary permutations ranging from learning to play musical instruments to manipulating the development of full length movies.

The worlds's first portable video CD-player (Jampoo Corporation of Taiwan)

Moving this technology into the cinema auditorium, Hollywood is trying to enhance even further the reality experience for audiences, although it is doubtful if the gains can equal the losses in creative cohesion. The acquisition of major studios by Japanese electronic companies such as Sony and Matsushita has provided a direct link between the traditional movie and video technologies and games. Some Hollywood directors such as Steven Spielberg have also set up companies where interactive and electronic expertise is becoming an influential element in production.

It is however difficult to accept that cinemagoers will really find the experience of interactivity with a movie an enhancement. The power of the cinema is in its ability to draw the viewer into the action by clever direction, editing and sound – in computer terms, providing a pre-programmed experience in which the audience has no choice. Immediately an element of choice is introduced, the viewer is separated from the action and becomes an individual again – not part of an inescapable atmosphere in the auditorium.

FUTURE DEVELOPMENTS IN THE MOVIES

Taking the story so far, it is clear that the evolution of cinema over the last 100 years offers a thread which may give some indication of possible future developments. The constant theme has been enhancing the realism and the spectacle of the cinema, despite the constant striving to produce quality films of creative calibre; critical successes, although at times making substantial contributions to the box office, have not been the major factor in the upturn in attendances.

The move of Japanese electronic manufacturers into Hollywood offers some indication of future developments. Their overall track record in backing outstanding films has not always been impressive, and the investment that companies such as Sony are making in Imax theatres and theme park attractions suggests that spectacle and sensation may either compete with the traditional cinema or even infiltrate it.

There is however room for improvement in the fortunes of conventional cinema, similar to the progress that has been made through the building of multiplexes and the upgrading of technical facilities. Video projection and electronic distribution will benefit the distributors and the exhibitors in running costs; the arrival of a genuinely practicable 3D system could transform the ordinary cinema experience with narrative films, even though the creative side of the industry may doubt this.

Much else is difficult to anticipate, apart from progressive change in the design of cinemas. More is being done in respect of the rake and perspective position of seating, in lighting and screen surrounds, in the overall comfort and associated facilities. But these are subtle improvements and unlikely to make a significant impact on cinemagoing.

The time scale for the introduction of video projection, and thereafter of electronic distribution, has been wrongly predicted in the past, but enough progress has been made for a safe estimate to now be made – probably video projection will begin to appear in new auditoria by the turn of the millennium, and in existing cinemas within the next ten years if not less.

Electronic distribution likewise could begin to arrive within the same time, particularly now that digital transmission of television signals is established as a practical technology and will be providing vast additional capacity for new channels on satellites. The electronic manufacturers are also trying to introduce the concept of home cinema, a fancy name for larger television screens with video disc playback of movies complete with stereo sound. But such systems are limited by the bulky cathode ray tube in television sets, and the concept will only have some credibility when 'hang-on-the-wall' television screens are available – not likely as a practical and inexpensive consumer product for at least another ten years. In any event, the apparent advantages of larger screen viewing in the average living room are spurious – the angle the eye subtends with an average size television screen at typical living room distances is not much different from that in a cinema, so the apparent screen size is similar.

The ultimate cinema experience in the future must remain the experience of being removed from the environment of the home, even the fairground, into a different world. Developments which achieve that will be the ones that survive and keep the cinema genuinely different from the competition of video and television. A BBC television producer, David Thompson, expressed it exquisitely: 'People go to the cinema to be transported out of themselves'. Indeed, just like the viewers of 100 years ago, who were able to witness and experience events and places in the world which before they had only dreamed about.

23 WHAT IS CINEMA?
The Sensuous, the Abstract and the Political

Sylvia Harvey

It seems appropriate in this cinema centenary year to reflect upon the continuing significance and value of cinema as both textual form and institutional practice, and to review some of its particular qualities as a medium of communication. Such a review is especially necessary in these last few years of the twentieth century since, in the context of an ever-expanding audio-visual realm, large screen cinema has increasingly been cast as an endangered species. This essay addresses the question 'what is cinema?' and the related issue of why it might continue to matter as an institution, through the 'twin track' approach of recognising some of the hard facts of its economic and industrial existence to-day, while also re-visiting the contributions made to our understanding of the nature of the cinematic image by the sometimes competing Bazinian and semiotic paradigms. I hope in the process to introduce some unexpected actors and ideas, injecting new life into long-standing (and now perhaps somewhat neglected) debates within film and cultural studies concerning the nature of the cinematic image, the appropriate methods for a materialist cultural analysis, and the most intellectually robust ways of linking the realms of politics and of cultural production.

In the first part of this essay I reflect upon André Bazin's question 'What is cinema?' considering in particular some of the continuing implications of the desire which he expressed in his early work to establish an 'ontology' of the photographic image. In the second part I briefly examine what seem to be some of the key facts and statistics of contemporary cinema, sketching out the broader audio-visual environment for this still surviving European institution. Finally, I add to this reflection upon conceptual and institutional questions a brief analysis of some recent films which seem, in their different ways, to exemplify the continuing power and strength of cinema.

1 ONTOLOGY AND AFTER

André Bazin's famous essay 'The Ontology of the Photographic Image' was published in 1945, just over a century after the invention and establishment of photography. Half a century later, we commemorate the hundredth anniversary of the birth of moving pictures, remembering 100 years of the cinema and of film as both institution and means of human expression. We stand also on the threshold of the new high definition and digital technologies which are likely to make significant changes to cinema's mode of distribution and exhibition and to bring about (at least to some extent) the convergence of the two small screens of the computer and the television. This short essay pays homage to the work of Bazin but seeks a different language to identify the social being of cinema and to reflect upon its position in both a 'universe of hours', of facts and figures, and in a 'universe of meanings', of emotional response and of cultural significance.

Bazin's formation was Christian and Catholic but also pluralist and liberal. From 1945 he wrote regularly about film for the journal *Esprit* which from its inception in 1932 had become fertile ground for an often explosive mixture of Marxism and Catholic humanism. Treated with suspicion by both the Communist left and the conservative right, *Esprit* had marked out a distinctive agenda with some interesting resonances for the centre ground of European politics in the 1990s. Their objective was:

> to mark out between the bourgeoisie and the collectivism of the State an avenue by which the transformation of structures can promote the enrichment of the individual and can lead to the 'civilization of labour' which will free men from the tyranny of money...to denounce oppression and falsehood, and to break loose from both Christian order and established disorder. [1]

Bazin's own commitment to the 'civilization of labour', combined with a passion for spreading as widely as possible the benefits of film education, led him, after the liberation of France, to work with the Communist-dominated organisation Travail et Culture. Here, in the period immediately after the Second World War, he worked to set up film clubs, screenings and discussions for working class audiences, providing the analytical tools for a critical engagement with the medium and offering some means for the practical realisation of Walter Benjamin's vision of mass participation in the age of mechanical reproduction. But if a sometimes militantly anti-establishment Christian socialism was one line of influence, the other key influence was religious and mystical, drawn from the writings of the Jesuit priest and scientist Teilhard de Chardin. Bazin's American biographer, Dudley Andrew, notes a key passage from Teilhard – one which links the material world to the immaterial realm in a way which, arguably, indicates the method to be adopted by Bazin in his analysis of the cinematic image. Teilhard writes of '..the purple flush of matter fading imperceptibly into the gold of spirit, to be lost finally in the incandescence of a personal universe'. [2]

In Bazin's writing about cinema a practical, open-minded, enquiring and rational approach is matched or shadowed by a less explicit but no less formative concern with the spiritual, with the presence of the divine in all things. It is this which underpins his conception of the cinema's vocation for realism and his philosophical ontology of the photographic image. For Bazin, as a theologically sophisticated Catholic, both the cinematic image and the real world share in the divine presence and the divine voice; matter is a bridge which 'fades into' but also carries the world of the divine. It is a comparable nexus of duality that Hannah Arendt had in mind when she wrote of Walter Benjamin's fascination with metaphor as the linguistic transference which 'enables us to give material form to the invisible'.[3]

For Bazin the most significant instance of invisibility is the divine, and a more ghostly and continuing presence than that of mere mortals is suggested by his imagery of the photograph likened to the touch of a finger or the imprint of a face: '..the creation of an ideal world in the likeness of the real'.[4] His confidence in the transfigurative power by which the enormous pulsation of reality itself might come crashing through the narrow, mechanical aperture of the camera lens is rooted, ultimately, in a belief in the omnipresence of the divine. For Bazin the cinema – no less than reality – is one more place for the recognition and expression of this omnipresence, it is one more place for the extraordinary Christian epiphany of 'God made human', 'the Word made flesh', for the mystical alchemy of the mundane become divine.

From the 1960s, the language of the 'human sciences' and in particular the analytical methods of psychoanalysis and of semiotics constituted a significant and deliberate challenge to what were regarded as the unscientific, subjective and impressionistic methods of earlier schools of criticism. The 'linguistic turn' in cultural studies, drawing on the work of Charles Sanders Peirce and Ferdinand de Saussure, sought to replace any previous confidence in the 'transparency' of human communication with a recognition of the material presence of the ubiquitous and irreducible sign. Henceforth the object of cultural analysis (and of film studies) was to be the material world of visual and verbal sign systems and not the immaterial world of pure expression – the spirit unclothed by the form of language. The process of representation was foregrounded and more-or-less replaced any search for 'essence', 'being' or 'ontology'. Likewise the Bazinian celebration of cinema as the language of reality, and the ecstatic claim that the photographic image might 'share a common being'[5] with its object were countered by the new critical terminology of codification and construction. These developments in intellectual history, combined with the now unfashionable anti-humanism of Althusserian Marxism, succeeded in almost completely marginalising the work of Bazin, pushing it into the shadowlands of film theory and of the film studies curriculum.

This essay does not seek to return to an innocent and Edenic garden before the 'fall' occasioned by the advent of semiotics, nor to restore Catholic theology to the heartlands of film theory. However, a recognition of Bazin's sense of the special, even 'sacred' nature of the photographic image, does now seem important for a re-evaluation and re-designation of the special qualities of the cinematic image.

It is not that cinema semiotics has failed in its important task of identifying the language or signifying practices of cinema, more that its roots in linguistic analysis and its association with a certain kind of radical and supposedly anti-bourgeois critique have resulted in insufficient attention being paid to both the visual and to the entertaining qualities of the medium. The number-crunching of syntagms has, as it were, restricted, not illuminated the potential field of recoverable meanings. Of course these are not original observations. The subtle semiotician, Roland Barthes, grappled with a complex sense of the extra, the special, the excessive meaning and quality of the image which connects both to the rich personal universe of emotions and to the lived reality of cultural and social meaning. He distinguished an additional 'third' or 'obtuse' meaning, and in his later writings the photograph is even 'a *magic*, not an art'.[6]

There is no doubt that film studies will continue to operate within the broad framework provided by semiotics; they cannot go back to a time before that 'linguistic turn' which characterises so much of contemporary intellectual life. But the particular cluster of ideas associated with the insights of semiotics as these affected studies of the visual domain requires closer and more critical scrutiny. Martin Jay has recently embarked upon an ambitious and extensive analysis of what he calls the 'denigration of vision' in twentieth century French thought. He traces a gradual process of the disintegration of confidence in the light of enlightenment rationalism (when sight was regarded as the noblest of the senses), from the subjectivism of the romantic movement with its rejection of the detached observational methods of science to the resurgence of iconoclasm, the work of Foucault on the savage surveillance of the panopticon and the critique of the 'society of the spectacle' developed by Guy Debord and the Situationists. The Situationist view he relates to the 'long-standing suspicion of theatrical illusion evident in Rousseau and before'.[7]

Jay contrasts Debord's views with Althusser's 'antiocular critique of ideology', noting their 'shared distrust of the hegemony of the eye'.[8] This suspicion of the visible is then traced in the work of radical film theory in the period after May 1968. He notes Serge Daney's 1970 criticism of 'a truly blind confidence in the visible', Jean-Louis Comolli's attack on the 'ideology of the visible'[9] and the argument developed by the journal *Cinéthique* that the film camera itself is 'an ideological instrument in its own right, expressing bourgeois ideology before expressing anything else'.[10]

This extreme mistrust of the fruits of the camera's labours, a highly reductive and apparently Marxist materialist form of technological determinism – as though the camera lens were condemned forever to the instrumentalism of registering 'bourgeois ideology' – also had an impact on the second stage of Christian Metz's analysis of cinema. In 'The Imaginary Signifier' of 1977 Metz proposes that 'to be a theoretician of the cinema one should ideally no longer love the cinema'.[11] It is this and other observations which lead Jay to the view that Metz has become a 'cinephobe' with a politically-motivated and puritanical belief that the 'cinephilic love affair with the medium..must be disrupted if the ideological effects of the apparatus are to be overcome'.[12]

To this generalised fear and loathing of the visible world of bourgeois ideology we might add a related dislike of the function of entertainment – perceived as one more weapon in the armoury for the reproduction of the status quo. Other traditions of thought – for example the ideas about entertainment and pleasure in art developed by Bertolt Brecht – would lead both critics and cultural producers in a very different direction. As Terry Lovell notes in her penetrating critique of those approaches to art which emphasise primarily its cognitive and ideological aspects, the pleasurable and entertaining aspects of art should also be valued in their own right. Indeed the force of her argument leads her to be critical of Brecht's own work which, despite its welcome emphasis on the importance of entertaining an audience, has in her view too instrumentalist an approach to pleasure as something to be harnessed to the interests of knowledge production.[13] For Lovell art may have a cognitive dimension in one of its aims, to 'show things as they really are', but this is not its only purpose and pleasure in art should not be 'always at the service of knowledge'. In the context of a discussion of the role and significance of visual sign systems, the validity of visual pleasure and the production of the beautiful, must also be recognised – even as this recognition is linked to historically specific questions about 'who finds what beautiful?'

While a healthy scepticism concerning the devices and purposes of visual communication and of entertainment might seem to be a useful stock in trade for the thoughtful fim critic, the particular 'antiocular' tradition of thought outlined by Jay seems to lead to the dead end of negation and despair, offering neither a more subtle understanding of visual language nor a basis from which visual or ideological innovation might be recognised.

The secular societies of enlightenment and post-enlightenment philosophy have refused the validity of the Bazinian sense of the sacred, the ineffable, of the presence of the divine in all earthly things.

Although the onward march of a reductive rationalism had already been thrown a little off course by the philosophical challenge of the romantic movement, rejecting the limitation of human intelligence to the activity of measuring the natural world and finding among the peaks and clefts of the human spirit an all but immeasurable realm; hence William Blake's denunciation of the figure of Isaac Newton seen as the archetypal measurer trapped by his own activity of mundane quantification. In place of this Blake posits a different kind of dynamism, of the contraries without which there is 'no progression', of those other dimensions – eminently representable within poetic language – where 'eternity is in love with the productions of time'.[14]

The subsequent combination of theories of relativity in the natural sciences together with the 'linguistic turn' in the human sciences has shaken enlightenment confidence in the knowability of an objectively existing real world without reinventing any more secular sense of the sacred or of the immortal (the passions which drive Bazin's account of cinema). Hannah Arendt notes that one of the consequences of Cartesian doubt is the modern loss of faith and of the 'certainty of immortality', accompanied by a sense that the physical world – 'less stable, less permanent and hence less to be relied upon than it had been during the Christian era' – offers no compensating security:

> Modern man, when he lost the certainty of a world to come, was thrown back upon himself and not upon this world; far from believing that the world might be potentially immortal, he was not even sure that it was real.[15]

She identifies the paradox that post-Cartesian rationalism, far from resulting in a confident human celebration of the material and objective world, in fact entails a deeply subjective form of secularism. Human beings are caught in the often bleak isolation of the rationalist: 'I think therefore I am' or, as she puts it, 'thrown into the closed inwardness of introspection...the empty process of reckoning of the mind, its play with itself'.[16]

It is one of the challenges for current secular criticism to reconstruct or re-invent a sense of the sacred and of the immortal, and perhaps to find other words than these to refer to the constant presence of the extraordinary within the ordinary, to foreground significance which is present without words, meaning that exceeds the mundane, value that is not monetary or market-based, experience that seems to make time stand still or to take place outside of time. As Susan Sontag points out in one of her essays on photography, the ordinary and the extraordinary achieve a special coming together in the term 'cliché' ('..the French word that means both trite expression and photographic negative'[17]). This world of the cliché is also, of course, the world of mechanical reproduction which moves millions of people to tears, to the box office and the video store.

The challenge to reinvent the sacred within the social and the secular cannot draw innocently upon the idealist and mystical traditions of thought that predate the various materialisms which have convincingly peopled the last three centuries of European intellectual life. Agnostics and unbelievers will certainly wish to identify some meaningful alternative to the promise of divine presence, perhaps finding this in Hannah Arendt's celebration of the plurality of the human condition and the significance of human agency:

> Plurality is the condition of human action because we are all the same, that is, human, in such a way that nobody is ever the same as anyone else.[18]

To this constant and unpredictable quality of pluralism in human action she matches the reassuring and enduring quality of the work of art, one of the products of human agency which has '.survived gloriously its severance from religion, magic and myth'. 'Worldly stability' becomes

> ..transparent in the permanence of art, so that a premonition of immortality, not the immortality of the soul or of life but of something immortal achieved by mortal hands, has become tangibly present, to shine and to be seen, to sound and to be heard, to speak and to be read.[19]

Two twentieth century writers who have in their different ways addressed the relationship between politics and cultural production, from a rationalist perspective, have also grappled with the limitations of a rationalism that has found it difficult to acknowledge the special, the sacred, the experience of that which is 'out of time' in a way that is either beautiful or terrifying.

In the *Buckow Elegies*, a series of late poems, Bertolt Brecht recalls a certain clarity and precision of seeing that persists across the movement and the changes of time:

> In the early hours
> The fir-trees are copper.
> That's how I saw them
> Half a century ago
> Two world wars ago
> With young eyes.[20]

The Czech dramatist, dissident and latterly politician, Vaclav Havel, writes of the importance of ancient myths which predate the emergence of a rationalist consensus but which also point to truths about the potential destructiveness of human irrationalism :

> It seems to me that with the burial of myth, the barn in which the mysterious animals of the human unconscious were housed over thousands of years has been abandoned and the animals let loose –

on the tragically mistaken assumption that they were phantoms – and that now they are devastating the countryside.[21]

Cinema can and has represented such phantoms, for unlike literature, which offers us the metaphors of vision, cinema offers us vision itself. Though the offering is neither simple nor entirely concrete, for just as one meaning of vision is 'something which you see that is not really there' so it is with the cinematic image. This may be what gives cinema its power: precision, clarity and intensity of vision, the extraordinary presence of that which is not present and an associated and uncanny ability to represent the 'mysterious animals of the human unconscious'. Moreover, visibility as the particular material of expression of cinema offers us the specific sensuous quality of the medium; and we spectators of cinema, visionaries in our millions, cross this bridge of material, sensuous form towards the immaterial and the abstract.

The density of meaning of the visual sign, and its 'bridge-like' character, recall both the religious idealism of the early Bazin (the visible world as the work of God) and – in a related but contrary trajectory – the traditions of materialist thought which struggled to draw abstract generalisations out of concrete and sensuous particularities. The examples cited here from the work of Brecht and Havel give us instances of thinkers who are also cultural producers struggling at the edges of traditional materialist thought.

For one further example of the materialist tradition engaging with the difficult problem of the relationship between 'material' and 'immaterial' in the practice of image production and in the theory of visual meaning, we might turn to the work of Sergei Eisenstein. As early as the 1920s, when cinema was still a young and developing form, Eisenstein had, through a passionate and idiosyncratic engagement with Marxist philosophy, mused over the problems of appearance and essence, confronting the difficulty of the relationship between the concrete particularity of sensuous form and the abstraction of ideas.[22] If the great burden of cinema was its very sensuousness, its pedestrian anchoring to the concreteness of things that can be seen, its ambitious aim was to offer the spectator something more than the immediate fruits of sight. Eisenstein developed his theory and practice of montage as a solution to the perceived limitations of sensuous form, struggling to provide for the spectator a means whereby to move from the immediacy of visual perception to the complexity of conceptual analysis. For Eisenstein the montage juxtaposition of images facilitates this process, generating in the mind of the spectator a 'third term' or 'extra' meaning beyond that which can be seen on the screen. Thus it was through the methods of montage that he hoped to achieve the ambitious objective of a cinema of ideas whose material was the sensuous form of images.

Montage theory with its presumption of the construction of meaning at different levels has fitted in well with semiotic approaches, comfortably echoing the theory of the articulation of verbal signs. Conversely, the Bazinian dislike of montage is well-known and is not defended or discussed here. However, it will be one of the purposes of the last section of this essay to consider the ways in which the cinematic image generates meanings at different levels quite apart from the use of montage. This is the special, even 'sacred' quality of the image, operating beyond the first order level of literal designation.

The route from Bazin's arguably theological ontology of the photographic image to the mode of semiotic enquiry which has dominated much of contemporary film studies is a long and difficult one. Indeed, perhaps the route is imaginary – involving not so much a journey as a transmutation from one paradigm (idealist, existentialist, Christian and catholic in both senses of the word) to another (materialist, scientific, often dull). But his work remains a landmark and point of reference for any serious study of the production and consumption of visual meaning, constantly to be re-evaluated and re-positioned as our intellectual landscape and the methods of visual production themselves change. Here the shift from photochemical and analogical systems of recording to digital ones may signal an important change or at least the occasion for a humorous reprise of the argument about photographic ontology.

For the celebrants of the specificity of visual communication – Pasolini, Barthes and others – the visual sign, the icon, was characterised by continuity of shape, not by the radical discontinuity, the 'bits' or phonemes – the more digital system of verbal communication. It was the analogical characteristic of visual sign systems (both painting and photography) which made them relatively unamenable to analysis in words, to assessment by a verbal, digital system of communication.[23] Barthes grapples with the particularity of photography as a non-verbal system of communication:

> Certainly the image is not the reality, but at least it is its perfect *analogon* and it is exactly this analogical perfection which, to common sense, defines the photograph. Thus can be seen the special status of the photographic image: *it is a message without a code*; from which proposition an important corollary must immediately be drawn: the photographic message is a continuous message.[24]

For some theorists this communicative system of analogies and continuities, with its specifically photographic indexical qualities, was incapable of lying in the sense that verbal communication can lie. For words can 'actualise' things which never happened whereas the photomechanical process required at least a pretty hefty trigger in the world outside the world of photographic technology, in order to produce its image. This is of course no longer so, though arguably the introduction of digitalisation in the production of images merely continues a long tradition of 'special' (that is, 'lying') 'effects' in photography, when for decades photographers from Méliès onwards had crept into the laboratory or 'interfered' with the mechanisms of the film camera in order to astonish an audience by breaking the causative, indexical bond.

There is something about the new potential opened up by the digitalisation of the film image which confirms and reinforces an increasing public scepticism about the truth status of the photographic image, though without, in my view, diminishing a continuing and felt need to distinguish between fact and fiction. In the age of digital imaging it becomes increasingly difficult to sustain Bazin's view:

> No matter how fuzzy, distorted or discoloured, no matter how lacking in documentary value the image may be, it shares by virtue of the very process of its becoming, the being of the model of which it is the reproduction; it is the model. [25]

For audiences today, one of the distinctive pleasures of the text may be a pleasurable recognition of the imbrication of the 'reality/unreality' duo. A recognition that has reached perhaps its most obvious point with the digital re-touching of documentary footage in the fiction *Forrest Gump* (1994). Though, contrary to the views of some post-modern theorists, this neither feeds nor produces a crisis in the reality/representation relationship, nor does it blur the boundaries of image and reality in a flickering field of endless and undifferentiated representationalism. The audience is in no doubt about the truth status of the black and white documentary sequences which show actor Tom Hanks 'meeting' with John Kennedy, George Wallace, Lyndon Johnson and Richard Nixon. However, this new composite iconography, far from elevating the ordinary person through association with the great, has the more comic and distancing effect of marginalising the great in the drama of everyday living and surviving.

I shall return to some of these issues concerning the nature of the cinematic image and the processes of meaning production and consumption in the last section of this essay.

2 SIZE AND SIGNIFICANCE

Cinema may be a visionary form but, like all visionaries, it needs a home beyond the desert or the mountain top. In this section of the essay I shall offer a brief sketch of its institutional home in Europe today, examining its situation, context and audio-visual neighbours, and considering some of the economic imperatives which delimit its terrain and differentiate it sharply from its ancestor: the cinema of the 'golden age' before the advent of television. This brief exploration of the current institutional context of cinema will serve as a prelude to the examination of some recent films, since it seems wise finally to try to understand the house through a small selection of its inhabitants.

The first thing to be said, of course, is that cinema is not what it was; the most cursory review of attendance figures demonstrates this. In 1946, a peak year for cinema-going in the United States, there were on average 36 visits to the cinema per head of the population.[26] The comparable per capita figure for the United Kingdom in the same year was 34 visits.[27] Some 40 years later, with the birth of television and the growth of a richly diversified and commodified leisure culture, the picture had changed radically. In 1984, the lowest recorded year for cinema attendances in the U.K., the annual figure was down to one visit per year.[28] By 1993, after a vigorous decade of new investment and multiplex building, the figure had barely doubled to an average two visits per year. The comparable figure for France was higher at 2.3 visits.[29]

The splendid statistical publication of the European Audiovisual Observatory tells us that Russia had one of the highest figures for cinema-going in 1993 with an average 4.3 visits per capita (with an extraordinary nine visits recorded for the previous year), only just outdoing the performance of the United States, home of Hollywood, where the figure was 4.2. Along with France, only Switzerland, Spain, Ireland, Norway and the Czech Republic can muster more than an average two visits per year.[30] A view beyond the boundaries of Europe tells us that cinema-going in India is significantly more popular with a figure of 5.8 visits per head, though it would also be wise to note the difficulty of obtaining accurate figures which can be compared from country to country.[31]

It is clear from the figures we have that cinema-going now represents a very small part of people's available leisure time and expenditure. However, the dizzying fall from 34 annual visits to one or two pales into insignificance (at least on a scale of hours occupied) by comparison with television. If we estimate that each visit to the cinema lasts about two hours we discover that even at the height of cinema's popularity in 1946 this represented an annual, average 'investment' of around 64 hours in the U.K. This figure then drops to *four* hours by 1993. By contrast, average annual television viewing in the U.K. per person amounted to over *1,300* hours in 1993, with a comparable figure for television viewing in France of over 1,000 hours.[32] So, while a trip to the cinema might have been the high point of the week, even at its height this activity had acquired nothing of the effect of the pervasive daily presence later to be established by television.

We might gain a fuller sense of the basic contours of cinema as a contemporary European institution if we go on to ask some questions about the the origin of films watched and the relative level of expenditure on the rival pleasures of video and pay television.

Pay TV is a relatively new form in Europe, video is more established, and cinema box-office, after a period of crisis, appears to be steadily growing (at least in western Europe), albeit from the very low base established in the early 1980s. A report produced for the European Commission's Media Salles programme gives us this percentage breakdown of European expenditure in these three areas in 1992:[33]

Cinema Box Office	23.8%
Home Video	51.3%
Pay TV	24.9%

It is clear from these figures that the combined value of the Pay TV and video markets, in terms of income which might eventually find its way back to film producers, is now worth three times the value of the cinema box-office.

A closer scrutiny of the figures for 1992 reveals some interesting differences of emphasis in different countries. Three countries spend a significantly higher proportion of their total on cinema; the figures for Belgium, Greece and Italy are, respectively, 36.5%, 55% and 36% – though the especially high figure for Greece should be related to the fact that there is *no* recorded expenditure for Pay TV. Proportionately higher spenders on video – all over 60% – are to be found in Germany, Ireland, the Netherlands, Portugal and the United Kingdom. While Pay TV is, proportionately, a more favoured market in France, Luxembourg and Spain with figures of, respectively, 46.7%, 32.3% and 30.9%. The success of Canal Plus has given a strong headstart to the phenomenon of Pay TV in France, and through careful policy and planning this television development has also been used to foster indigenous film production. In Europe-wide terms Pay TV is likely to be the most rapidly growing market in the next few years, though unlike the home video market which is predominantly a vehicle for feature films, it is likely to be more catholic in its range of genres, including sport and news among its key attractions.

With some important exceptions (Canal Plus in France, Channel 4 in the United Kingdom) television has been seen as the adversary, not the saviour of film. And, generally speaking, the volume of indigenously produced films has been low as cinema screens have continued to be dominated by imported American films. By 1993 only three western European countries could demonstrate over a 15% market share for nationally produced films, and this included co-productions. The figures are as follows:[34]

MARKET SHARES OF NATIONAL FILMS
(INCLUDING CO-PRODUCTIONS) 1993

Denmark	16.0%
France	34.6%
Italy	18.0%

The figures for market share of American films are correspondingly high. In five countries this figure stood at over 75%:[35]

MARKET SHARES OF U.S. FILMS 1993

Germany	87.8%
Luxembourg	80.0%
Netherlands	89.3%
Spain	75.5%
United Kingdom	94.1%

The figure for market share for indigenous films in France is striking at around 35%, and the result of a strong tradition of interest in cinema combined with a series of sustained measures on the part of the French government to foster a national cinema. But it would be difficult to argue that there is any clear correlation between the successful market exposure of national films and the relative popularity of the cinema in any given country. This becomes apparent if we look at the top eight countries in terms of average annual cinema attendance and compare this with the national market share of films screened. The following figures are for 1993:[36]

COUNTRY CINEMA ATTENDANCE
MARKET SHARE OF NATIONAL FILMS

	PER INHABITANT	(%)
Belgium	1.9	5.5
Denmark	2.0	16.0
France	2.3	34.6
Ireland	2.4	2.0
Norway	2.5	9.4
Spain	2.2	8.5
Switzerland	2.3	5.3
United Kingdom	1.9	2.4

The highest attendances are in Norway and in Ireland, although the indigenous market share in Norway is under 10% and in Ireland only

2%. Italy, which has a relatively high market share at 18%, records average attendances at 1.6 per year (lower than in the United Kingdom and therefore not included in the above 'top seven' table). In the cases of both Denmark and France it might be argued that the relatively strong presence of national films helps to sustain higher attendance figures, but it may be that other factors, for example a shared language, climate, level of investment in cinemas and availability of alternative audio-visual services are equally significant. Although a counter-factual argument presents itself in the case of the United States where cinema-going is almost twice as popular as in Europe and where the films screened are overwhelmingly indigenous in origin.

Finally, and from a demographic point of view, published data on the composition of the cinema audience is currently quite inadequate. Though figures provided by the British Film Institute indicate the perhaps obvious truth that the majority of the cinema audience is under the age of 35 and that, in social class terms, there is a skewing towards higher income professionals (ABC1s) and away from lower income manual and craft skill groups (C2DEs).[37]

Of course, like all naked figures, these statistics on average frequency of attendance, on market share and (with less precision) on audience composition may be seen to hover on the edge of the ridiculous. For they help us very little when it comes to the business of analysing and assessing the significance of individual films and of cinema as a cultural form. Nonetheless what they do give us is a kind of framework, a sense of context and of the scale and scope of cinema as a contemporary institution.

It would be appropriate now to return to a consideration of the relative amounts of time spent before the large and the small screen, and to reconsider the significance of this time from the point of view of quality rather than quantity. For if there is to be a defence of cinema in relationship to television it must be related to the particularity of the cinematic experience which also provides a basis for the particularity of the cinematic image. It is here that we might start to link arguments about image quality made in the first part of this essay, to the details of the 'universe of hours' offered in the second part, noting that duration and frequency cannot be assumed to correlate with impact in the 'universe of meanings'. It would be absurd, of course, to suggest that cinema was in some way more impactful than television, but reasonable to note that the 'big picture' has a cultural force and resonance connected to its mode of exhibition and even to its scarcity. Moreover, any attempt at delineating the qualities of cinema must begin with this mode of exhibition, noting that its promise is a paradoxical one: offering since its earliest days a social space which fosters the most intensely private experience.

trader and railroad magnate; first and only Grand Wizard of the original Ku Klux Klan and leader of a famous and finally defeated force of Confederate cavalry.

The fictional Forrest, brought up in Greenbow in the southern state of Alabama in the 1940s, offers us a 'second take' on the history of white supremacism: not challenging the language and practices of racism, but simply failing to recognise them and therefore unable to reproduce them. His best friend is Bubba, black man and fellow Alabaman, whose dream of becoming the captain of a shrimp boat is taken up and finally realised by Forrest after Bubba's death in the killing fields of Vietnam. The shrimping business, following a freak typhoon which wipes out all the competitors, makes Forrest a millionaire and becomes a kind of terrible monument to his dead friend.

Forest Gump, 1994

Forrest's other and perhaps primary relationship is with Jenny, the love of his life, terrorised and abused by her father in childhood. Jenny is more absent than present in the story but it is she who connects the film to its other great theme: the liberalism and sexual licence of the sixties. Losing her, he loses a part of himself and expresses his inarticulate loss through the language of the body: embarking on a lonely marathon race, running from coast to coast, dogged, determined, and attracting followers in a silent ritual that is at once grand and absurd. It is this mixture of the grand and the absurd rendered through wordless gesture that gives us, perhaps, a feeling for the film as a whole. For the endless running, moved by hurt and motivated by desire, together with the digital dodging in and out of a documentary picture space occupied by the great, offers us a secular and modest celebration of human integrity. Though this celebration is itself wary and provisional, linked to a mistrust of politicians and leaders and bound to a solitary individualism that is transcended only by a commitment to the next generation, to the expression of loving support for a child.

The simile of life being 'like a box of chocolates, you never know what you're going to get', offered as a pragmatic and stoical guide to living in *Forrest Gump*, provides a pointer towards the themes of chance, accident and unpredictability as these are developed in Krzysztof Kieslowski's *Three Colours Red*. And if neither film has the kind of deep pessimism of Shakespearean tragedy – 'as flies to wanton boys are we to the gods, they kill us for their sport'[41] – yet they share an apprehension about the role of chance in human history, and a deep scepticism about the political realm. It is as though the alienation generated by the experience of Stalinism on the European continent now offers itself as a deadly partner to the widespread sense of political disillusionment in capitalist democracies. In this respect a recent popular film from Hollywood and an arguably élite product of the European art cinema share a similar ideology or 'structure of feeling'.

The revulsion against politics seems to be a general feature of late twentieth century life in North America, Europe and Russia. Tom Hanks offers this account of *Forrest Gump*: 'the film is non-political and thus non-judgmental. It doesn't just celebrate survival, it celebrates the struggle.'[42] A British critic, interviewing Kieslowski, notes: 'Asked what puts him off making a political film, he replies "Politics" ', and goes on to cite Kieslowski's observation:

> When we talk about politics we immediately start separating ourselves. I found it absolutely necessary to look for things which bring people together.[43]

Politics is the realm where humans beings act in concert and in conflict to remake their social environment. But, as the title of Arthur Koestler's book *The God That Failed* so graphically illustrates, the grand aspiration of collective action designed to build a better world (a 'new Jerusalem', a communist society, a paradise on earth) has come under pretty heavy fire. And when human beings come to fear that collective action is impossible or undesirable then the role of chance and accident returns with a new, if rather desperate, explanatory force. The two great recipes for the good life appear, from our *fin-de-siècle* perspective, to have been defective. On the one hand Stalinism and, to some extent, the command economy, deformed people and their lives, while on the other capitalism continually fails to 'deliver the goods' to significant sections of the population and to large parts of the world. The result is a diminution of political confidence and of hope. It is in this context (and not because of the forms of political self-censorship characteristic of earlier periods of film production) that a key aspect of the pleasure of contemporary cinema is its avoidance of the official discourses of politics; and yet its stories so clearly continue to embody the values and conflicts of our time.

The generalised feeling of 'not knowing what fate has in store' may, in America, have older and deeper roots in the experience of the Great

Depression of the 1930s. But, in a contemporary European context, the more appropriate points of reference are the fall of the Berlin Wall and the radical and largely unpredicted changes in the Soviet Union and in Eastern Central Europe. After an initial moment of exuberant celebration these changes have ushered in an era of uncertainty and fear and it is this nervous sense of disconnection and apprehension that to some extent characterises the Kieslowski film. In the opening shot of *Three Colours Red* a cluster of telephone lines plunges into the sea, signifying the radical separation of the people thus technologically linked. The potential intimacy of the telephone call is negated by the despairing voyeurism of the eavesdropping judge, and the central character, Valentine (played by Irène Jacob), is increasingly objectified by the agressive jealousy of her long-distance lover.

Valentine's face shares something of the blankness and bleakness of Tom Hanks playing Forrest. She is a model whose looks are constructed by others, and for the photograph where she is positioned before a huge and billowing red flag, she is directed to 'look sad'. This icon of a beautiful and sad face with an intense red background is given the slogan: 'a breath of life'. It is this breath, and a reason for living, that she later tries to give to the alienated and misanthropic judge (played by Jean-Louis Trintignant). Valentine's encounter with the judge's dark house of self-hatred awakens her disgust and subsequently her compassion as she shares his memory of betrayal and his sharp and deeply relativistic sense of the impossibility of judging others: 'Given their lives, I'd steal, kill, lie'.

We never discover what product is being advertised by the great red poster which is raised like the sails of a ship above the streets of Geneva. At its centre, before a pulsating and undifferentiated background of deep red, Valentine's face appears in sharp focus, strands of bedraggled, wet hair giving her the appearance of a shipwreck survivor. But it is this iconography of shipwreck which recurs at the end of the film. As the judge watches a television screen, the news reports a disaster at sea: the cross-channel ferry carrying Valentine has capsized, drowning hundreds of people. And so the hand of an unpredictable and malign fate strikes.

The terrible image of the over-turned ship has both a referential and a broader cultural significance comparable, perhaps, to the great history painting of Théodore Géricault: *The Raft of the Medusa* (1819), which both referred to a particular event and contributed to a broader public debate. The shipwreck represented by Kieslowski may be taken to have broader references to the 'shipwrecked' societies and economies of Eastern Central Europe. The previous film in his trilogy, *Three Colours White* (1993), had sketched some of the brutalities and uncertainties of contemporary economic life in Poland.

But in *Three Colours Red*, the concluding film, the all-powerful and omniscient story-teller also has a hand in things, and the director invokes and imposes the ancient 'deus ex machina' of a happy ending. We see, among the few survivors of the disaster, the faces of the principal characters from all three films of the trilogy. Thus one arbitrary power replaces another, inducing – along with a foregrounding of the deliberate artificiality of the narrative device – a sense of uneasy resolution. In the narrative terms that the film has set for itself this happy ending is hard to believe; here the fickle gods of Chance and Fortune are in the ascendant.

Despite the modest hopefulness of the maternal father (Forrest) and the woman with redemptive powers (Valentine), neither *Forrest Gump* nor *Three Colours Red* offer much promise of satisfaction for individuals or communities. Rather these films share a powerful sense of disquiet and anxiety, uncertainty and disconnection: reflecting upon lost and obsessive loves, bleak and difficult histories. By contrast, Jane Campion's film *The Piano* introduces – in the unexpected form of

a tale from the wilds of nineteenth century New Zealand – an iconography of erotic pleasure and of female satisfaction. A new and striking repertoire of pleasures is thereby offered to the cinema audience in general and to women viewers in particular.

The protagonist of *The Piano*, Ada (played by Holly Hunter), is mute; her daughter, Flora, translates her sign language when necessary. Ada's silence seems to signify enormous and pent-up reservoirs of inner strength and, as a narrative device, intensifies the visual expressivity of the film. Her piano, transported with diffi-

Three Colours Red, 1994

culty to the shores of this new world, becomes her voice, and her playing is an expression of her sense of self and a celebration of sensuous pleasure which only gradually acquires a sexual component. The stifling tempo of her unsatisfying marriage to landowner Stewart (played by Sam Neill) gives way to the slowly realised excitement of an attraction to her husband's neighbour, Baines. It is Baines (played by Harvey Keitel) who, unlike her husband, recognises and respects her need for the piano and whose inarticulacy and illiteracy find an echo in the muteness of Ada. The tattoos on his face are a sign of his association with Maori culture, a culture rejected and derided by Stewart but adopted and respected by Baines.

With various light and precise touches the film sketches Baines as 'the other' in terms of race and of class. Despite his obvious energy and determination he is associated with the suppressed, the misrepresented, the silenced. His helpless distress at Ada's lack of response to him both recognises the strength of her position and is a part of the process of erotic attraction which finally leads her to him. Their alliance, achieved in the face of social disapproval and opposition, resonates with the political values of the 'new social movements' of the late twentieth century. Indeed it is the existence of communities holding these values, in many parts of the world, which makes the film possible. Thus the sensuous forms which represent the attraction between two fictional characters speak to a community and are made possible by the existence of that community outwith the world of the film.

In the early part of the film Ada's face is encased in the black and white of a severe and delicate bonnet, her body in the imprisoning structure of a crinoline. Only later, as she fulfils her part of the bargain with Baines, are her face and hair, her arms and breasts fully revealed. But as the tragedy and violence of marital possession begin to unfold, the soft and filtered play of light on the bodies of the lovers is replaced by the dull light of a rain-filled sky as Ada and Flora trudge through the muddy landscapes that separate the dwellings of husband and lover.

The growing claustrophobia and the rules of sexual ownership in white society reach their culmination and final expression in the rage of the husband who mutilates his wife. And, of course, the mutilation must be connected to her means of expression: to her playing of the piano. Later, as the twists of the narrative allow Ada to depart with Baines and to survive a half-accidental plunge into the ocean, we hear in her playing the sound of the metal-tipped finger which is the sign of her mutilation. In a powerful metaphor, which links liberation and deformation to the activity of expression, we are given, in the sight of the hand and the sound of the music, an image of that which is lost and that which is found, that which is deformed and that which transcends deformity.

Charles Burnett's film, *To Sleep with Anger*, also draws upon the imagery of playing a musical instrument and transforms this into visual metaphor in order to (in Arendt's terms) 'give material form to the invisible'. We may see the mutilated finger in *The Piano* as having an ambitiously referential purpose, alluding to the long history of control and deformation of women's bodies and minds. The iconography of the young boy learning how to play the trumpet in a black suburb of contemporary Los Angeles has a similarly broad referential purpose. Like the Géricault painting, the shipwreck in

Three Colours Red and the mutilation in *The Piano*, this icon has something of the grandeur of the history painting infused with contemporary subject matter. The boy is never named, he is simply a neighbour to the film's main characters: Gideon and Suzie. But his playing improves as the story unfolds until, at the end, it merges into the non-diegetic music of the film's final credits sequence.

The film is a deceptively simple account of contemporary family life, reflecting the conflicts, internal and external, contemporary and historical, that have shaped the lives of African Americans. Gideon and Suzie are of the generation who settled in California, moving away from painful roots in the Deep South. In the opening image of the film a bowl of fruit appears to catch fire, and the fire spreads, burning Gideon as he sits below the photographic portrait of an ancestor. This image of pain, the inheritance of slavery, the consequence of sleeping night after night without speaking one's anger, accompanies the notes of a gospel song: 'Precious Memories'. And as the inflicted pain and the inner rage combine these have the potential to convert to violence and inhumanity, and to the flames of destruction and self-destruction.

In its 'surrealism' (subsequently anchored as a dream image) the opening sequence sets the scene for a tale that draws constantly on unseen threat, rendering this threat apparent through narrative structure and the use of metaphor. When Harry, an old friend from the deep South, knocks on Gideon's door and enters the life of the family, the threat is embodied in human form. His presence is mysteriously coincidental with Gideon becoming seriously ill, and the 'spell' that he casts on the younger son has the effect of exacerbating tensions both between brothers and between the different generations of the family.

Harry's presence seems to be a concrete manifestation of the danger of 'man being wolf to man'. His power within the narrative is finally countered by the wonderfully funny sequence of his accidental death, but also by a challenge issued by the mother, Suzie: 'I have to know who is in my house'. A context for this challenge has already been provided by a family friend reflecting upon Harry's nature and influence: 'if you're made to feel half a man what do you think the other half is?' Alternative images of human nature are offered by the activity of growing, nurturing, learning: as the un-named boy learns to play his music, as Suzie roots and grows new plants on the windowsill of her kitchen. *To Sleep with Anger* might be viewed as a poignant reprise of John Ford's *How Green Was My Valley*, with its similarly luminous family interiors. But this is a reprise with all of the weight of a real and remembered history, with characters moved by the conflicts and contradictions of contemporary society, not by the sentimentalism of a drama whose skilfully crafted and 'universal' characters are at once from everywhere and from nowhere.

CONCLUSION

The position and significance of cinema as an institution has changed radically over the last fifty years. In 1946, a peak year for attendances, there were an average *34* visits per person per year to cinemas in the United Kingdom. Cinema-going was at least a weekly habit, and some people went more frequently than this. By 1993 the figure was down to an average two visits per person, per year, in a period when average annual television viewing amounted to 1,300 hours. It is interesting to note that average cinema attendances in the United States are at more than twice the UK level, though in almost all European countries attendance figures remain extremely modest. So it is clear that, despite the continuing importance of movies in both the television and video markets, and despite the slow but steady increase in cinema-going (attendance figures doubled between 1984 and 1993 in the UK), this cultural activity has still been drastically reduced in scale and scope, and significant sections of the population do not attend cinemas at all.

I have tried to suggest that the cultural significance of cinema as an institution should be explored (and if necessary defended) not in terms of quantity of visits but in terms of the quality of the viewing experience, and its broadly social and public character. The quality of the viewing experience has to do both with the size and density of the image and with the concentrated attention span which this image receives.

I have furthermore suggested that our attention to the specific quality of the cinematic image might benefit from a re-reading of Bazin's account of photographic ontology and from Barthes' recognition of the extraordinary and powerful nature of the photograph as sign. A recognition of the special, even 'sacred' character of the film image, its capacity in both emotional and rational terms to render visible that which is invisible and to lead an audience from the particularity of sensuous form to the abstraction of ideas must be an important element in our 'balance sheet' of commemoration and celebration in the period of the centenary of cinema.

In the context of the advancing 'revolution' of the information super-highway we might say that what cinema offers us is 'information with attitude', icons that are already dense with social meaning and that in combination build narratives, telling tales of modern life. Moreover, the special or 'sacred' quality of the cinematic image derives not from divine authority but from human response. Its special character is the product of the range of meanings which it has for the many people who view it and use it. For it is the viewers of the image who complete it, who in responding to it and appropriating it both enter and construct a shared and social world of meaning. In this respect we might think of cinema as one small domain which contributes to the making, shaping and reflecting of what Hannah Arendt has called 'the human condition'.

NOTES

1. Cited in Dudley Andrew, *André Bazin*, Oxford University Press, 1978, p. 101.

2. ibid., p. 66.

3. Hannah Arendt, 'Introduction – Walter Benjamin: 1892-1940' in Walter Benjamin, *Illuminations*, translated by Harry Zohn, Jonathan Cape, 1970, p. 14.

4. André Bazin, 'The Ontology of the Photographic Image' in *What is Cinema?* Volume I, translated by Hugh Gray, University of California Press, 1967, p. 10.

5. ibid., p. 15.

6. Roland Barthes, 'The Third Meaning: Research Notes on some Eisenstein Stills', in *Image-Music-Text*, essays selected and translated by Stephen Heath, Fontana, 1977, pp. 53-54; and Roland Barthes, *Camera Lucida – Reflections on Photography*, translated by Richard Howard, Jonathan Cape, 1982, p. 88.

7. Martin Jay, *Downcast Eyes – the Denigration of Vision in Twentieth Century French Thought*, University of California Press, 1993, p. 420.

8. ibid., p. 430.

9. ibid., p. 470.

10 ibid., p. 473. The work of *Cinéthique* was reviewed from a more positive perspective – within the 1970s framework of the project of 'political modernism' – in Sylvia Harvey, *May '68 and Film Culture*, BFI, 1978, pp. 36-40.

11. ibid., p. 479.

12. ibid., p. 483.

13. Terry Lovell, *Pictures of Reality – Aesthetics, Politics and Pleasure*, BFI, 1980, p. 95.

14. William Blake, from 'The Marriage of Heaven and Hell', in ed. J. Bronowski, *William Blake*, Penguin, 1965, p. 96.

15. Hannah Arendt, *The Human Condition*, University of Chicago Press, 1958, p. 320.

16. ibid.

17. Susan Sontag, *On Photography*, Dell Publishing Company, New York, 1977, p. 173.

18. Hannah Arendt, *The Human Condition*, op. cit., p. 8.

19. ibid., p. 167 and p. 168.

20. Bertolt Brecht, *Poems 1913-1956 – Part Three 1938-1956*, edited by John Willett and Ralph Mannheim, Eyre Methuen, 1976, p. 442.

21. Vaclav Havel, 'Thriller' in *Living in Truth*, edited by Jan Vladislav, Faber and Faber, 1987, p. 161.

22. See Sergei Eisenstein, 'The Cinematographic Principle and the Ideogram', in *Film Form – Essays in Film Theory*, translated by Jay Leyda, Harcourt, Brace and World Inc., New York 1949, p. 32.

23 For an elaboration of this debate see the essays by Pier Paolo Pasolini, Ron Abramson, Umberto Eco and Bill Nichols in ed. Bill Nichols, *Movies and Methods – An Anthology* (Vol. I), University of California Press, 1976.

24. Barthes, 'The Photographic Message' in *Image-Music-Text*, op. cit., p. 17.

25 Bazin, 'Ontology', op. cit., p. 14. For an incisive discussion of the weaknesses of Bazin's ontology see Noel Carroll, *Philosophical Problems of Classical Film Theory*, Princeton University Press, 1988.

26 ed. Terry Ramsaye, *International Motion Picture Almanac 1947-48*, Quigley Publications, New York, 1946, p. xv. With weekly attendances of 98 million, and a population recorded as 141.9 million by the U.S. Bureau of the Census, average annual attendance, per head, was 35.9.

27. eds. David Leafe and Terry Ilott, *Film and Television Handbook* 1994, BFI, 1993, p. 34.

28. ibid.

29. ed. André Lange, *Statistical Yearbook 1994-1995 – Cinema, Television, Video and New Media in Europe*, European Audio-Visual Observatory, Strasburg, 1994, p. 97.

30. ibid.

31. ed. Nick Thomas, *Film and Television Handbook* 1995, 1994, p. 34.

32. *Statistical Yearbook* 1994-1995, op. cit., p. 148.

33. *White Book of the European Exhibition Industry – Synthesis*, a Report by London Economics and BIPE Conseil for MEDIA Salles, MEDIA Salles, Milan, 1994, p. 9.

34. *European Cinema Yearbook – a Statistical Analysis 1994*, MEDIA Salles, Milan, 1994, p. 33.

35. ibid., p. 34.

36. *European Cinema Yearbook* 1994, op. cit., p. 24 and p. 33. The market share figures for the U.K. and Ireland are taken from the *Statistical Yearbook 1994-1995*, op. cit., p. 105; in the absence of a figure for 1993, the market share figure for Ireland is from 1991.

37. *Film and Television Handbook 1995*, op. cit., p. 35.

38. Charles Burnett, 'Inner City Blues', in eds. Jim Pines and Paul Willemen, *Questions of Third Cinema*, BFI, 1989, p. 225. The Arendt citation is from *Men in Dark Times*.

39. Box office figures are from ed. Eddie Dyja, *Film and Television Handbook 1996*, BFI, 1995; *Variety*, January 24-30, 1994; Richard Sean Lyon, *Top Grossing Films of All Time – the 1990 Survival Guide to Film*, Lyon Heart Publishers, Los Angeles, 1989.

40. J. Hoberman in *Village Voice*, July 12, 1994; British Film Institute, microfiche collection, *Forrest Gump*.

41. William Shakespeare, *King Lear*, Act IV, Scene 1, various editions.

42. Tom Hanks interviewed by Richard Corliss in *Time*, August 1, 1994; BFI microfiche collection, *Forrest Gump*.

43. Krzysztof Kieslowski interviewed by Tom Shone in the *Sunday Times*, November 6, 1994; BFI microfiche collection, *Three Colours Red*.

I should like to thank the Lumière Institute, Lyons, and the University of Versailles (San Quentin-en-Yvelines) for their invitation to participate in the seminar *L'invention d'une culture – une histoire de la cinéphilie*, where this essay was presented in the form of a paper in October 1995.

NOTES ON CONTRIBUTORS

John Barnes MBKS, is the author of the series of books on early cinema in Britain: *The Beginnings of the Cinema in England* (1976), *The Rise of the Cinema in Great Britain* (1983), *Pioneers of the British Film* (1988), *Filming the Boer War* (1992) and *The Cinema in England, 1900* (1996). For more than 50 years he and his twin brother William have been collecting the artefacts of cinema archaeology which now form the Archives of the Barnes Museum of Cinematography.

Stephen Bottomore is a television director and independent film historian based in London. He has published a range of articles and is researching early cinema and its social and cultural contexts.

Richard Brown has a particular interest in early British cinema. In 1994 he received a Kraszna-Krausz grant to research the history of the Kinetoscope in England, and has worked with the National Film and Television Archive and the Public Record Office to catalogue a unique collection of copyrighted British films dating from 1897 to which he first drew attention. He is co-author (with Barry Anthony) of *A Victorian Film Enterprise – a History of the British Mutoscope and Biograph Company* (1996).

Michael Chanan is a film-maker and writer who teaches in the Media School, London College of Printing. His most recent books include *Musica Practica* (1994, on the social practice of music) and *Repeated Takes* (1995, on the history of sound recordings).

John Chittock OBE, FRTS, FBKSTS, FRPS, is Chairman and founder (1971) of *Screen Digest*. For 24 years he was *Financial Times* columnist on the moving picture media, has been Chairman of the British Federation of Film Societies, a founder and Deputy Chairman of the British Screen Advisory Council, founder and now Chairman of the Grierson Memorial Trust, and trustee of the Kraszna-Krausz Foundation. He is involved in various other industry activities spanning television, film and cinema, including BKSTS, the Royal Television Society and the Advisory Committee of the National Museum of Photography, Film and Television.

Roland Cosandey teaches at the Ecole cantonale d'Art at Lausanne, Switzerland. The recipient of a grant from the Fonds national suisse de la Recherche scientifique, he has specialised in early and Swiss film history. He is the author of *Welcome Home, Joye! Film um 1910 – Aus der Sammlung Joseph Joye* (NFTVA, London) (1993) and co-editor of the first two volumes of Domitor Conference proceedings; with André Gaudreault and Tom Gunning, *An Invention of the Devil? Religion and Early Cinema* (1992) and, with François Albera, *Cinéma sans*

Frontières 1896-1918 – Images across Borders, Internationality in World Cinema (1995).

John L. Fell is the author of *Film and the Narrative Tradition* (1974), *Film, an Introduction* (1975) and *A History of Films* (1979) and the editor of *Film before Griffith* (1983). He participated in the development and administration of the Cinema Program at San Francisco State University and has taught in several other universities. Now retired, he teaches jazz at the College of Marin and recently completed a book on Stride Piano.

André Gaudreault is Professor of Cinema at Université de Montréal, Canada. He is one of the five founding members of Domitor (the association to promote research into early cinema) and has been its president since it was founded. He has published many books, including *Du littéraire au filmique* (1988), and, with François Jost, *Le Récit cinématographique* (1990) and articles in journals (*Cahiers de la Cinémathèque, Iris, 1895, Framework, Cinema Journal, CINéMAS*, etc).

Sylvia Harvey is Reader in Broadcasting Policy at Sheffield Hallam University. She is the author of *May '68 and Film Culture* (1978), co-editor of *Enterprise and Heritage* (with John Corner, 1991) and *The Regions, the Nations and the BBC* (with Kevin Robins, 1993) and has published many articles on film and broadcasting issues.

Mervyn Heard is a professional magic lantern showman. Since the mid 1980s he has devised and presented a variety of 'antique' picture-show entertainments and special lantern sequences for theatrical venues, film festivals, museums, and film and television companies.

Stephen Herbert is Co-ordinator of Special Events at the Museum of the Moving Image, London, a consultant in visual technologies and contributing co-editor (with Luke McKernan) of *Who's Who of Victorian Cinema* (1996).

Joost Hunningher is Principal Lecturer in Film and Television Production at the University of Westminster. He has a wide range of profesional production experience as a producer, director, writer, lighting cameraman and editor.

Roberta McGrath teaches photographic history and theory at Napier University, Edinburgh. She is writing a book which examines the relationship between nineteenth century medical photography and the pathologising of the female body.

Luke McKernan is a cataloguer at the National Film and Televison Archive in London and contributing co-editor (with Stephen Herbert) of *Who's Who of Victorian Cinema* (1996). He has presented programmes of Victorian film at the NFT and other locations.

David Mingay co-produced and wrote the film *A Bigger Splash* and co-directed *Rude Boy* (1980). For television he has directed the series *The Amazing Years of Cinema 1895-1916* (1977) and *Sophisticated Lady* (1990). In the last three years he has developed and produced the *Virtual Nightclub* CD-ROM.

Roberta E. Pearson teaches Mass Communications at the Centre for Journalism Studies, University of Wales, Cardiff. She is the author of *Eloquent Gestures* (1992) and co-author of *Reframing Culture* (1993). Also with William Uricchio she is writing a history of New York City's nickelodeons entitled *The Nickel Madness*.

Simon Popple teaches the history of film and visual media at Manchester Metropolitan University. He has published several articles on early cinema and is researching a project on the Boer War.

David Robinson is a cinema critic and historian. His numerous books include *World Cinema* (1972, 1985), *Chaplin, His Life and Art* (1985), *Masterpieces of Animation/Capolavori dell' Animazione 1833-1908* (1991), *Lantern Images – Iconography of the Magic Lantern 1440-1880* (1993), *Musique et Cinéma muet* (1995), *Light and Image: Incunabula of the Motion Picture* (with Donata Pesenti Compagnoni and Laurent Mannoni, 1996), and *Peepshow to Palace* (1996).

Barry Salt teaches at the London International Film School and is the author of *Film Style and Technology: History and Analysis* (2nd revised edition 1992).

Paul Schrader is one of America's most highly regarded writer-directors. He wrote the screenplays for *Taxi Driver* (1976), *Raging Bull* (1980), *The Last Temptation of Christ* (1988), wrote and directed *Blue Collar* (1978), *Hardcore* (1979), *American Gigolo* (1980), *Mishima* (1985), *Light Sleeper* (1992), and directed *Patty Hearst* (1988) and *The Comfort of Strangers* (1990). His critical work includes the book *Transcendental Style in Film: Ozu, Bresson, Dreyer* (1972, reprinted 1988).

Mark Shivas is Head of Films at BBC Television.

Martin Sopocy is an unaffiliated historian who writes about early film. His book on James Williamson will be published in 1996. He lives in Brooklyn, New York.

Christopher Williams is Reader in Photography, Film and Video at the University of Westminster. He chairs the Criticism and Creativity Research Group and edited *Realism and the Cinema* (1980).

INDEX

ACKNOWLEDGEMENTS

We are grateful to the following institutions and people for allowing us to reproduce the visual material in this book.

The Lumière Institute, Lyons, page 8; BFI Stills, Posters and Designs, pages 11, 44, 55, 57, 61, 73, 78, 89, 115, 155; the Theatre Museum, London, pages 18 and 19; Mervyn Heard, pages 27, 30 and 31; the David Robinson Collection, pages 35, 36, 39, 108, 112 and 166, Dr David Pizzanelli, page 37; the Archive at the University of Westminster, pages 42 and 43, 48, 51 and 84; Joost Hunningher, page 45; Stephen Bottomore, pages 46, 66, 142 and 143; The Photographic Journal, pages 47 and 65; The National Museum of Photography, Film and Television, pages 99, 102 and 103; Luke McKernan, page 110; Martin Sopocy, pages 128 and 129; Valerie Williamson, page 137; Stephen Herbert, pages 158 and 163; the Kingston Museum, pages 160 and 161; Screen Digest, pages 169, 218 and 219; Barry Salt, pages 173, 175, 177 and 179; Mark Shivas, page 186; BBC Films, pages 187 and 188; Channel 4 Television, pages 196, 198 and 199; Prospect Management, pages 210, 211 and 213; Imax Corporation, Toronto, page 221; Jampoo Corporation, Taiwan, page 225; CIC/Paramount, page 244; Artificial Eye, page 247.